PRAISE FOR
GRANNY THORNAPPLE'S BOOK OF CHARMS

"Every bit as entertaining as it is informative, *Granny Thornapple's Book of Charms* brings the time-honored traditions of Ozark charming to life. Following the story of the titular character, readers are presented with dozens of useful, and at times quite whimsical, charms for everything from health to hexing. Brandon Weston has once again provided an invaluable collection of folk magic, and readers of this volume are sure to be both delighted and charmed by the fabulous Granny Thornapple."

—**Kelden,** author of *The Crooked Path* and *The Witches' Sabbath*

"This book offers a unique exploration of Ozark charming traditions through examination of regional storytelling tropes, tales, and narratives.... Brandon's careful analysis grounds these witch tales in the craft-logics and operative techniques of Ozark magical practices, offering supplemental advice, spell-craft, and formulary for working these storied charms in one's own work. In so doing, the author traces (amongst many other things) the oft-crossed hedge-lines between healer, charmer, granny, and witch and the uneasy folkloric tensions between communal fears of harmful witchcraft and the fondness for telling of the exploits of this larger-than-life granny / witch figure."

—**Dr. Alexander Cummins,** author of *The Starry Rubric, An Excellent Booke of the Arte of Magicke* (with Phil Legard), and *A Book of the Magi*

"Brandon Weston masterfully takes us into the world of Granny Thornapple, where we learn about her life and the spells she casts to help her community. Storytelling in magic is a long-lost art that not only teaches us enchantments but also helps us understand the person who is conjuring the magic. Step into the world of Granny Thornapple, pull up a chair, and ask her to teach you the magic of the Ozarks."

—**Chris Allaun,** author of *The Black Book of Johnathan Knotbristle*

T0006828

"Weston weaves the reader into the flow of Ozark folk charming practices, showing how they move and change over time to meet the needs of those using them. Charms for healing and harm, charms for love and beauty, charms for knowing what others don't and speaking to the spirits others won't all fill this hearty compendium.... The research we expect from Weston is still here but tempered by modern twists on old charms, linking the lore of the past to the world of the present."

—**Cory T. Hutcheson,** author of *New World Witchery*

"A rare volume, not merely a collection of tales or raw folkloric data, but a whole landscape populated by characters you will come to love by the end. Weston's teachers, neighbours, and friends all find their voice in this deeply personal work, their stories supporting the magical practices outlined. So often in magical books we get the practices divorced from culture, but in this book we have all of it right in front of us. Weston gives us rituals, charms, prayers, and all manner of magical practice.... and supports almost every single one with a story.... This book will appeal not only to those interested in the Ozarks, but to all who want to connect to their own landscape as deeply as Weston has."

—**Ben Stimpson,** author of *Ancestral Whispers*

"As a lifelong Ozarker as well, I was immediately drawn into the story of Granny Thornapple. She is the Granny woman we all wished we'd had in our life. Brandon Weston has given us a connection to those healers, teachers, and workers that many of us missed in our youth. He demystifies the charm practice, allowing us to give ourselves permission to explore this path. He shows us that anyone who is willing to do the work can fold this practice into their own."

—**Debra L. Burris PhD,** professor, farmer, and author of *Weather Magic*

✳ GRANNY THORNAPPLE'S ✳
BOOK OF CHARMS

ABOUT THE AUTHOR

Brandon Weston (Fayetteville, AR) is a healer, writer, and folklorist who owns and operates Ozark Healing Traditions, an online collective of articles, lectures, and workshops focusing on the Ozark Mountain region. As a practicing folk healer, his work with clients includes everything from spiritual cleanses to house blessings. He comes from a long line of Ozark hillfolk and is also a folk herbalist, yarb doctor, and power doctor. His books include *Ozark Folk Magic*, *Ozark Mountain Spell Book*, and *Granny Thornapple's Book of Charms*. Visit him at www.OzarkHealing.com.

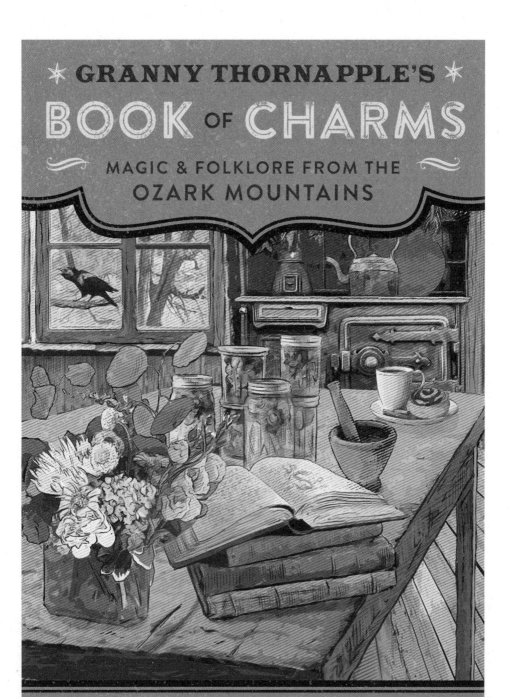

GRANNY THORNAPPLE'S
BOOK OF CHARMS

MAGIC & FOLKLORE FROM THE OZARK MOUNTAINS

BRANDON WESTON

Llewellyn Publications
Woodbury, Minnesota

FIRST EDITION
First Printing, 2024

Cover design by Kevin R. Brown
Cover illustration by Jerry Hoare
Zodiac Man (Man of Signs) illustration © Mary Ann Zapalac

Unless otherwise noted, the New Revised Standard Version Updated Edition (NRSVUE) of the Bible was referenced throughout.

Llewellyn Publications is a registered trademark of Llewellyn Worldwide Ltd.

Library of Congress Cataloging-in-Publication Data (Pending)
ISBN: 978-0-7387-7608-8

Llewellyn Worldwide Ltd. does not participate in, endorse, or have any authority or responsibility concerning private business transactions between our authors and the public.

All mail addressed to the author is forwarded but the publisher cannot, unless specifically instructed by the author, give out an address or phone number.

Any internet references contained in this work are current at publication time, but the publisher cannot guarantee that a specific location will continue to be maintained. Please refer to the publisher's website for links to authors' websites and other sources.

Llewellyn Publications
A Division of Llewellyn Worldwide Ltd.
2143 Wooddale Drive
Woodbury, MN 55125-2989
www.llewellyn.com

Printed in the United States of America

OTHER BOOKS BY BRANDON WESTON

Ozark Folk Magic

Ozark Mountain Spell Book

DEDICATION

To Granny Thornapple, "Pauline," Gram French, Gram Wasset, Granny Nallow, Doc Green, Gram Watson, Aunt Hazel, Uncle Bill, and all Ozark charmers of fact and fiction.

CONTENTS

DISCLAIMER

The old-fashioned remedies in this book are historical references used for teaching purposes only. The recipes are not for commercial use or profit. New herbal recipes should be taken in small amounts to allow the body to adjust.

Please note that the information in this book is not meant to diagnose, treat, prescribe, or substitute consultation with a licensed healthcare professional. This book is not intended to provide medical advice or to take the place of medical advice and treatment from your personal physician. Readers are advised to consult their doctors or other qualified healthcare professionals regarding the treatment of their medical problems. Neither the publisher nor the author take any responsibility for possible consequences of any person reading or following the information in this book.

Introduction

Let's begin with a story ...

Little Ann was born on the same night her grandmother died. It was on May Day, just after midnight, and in a thunderstorm so strong it flooded ol' Paul Landry's mill and killed at least ten cows out on Buffalo Ridge. A local midwife called Gram Watson was present, as she had been for many of the children born in Nelson's Holler. Besides the auspicious timing, she reported two unusual tokens, or omens, at the birth of Little Ann: one, she was born in the caul, meaning the placenta was fully covering her head and face at birth and had to be removed by hand, and two, she was born silent and remained so for three whole minutes until all of a sudden, she let out a banshee wail that shocked even Gram Watson. At the same time, a bolt of lightning struck a wild plum tree out in the yard and split it completely in twain. The ruckus woke up the old hound dog asleep beside the fireplace, who started to bark toward the cabin ceiling. Little Ann's mother grabbed hold of the bedsheets beneath her and gripped them tight with her fingers, wincing at the sudden cacophony of sounds. Gram Watson just laughed and rocked the baby in her arms. "Well, bless my soul, Lucy," she said, handing the swaddled newborn to her mother. "She's got some of her grandmother's gift in her!"

Lucy shook her head in disbelief. "Don't go puttin' that on her, Gram!" she shouted, pulling the baby to her breast.

The storm suddenly calmed. There was a silent moment while the crickets outside were still sheltering from the rain. The wooden ceiling above the two women creaked as though something was walking across it with careful steps. "Gram, what is that?" Lucy whispered, the words catching in her throat.

Gram had been gathering up blood-soaked rags into an old bucket when she heard the sound. She set the bucket down and loaded up her briarwood pipe with a good-sized plug of tobacco. Whatever was on the roof continued its path toward the chimney. "It's a monster," Gram whispered, "sent for the baby." The wild, chaotic universe could never allow such an auspicious child to be born.

The old woman lit the pipe and took two long puffs, then a third, which she held in her mouth. She stepped softly across the cabin floor, tracing the path made by the noise up on the roof. Then she stopped and blew a strong line of tobacco smoke up toward the ceiling. The creature on the rooftop scratched and clawed in place as though it was struggling against something trying to pull it away from the house.

"Remember this charm, child!" Gram said, grinning toward the baby, pipe clinched in between her sparse, yellowed teeth. "Carry him crow!" she yelled toward the ceiling, blowing another trail of tobacco smoke. "Carry him kite!" A third stream of smoke twisted an unnatural line toward the sound of frantic clawing and scratching on the roof. "Carry him away 'til the apples are ripe! And when they're ripe and ready to fall, bring him back, apples and all!"

The scratching intensified. It sounded to Lucy like whatever demon was on her roof was about to take the whole thing clean off. Then, all of a sudden, the clambering stopped. All she heard now was the popping of embers in the fireplace and Gram's heavy breathing. "Is it gone, Gram?" she asked, holding her baby closer.

"It is for now," the old woman answered as she stoked the fire with a metal poker.

"Ain't there nothin' we can do?"

"This'll keep her safe."

Gram rolled a charred piece of wood out of the fire and onto the hearthstones. She took a dipper of water from a pail nearby and quenched the smoking log. It sputtered and steamed. "Whittle this down into a chunk big enough for the child to wear on a necklace string. She's got to wear it all her life."

"Gram, and that'll keep her safe?" Lucy asked sternly.

"That'll keep her safe," the old woman nodded, reading some secret signs and tokens in the glowing fireplace embers.

Lucy named her baby Ann in honor of her own mother, who, unbeknownst to Lucy, had passed with grace in her home on the other side of Nelson's Holler at the very second little Ann was born.

★ ★ ★

The fireside tales you will read in this book all feature the same protagonist: Granny Thornapple. This is in keeping with the age-old Ozark storytelling tradition that features a common heroic (or antiheroic) figure throughout many different adventures. Perhaps the most famous of this type of story are the Jack tales. Many will no doubt remember Jack's adventures with the beanstalk, but do you know the story of Jack and the possum? Or how about Jack and the magic cow skin? These are only a couple examples amongst many found across the Ozarks as well as our sister culture in Appalachia.

My favorite Ozark story cycles all feature a protagonist who is a granny woman or witch. Folklorists like Vance Randolph, Mary Parler, and Otto Ernest Rayburn collected many of these witch tales from informants across the region. In my own travels across the Ozark Mountains, I've collected many modern versions of these wonderful tall tales. These stories represent an interesting area within Ozark studies and feature the witch as a *villainous-yet-somehow-still-relatable* character. Many of the stories of this type even present the witch as an admirable individual, which stands in direct contrast to traditional Ozark views about witchcraft. Culturally, witchcraft and witches were held in a negative light in Ozark communities. "Healers always heal and witches always hurt," as it was once explained to me. But the reality of the situation was often more complicated than this, especially when we look at the role of the granny woman in Ozark society.

The character of Granny Thornapple is my own creation, but she is based on one of my actual teachers. Her fanciful name derives from the thorn apple, or jimsonweed (*Datura stramonium*), which, according to Ozark legends, is a favorite herb of witches. She represents an amalgam of many Ozark granny women, charmers, healers, and witches, both from the storytelling tradition as well as reality.

That's a funny word, "reality." In the Ozarks, sometimes fact and fiction are closer together than outsiders are comfortable with. I remember one time I took a friend to meet an old-school storyteller I knew who lived out in the middle of nowhere, off a dirt road that, at certain times of the year, doubled as a creek bed. He told us many fantastic tales by the glow of the fireplace, most of which were from his own life. One in particular—my favorite—was a tale about how when the old man was much younger, he had a ten-year love affair with a fairy woman who lived in an ancient tree stump near his home. My friend sat with a puzzled but intrigued look on his face as the old man told the tale in great detail. When we were on our way back home the next day, my friend finally asked me, "Were those stories real or just made up?" to which I answered with a chuckle, "Yes."

Granny Thornapple's stories are just like this: they blur the line between fact and fiction, like so many things do here in the Ozarks. I don't know how many times I've talked to Ozarkers who outwardly didn't seem like they would believe in ghosts and the Little People (Ozark fairies) but who told elaborate and heartfelt tales about encounters with these very beings. Famous Ozark witches from local legends are incorporated into the figure of Granny Thornapple. Many of their stories were published by folklorists like Vance Randolph: figures like Gram French, Gram Wasset, and Granny Whittiker, who once turned herself into a spectral turkey to haunt a neighbor girl who called Granny Whittiker's grandbaby ugly.[1] Granny Thornapple also represents many of my own teachers who would have been considered granny women had they lived in the old Ozarks. In this way, I'm proud to be able to honor their memories—as well as the memories of all Ozark healers and magical practitioners—through this book.

THE CHARMING WAY

You might already be familiar with Ozark folk magic and healing practices. Some of you might have grown up with these beliefs, or maybe even been passed something by healers like Granny Thornapple. Others of you might have read about these traditions in my other books, *Ozark Folk Magic: Plants, Prayers & Healing* and *Ozark Mountain Spell Book: Folk Magic & Healing*. Whether you're a seasoned practitioner or just starting out, I'd like to introduce you to a unique tradition within this tradition. It's just as important as the more complicated methods of magical divination, diagnosis, and ritual procedure I've spoken about elsewhere in my works. I like to call it the "Charming Way" of rhymes, poems, and verses. Many of these are treasured and passed down from charmer to student. Others are born from within the womb of one's own inborn inspiration, imagination, and power. This

---

1. Randolph, *Ozark Magic and Folklore*, 298.

ancient path has been passed down for generations from Old World to the New, to this very day. This is a path that I'm now passing down to you.

I'm a multigenerational Ozarker. Both sides of my family have deep connections to the region, but like many Ozarkers, my family was disconnected from their culture. I really only discovered there was a deep stream of tradition here when I found Vance Randolph's *Ozark Magic and Folklore* in my university's library. Reading Randolph opened my eyes to how much "Ozarkness" my family really had. The stories and traditions collected by Randolph in the 1920s and '30s felt like stories from my own family.

I don't come from a long line of healers and magical practitioners. I do have them in my family, but most Ozark families do if you look hard enough. One ancestor, Hazel, was gifted with the "second sight" and read fortunes in tea leaves. She could also see emotional states in the color of a person's aura. My great uncle Bill, who I did have the fortune of knowing while he was alive, was a known Wart Charmer and Blood Stopper. Specifically, he had the ability to buy warts off people. The process was simple: He'd walk up, look at your wart, then usually say something like, "That's a good one. I'll buy it off you," and then hand you a penny or dime. We knew to take the money, and then overnight, the wart would disappear. I never got to experience his role as a Blood Stopper, which—along with wart charming—was once a highly prized healing ability in the old Ozarks. As with many of these traditions, folks only know they're special and worth recounting after the healer is long gone.

The charming tradition has been the heart of my personal practice for years now. I immediately took to the simple approach to magic that is offered by this tradition. I've always had a mind for rhymes, songs, and verses. My family likes to recall how when I was a kid, I used to memorize commercial jingles off the TV and sing them endlessly. As one of my teachers said, this was an early token or sign that I have a gift for this work. Charmers especially often look for good memories in their students, as many of the verbal charms and prayers used in this work have traditionally been passed down orally. Of all the practices of Ozark folk healing and magic, the Charming Way has traditionally held the most taboos surrounding holding and passing down this unique gift. These taboos have been put in place to prevent the tradition from dying off. Tradition can be a tricky thing, though, especially in the modern world.

PASSING DOWN THE CHARMS

In the old days, charms like you'll find in this book were only passed down to others who were identified as having "the gift." These folks included both those born with the gift and those who had already been passed the gift by another. This gift is difficult to explain in modern terms, but perhaps the best way to think of it is as an *aptitude*. In the old days, having this inborn gift meant that you were more likely to become a talented healer or magical practitioner. The gift was only a marker, however, not a set-in-stone destiny. One could choose not to embrace their gift. Amongst more traditional Ozarkers, however, this has been considered squandering something valuable in the community. Unlike the old ways of viewing the gift, I believe that *everyone* possesses the ability, but everyone also has specific magical talents, capacities, and leanings. Consider a talented painter and a talented sculptor: both have aptitudes to create art, but they use very different mediums.

There were once many taboos surrounding passing down verbal charms, remedies, and rituals, the most important being that such things could only be passed down to someone who has been identified as already having the gift inside of them. This could be identified through various traditional methods; for example, peculiar circumstances around the individual's birth or certain birthmarks on the body. One of the most common ways of identifying the gift was to have someone with the second sight "see" it inside the person. Other taboos surrounding passing down charms and healing methods included that they could only be passed down orally, across genders (man to woman, woman to man), from an older person to a younger, and, in some cases, charms had to stay within a bloodline.

One of my favorite teachers taught me a different way. This isn't a more modern way nor a way that deviated from any of the foundational Ozark methods of working; it was just *different*. According to my mentor, charms love an open heart. Openness on the part of the magical practitioner creates a little nest, or home, inside of their own spirit where these charms will live out their days. So, first and foremost, this openness becomes the foundation for receiving any verbal charms, prayers, verses, etc. After that, there are some traditional practices of passing down power that you can use. Many of these I use in my own practice.

Verbal charms were traditionally passed down only by word of mouth from one practitioner to another, or from a practitioner to their student. There are still verbal charms that I've received that I will never write down; I only pass them along orally. This is a deep connection that goes back to our ancient ancestors, most of whom were illiterate. In the Ozarks, literacy didn't become commonplace until well into the twentieth century. Even when most folks could read and write, healers and magical practitioners often chose to stick with the old ways and only pass things down by word of mouth. This practice also traditionally applied to passing down herbal and home remedies.

In many cases amongst Traditionalist practitioners, a person is only able to pass down verbal charms to a certain number of people (usually three). After that, all of the power will be lost for the original holder of the charm and will now reside in the person the charm was passed to. Because of this, it's traditional for many healers and magical practitioners to keep their verbal charms secret until they reach retirement age. Then they pass the charms down to members of their family, students, or others with the gift. In some cases, writing down a charm might be allowed only for the purpose of memorizing the words. Once the words are committed to memory, the paper is burned. Often, the same limitation for how many people can receive the charm still applies to the writing-down method. For this reason, many Traditionalists look at the charms published by folklorists as being "dead" or no longer usable.

Modern healers (as well as most of my personal mentors) tend to approach the charming tradition in a different way. I was taught that there are verbal charms you can share as well as those you should keep secret. The shareable charms are the ones commonly known throughout the region that are passed back and forth amongst healers, practitioners, and even ordinary folks. These include charms like the blood-stopping verse in the Bible, Ezekiel 16:6 ("I passed by you and saw you flailing about in your blood. As you lay in your blood, I said to you, 'Live!'") as well as all the charms I've included in this book.

Secret charms, as I was taught, are the ones we pull out of our own wellspring of magical power and breathe into the world. These are charms that might be spoken in the moment, or delivered to the practitioner by way of divination, dreams, trances, visions, or other magical methods. One of my teachers always told me that the charms that just suddenly appear fully formed in your mind are deeply special and magical. These charms are commonly kept secret in order to sustain the inborn magical power that gave them life.

As a folk character, Granny Thornapple is a great example of a bridge between the old ways and modern practices. Like many real-world Ozark magical practitioners, she keeps her own charming book. This is a secret patchwork collection of rhymes, verses, poems, songs, and prayers she's collected from other healers, from books she found in the library, or from the Bible. Charming books are more common in the modern world; in the old days, charmers would have needed to memorize everything. This book is based on charming books from several of my teachers. It too is a patchwork of pieces I've collected from charmers, granny women, healers, practitioners, and commonfolk across the Ozark Mountains.

The inspiration for the chapter structure of this book came from a blessing charm my teacher sang to me one night. I give these words to you now. My hope is that all the charms in this book will live inside of you and be good little helpers for you and your work.

> I've got charms aplenty to give to you.
> Charms to bless you through the holy year.
> Charms to grow you like a green tree.
> Charms to tie your ills upon a stone.
> Charms to bring you love, if it be true.
> Charms to set a watch on house and home.
> Charms to right all wrongs that you might see.
> Charms to pass beyond and back again.
> Charms to see in dreams and visions too.
> Yes, I've got charms aplenty to give to you.

CHAPTER 1
The Ozark Charming Tradition

No doubt many of you already know some of the verbal charms contained in this book. Quite a few of them have been a part of our shared cultural experience for centuries—like one famous burn charm, for example:

> Two angels came out of the east.
> One brought fire, the other frost.
> In frost, out fire!

Or perhaps you know many of these spells by another name—nursery rhyme. These are the Mother Goose rhymes and fairytales many of us grew up hearing and memorizing as small children. Charms that today seem like nothing more than nonsense babbling in many cases originated within practices of folk healing and magic. Like the old rhyme that can double as a charm to cause tension and anger between two people:

> There were once two cats of Kilkenny.
> Each thought there was one cat too many;
> So they fought and they fit,
> And they scratched and they bit,
> Till, excepting their nails,
> And the tips of their tails,
> Instead of two cats, there weren't any.

Or the milking charm that I've heard repeated by a number of Ozarkers. I can even remember it from my own childhood. This rhyme can double as a charm that links offerings in exchange for prosperity and health, symbolized by milk:

> Cushy Cow bonny, let down your milk,
> And I will give you a gown of silk,
> A gown of silk and a silver tee,
> If you'll let down your milk to me.

There are so many others that will fill the later pages of this book. Charmers are very clever in their use, repurposing, and creating of verbal charms and prayers. With the right intention, one person's nursery rhyme could easily be another person's spell. As magical practitioners, witches, healers, or whatever we choose to call ourselves, we tend to get lost in complicated rituals and lengthy spells, mistakenly equating complication and effectiveness. We've forgotten many of the older, simpler charms that practitioners of the past would have cherished for centuries. One of the famous Ozark charms for stopping a bleeding wound is a meager twenty words long:

> Upon this grave
> Three roses grew,
> Stop, blood, stop!
> From wound to wound
> The pain [he / she / they] drew,
> Stop, blood, stop!

And yet, it's believed that this simple charm, easily memorized, has the power to heal if one *believes* in that power.

Verbal charms are often hard to define, but if I could try, I'd posit them as short recitations, poems, or even verses from the Bible that are memorized, kept secret (relatively), and used on their own as part of a healing or magical act. Someone who uses these verbal charms as the principle method of working is then called a *charmer*. Verbal charms can be just a small part of a more elaborate ritual, but in this work, we're going to be looking at charming as a path of its very own.

Charming is often viewed as a fast-acting magical method, when compared to the much lengthier and more complicated rituals and diagnosis processes that many healers choose to utilize. The charmers and granny women who I count as my teachers often pushed aside magical timing in favor of observing *tokens*, or omens, in the world around them. For those unfamiliar with the practice, magical timing refers to formulating rituals based upon the cycles of celestial bodies, specifically the moon phases, zodiac moon days, and days of the week (planetary signs). This astrological tradition often yields very specific, but very complicated, magical rituals—the idea being that by connecting with the innate flow of magic by way of nature's cycles, your magic will be more effective.

It's not that charmers have disagreed with this concept. Some that I've met do, in fact, work with magical timings. Generally speaking, though, charmers have traditionally been in the role of providing "quick magic." For example, someone cuts their hand while working out in the field and the nearest doctor is hours away. What can they do? Well, this is when the role of the charmer becomes vitally important. Blood stoppers in particular were individuals who held charms that could stop a bleeding wound. They would be called in at times like this to help save people. Sometimes their work provided exactly the care needed in the moment or until more extensive medical care could be found.

The work of the charmer is often reactionary, as in the case of Gram Watson in the story that introduced this book. A clawing sound was heard on the rooftop and Gram reacted with a charm and simple ritual. These magical reactions and countercharms often fall under the traditional Ozark phrase of "taking the cuss," or curse, off a situation. There are many of these countermeasures in the Ozarks because in the old days, hillfolk had a lot of tokens that they watched out for. Today, when someone hears an owl hoot, they might think it's a pleasant sound. In the old days, however, when an Ozarker heard an owl, it meant some evil was outside their house, trying to get inside to cause mischief or harm. The countercharm for hearing an owl hoot is to throw a pinch of salt into a fire, usually in the fireplace or on the stove. Of course, charmers know many verbal charms that can act as counters to these ill omens as well.

Many of the old taboos and tokens have died out, like so many Ozark folk traditions. Charming, however, still remains a reactionary art for the most part, as well as being quite simple in its methods. There is rarely any sort of lengthy ritual that accompanies a verbal charm; the charmer might simply make three crosses with their thumb over a wound, in the case of a healing charm, or blow a stream of tobacco smoke out of their mouth, in the case of several specific protection and countering charms. But make no mistake: the charming tradition might not involve a lot of ritual, but it is still considered a vital part of traditional healing and folk magic.

WOMEN OF POWER

Traditionally in the Ozarks, women have primarily held the position of charmer. In many cases, these highly important community healers were called *granny women*. Terms of affection and respect like *Gram*, *Gran*, or *Granny* were given to these women despite their age and whether or not they actually had grandchildren of their own. I once met a twenty-eight-year-old midwife who many of the old-timers in her community affectionately called Gram. As members of the community, granny women were considered vital healers and midwives, especially in the old Ozarks where it was once considered taboo for male folk healers to work with "women's issues." The granny woman was then the only one who could heal the women of their communities until country doctors and pharmacists became more common in the region.

Amongst both the generalist and specialist healers in the Ozark tradition, granny women stood out as having training in all areas. At times the term *granny woman* was synonymous with the role of the midwife, but these figures were so much more than that. Granny women often took on the role of Yarb Doctor, or traditional herbalist (*yarb* being Ozark-speak for a medicinal plant). Granny women also often filled the role of Power Doctor, generalist healers who worked with ritual methods, divination, and amulet making as opposed to physical medicines. Granny women also served as skilled charmers who held prayers and recitations for all manner of ills that might afflict a person. In the old Ozarks, there wasn't a more well-rounded magical practitioner in the community than the granny woman. This situation has changed over the years. Nowadays, you are likely to find many generalists amongst the Neotraditionalist practitioners. Neotraditionalists are individuals who still have some connection to Ozark folk magic but who break from the older traditions in many areas, and who incorporate other systems of magic that would have been unknown in the Ozarks until after the 1950s.

Unfortunately, granny women were often the first people in the community to be targeted as witches. In the old days, there was a very fine line between a healer who used their God-given power to do good in the community and the figure of the witch, who was seen as someone who either stole their power or inherited it through a bond with the devil. Often this line was based solely off how the community viewed the healer's work; one bad review from someone important could label a practitioner as a witch. Being a witch in the old Ozarks meant exile from the society that was vital for the survival of the individual and their family. For this reason, healers, granny women, and other magical folk kept their practices secret and often bolstered themselves with piety. Local preachers, ministers, and *praying grannies* often doubled as healers and charmers because they were already seen as being closer to a divine source of healing and power. It's an unfortunate fact that granny women were sometimes the first ones to point the finger at others in the community for practicing the dark arts. This was often the only way someone could keep fingers from pointing at their own work.

Although the name has fallen out of use, the role of the granny woman as a magical and spiritual pillar of the Ozark community remains even today. As charmers, their work has shaped the tradition in countless ways. Of the fourteen individuals I consider to be my own mentors and teachers of this charming path, ten are women. This isn't to say that this work has any gender limitations in the modern world; I myself am nonbinary and have met many other Neotraditionalist practitioners across the gender spectrum. But the stories of healers in general (and women healers, specifically) have a history of going untold here in the mountains. In honoring the ancestors of this path, we can't forget that, by-and-large, it's been women who have healed the Ozark community, and women who have been the first persecuted within the Ozark community.

SIMPLE MAGIC

Ozarkers have famously been averse to anything overly complicated. This has historically fueled many stereotypes about the laziness of hillfolk, who were often recorded by tourists and folklorists alike sitting outside on the porches of their mountain cabins doing absolutely nothing. Outward appearances are often deceptive. It's not that Ozarkers have been do-nothings or lazy; it's just that maybe we know how to sit back and enjoy the present moment a little better than others. This outlook on the world has greatly influenced our traditions of healing and folk magic. In Ozark cosmology, all of nature is permeated by a stream of neutral, innate magic. More traditional folks never use the term *magic*, choosing instead to refer to this flow as *that-of-God* in all things. This flow includes human beings, who aren't traditionally separated from nature like some will try and tell you. This puts an entirely different spin on the old phrase "Go with the flow." For Ozark healers and magical practitioners, going with the flow of nature's magic is exactly how one should work. As I was taught, the best way to get down a river is to just fall back and let the current carry you. For healers that work in a Christian context, this often goes by the phrase of *working in the Spirit* or *working Spirit-led*. The *Spirit* here refers to the Christian concept of the Holy Spirit, a figure that is commonly credited by these more traditional healers as the very source of their gift.

Going with the flow means connecting to your own inborn power, imagination, inspiration, and intention above reliance on external rituals, tools, and ingredients. As I was taught, all the external work is just icing on the cake, to use a familiar phrase. Or, in the context of going with the flow, sometimes we need to get down the river quicker or maybe even run against the current. In this case, we can build ourselves a boat, which is using external tools, ingredients, and rituals as aids. Charmers have traditionally viewed this state of going with the flow as being of supreme importance to any act of magic. At its heart, the charming path means fostering a whole lot of faith in your own innate gifts as well as developing a clever mind that can work through all sorts of issues in a flash. Like I said earlier, charming is almost always reactionary, meaning that having eyes, ears, and intuition that are keenly fixed on all things in the world around you is seen as a great gift in and of itself.

In the old countries, many traditional healers were given names like *cunning folk* or *wise folk*.[2] In Denmark, they are called *kloge folk*.[3] In Finland, they are called *Tietäjä* or *knower*.[4] Even in the Ozarks, healers are still often referred to as people who "know things," hinting at the ability of the healer

---

2. Davies, *Cunning-Folk*, 163.

3. Davies, *Cunning-Folk*, 163.

4. Stark, *The Magical Self*, 43.

or magical practitioner to be able to work through problems in ways other people in the community can't. This cunningness is distinctly separate from what can be learned and is almost always considered a natural ability or connection that springs up when the individual is ready to embrace their inborn gift. As one of my teachers told me, "There's knowing and then there's *knowing*," making a firm distinction between the cunningness of the healer and perhaps the knowledge obtained by a medical professional or academic.

Charmers of old used to rely on their cunningness for almost everything in their practice. Rather than relying upon methods of divination, set ritual formulations, or even magical timings provided by the almanac, charmers often went inside themselves to find vital information or tokens surrounding a situation. For this reason, charmers are often said to naturally possess the "second sight." Because of this, many charmers also have the ability to see into the otherworld of ghosts and fairies.

WORKING SPIRIT-LED

When I was growing up, I loved a good spell book. I had several that I kept hidden away from my parents who, at that time, would have fiercely disapproved. I loved the formulas, the mixing and matching when it came to all the symbolic ingredients. I loved assembling my favorite bowls and wooden spoons, bringing them together on the kitchen counter like I was baking a cake. I still have a deep love for ritualistic spell work, and I still try and calculate the perfect auspicious timing for my more complicated work. But I also remember well the first time I met an Ozark charmer and the profound effect it had upon my work.

She was my first teacher and the one who identified the gift inside of me. I met her by real happenstance while chatting with another informant of mine in a rural café. As we finished up our coffee, an old woman whom I didn't recognize walked confidently up to our table. She was dressed in denim overalls and a flannel shirt. Her thin, gray hair was braided in two ropes that were tied and pinned across the top of her head in the popular Ozark "old German style," as one informant told me. I looked up at the woman and smiled. She smiled back and without any greeting or introduction said, "We need to talk."

I took this as a token from the universe that I shouldn't ignore. So, I agreed to meet her at her house later that day. While I brought out my notebook and pens, she flitted around her kitchen gathering provisions we might need for our talk. She heated up a percolator for coffee on the stove, cut some freshly baked banana bread, and poured some peanuts into a wooden bowl at the center of her dining table. Ozarkers often take hospitality as serious business. As one old belief goes, a stranger can be an angel in disguise. When we finally got to talking, she said that the Spirit had told her to be in that café at that moment, and that if she'd ignored it, we never would have met. I'd heard this phrase that she used many times before, but usually while talking to religious folks; "the Spirit" is commonly a reference to the Christian Holy Spirit.

After this, we talked about everything she knew, from plant remedies to a few old folktales and even a song or two. She immediately felt comfortable with me, which can be unusual with Ozark old-timers, who are often suspicious of outsiders. The Spirit always leads in a trusted direction, however; on more than one occasion, I've had informants open up to me because they "prayed on it" and the Holy Spirit told them I was a good person.

Soon we got onto the subject of magic-based healing practices, which she referred to as "trying" for someone, a term common amongst Ozark practitioners of German heritage. I asked her how she worked and what actions she used as a part of her healing process. I avoid the term *ritual*, as it often makes old-timers uncomfortable because of the connotations between ritual work and witchcraft. She just laughed and responded with her own question: "What actions *should* I be usin'?"

I responded that I didn't really know and that I figured it was completely up to her how she "tried" for people.

"So there's somethin' inside me that tells me how to try for people?" she asked with a grin. "I reckon it's the Spirit that leads me."

I finally recognized that she was attempting to break down all my preconceived notions about how people with the gift *should* be working. I automatically assumed she used some kind of ritual as part of her work, which is why I asked such a leading question to begin with. She immediately saw through this and returned with her own question, making me reconsider everything I'd planned on asking her previously. "All right then," I answered, returning her smile, "Why don't you tell me how you try for people?"

She nodded, proud that I had picked up on my original mistake so quickly, and then went on to explain her process. This was my first encounter with the deep and powerful simplicity at the heart of the charming path. It was also my introduction to the inborn leading or guidance that comes from within the charmer themselves. I refer to this as a person's cunningness, inspiration, or intuition. For others, this is the Spirit, Holy Spirit, or, in many cases, a spiritual entity of a different sort. I'm referring specifically to the tradition of charmers receiving their gift from the Little People, angels, or spirits of the dead.

In that moment, I knew I had to dig deeper with this stranger. Little did I know what sort of poetic inspiration and magic she would stoke inside me through our interactions.

POETIC POWER

Oral folk cultures traditionally hold the power of spoken word in the highest esteem. Today we often forget that our Ozark ancestors would have lived in an oral culture as well. Even to this day, many aspects of our folk culture are still passed down orally rather than through the written word. I've even met famed mountain cooks and bakers who prefer passing down recipes through word of mouth and observation, believing the resulting food tastes better than if it came from a written recipe.

The belief in the inherent power of words by no means popped up in the Ozarks of its own accord. This connection to imagination and inspiration has roots back into ancient days, especially the Gaelic cultures from Scotland, Ireland, Wales, Cornwall, and Brittany, which have had such an important influence upon Ozark folk practices. Across the Gaelic world, bards (called *Filí* in Ireland and Scotland) were often considered magicians who used their words to spin the raw, innate magic of the world like wool being spun into yarn. Praise and its opposite, satire, were once powerful tools of the poets for bestowing both blessings and curses.[5] This power, of course, didn't just stay in the past, but found its path to the Ozarks through folk cultures and

5. Breatnach, "Satire, Praise, and the Early Irish Poet," 63–84.

family traditions, where charmers and our very own poet-musicians have been continuing the work of the ancient bards well into the modern age.

Keeping in this storytelling tradition, I'd like to share a tale as an example. After our first meeting in that little café, I continued visiting the old charmer (whom we'll call Pauline) for more lessons about the tradition. She introduced topics by first saying that her teachings were "Spirit-led" and that other people might do things differently. I took this to heart, recognizing the deep truth that Ozark traditions are intimately connected to individuals, families, and small lineage groups.

One morning, I accompanied Pauline to the grocery store. While inside, we bumped into a smartly dressed older woman with dyed red hair that was permed into a mound of tight curls on top of her head. My own intuition immediately told me this was a local church gossip. She made a path toward us as soon as she spotted Pauline and wedged her shopping buggy in front of ours, blocking our exit. "Why, good morning! It's been so long since we seen you up at the church," the woman cackled at us with a fake, saccharine-sweet smile. "I was about to send someone out your way to make sure you were still alive!"

Pauline remained calm while the woman got out all the local news she figured Pauline hadn't heard living up on the mountain. "I just want you to know," the woman said, lowering her voice, "that you're always in my prayers."

"Why thank you, Kitty," Pauline answered with a smile. "You're in my prayers too."

The woman was clearly taken aback. "Well, with a good life like mine, I think your prayers would be better suited for yourself, or maybe that alcoholic cousin of yours?"

I thought for sure that Pauline was going to up and slap the woman across her painted face, but she didn't. She just calmly nodded. "Yes, my prayers can cover a lot of different folks, Kitty. And I have a special one for you, right now. Would you pray with me, Kitty?"

The woman couldn't resist being seen in public praying with someone. So, Kitty reached out and took the old woman's callused hands into her own, closing her eyes. "Dear Lord," Pauline started, "I pray your Holy Spirit would rise up in me and give me the strength to speak your words. To speak these words down upon your child, Kitty. Let them flow over her like a sweet-smelling water, like a balm of fine herbs. May Kitty see this power in her own life. May Kitty's insides be twisted up in curls, like her God-forsaken red hair. May Kitty's words stick in her mouth, like her rotten peanut butter pie. May Kitty walk forever away from me now, like her no-good husband walked away from her two years ago. Amen."

Miss Kitty stood in silent shock for a moment before turning and walking away from us without another word. Pauline nodded to me. "Hand me a can of them tomatoes," she said, pointing to a shelf out of her reach.

I occasionally asked my teacher about Kitty, and Pauline always said that after the incident at the grocery store, she never had to deal with Kitty or any of her cronies again.

When a charmer is going with the flow, there isn't a moment of their lives that isn't imbued with nature's magic or this sense of the Divine. A charmer's real power comes from their ability to draw from that wellspring deep inside themselves and fish out powerful words that can then be birthed into the world in the moment, just like how Pauline was able to birth her blessing-curse in the moment, without any need for external tools, ingredients, or ritual.

Pauline was the teacher who gave me my most important lesson. One day we were talking about rituals and tools, and she stopped me and said, "A healer should be able to do everything they need to do in a completely empty jail cell." This has stuck with me ever since, and I think it illustrates the power of the charmer perfectly.

TRY IT OUT: CONNECTING TO YOUR INNER CUNNING

Because what I teach is a practical magic, let's look at a method for getting in touch with your inner inspiration and cunning. I'd like you to read through the following section a few times before replicating the steps.

Take yourself to a quiet location. This can be anywhere you are most comfortable. Maybe it's your bedroom, or some secluded corner of the library, or even outside in nature. Absolute silence and stillness aren't required, unless these things help you still your mind. In general, just seek out a spot that is least distracting for you.

Next, close your eyes and let your mind wander. Don't worry about the thoughts; whether they are good or bad, just let them come and go naturally. Stay in the center of the whirlpool, however uncomfortable the stillness might be. Charmers are never afraid of the darkness but instead choose to harness the chaos around them to form new and beautiful creations. The cunning path makes use of all things, no matter their origin. We are recyclers of the world's energies. Swirl with the swirling thoughts, deeper and deeper, until the cascading rapids naturally smooth out. Until the swiftly flowing river becomes a gentle brook. This flow is the current of your magic.

Remember how this moment feels both inside and outside your body. Remember how it feels to recline back into this lazy current and let it carry you. Thoughts rise to the surface, then fall back down below. You can use this meditation to help recharge your energetic batteries anytime you're feeling low. For many charmers, this is the very heart of all inspiration and cunning. In returning to this state, one can even fish out charms from this flow and speak them into existence.

Try it out yourself. Let your mind naturally find that point of complete equilibrium. Float along with this calm current, not focusing or worrying about the thoughts that rise up. The thoughts themselves *are* the stream, just like you are. Then, when you're ready, reach into the stream and see what you can pull out. Maybe it's a song, poem, charm, image, vision, or prophecy. Maybe it's all of those things all at the same time. Try not to label, explain, or examine what you pull out—just let it be. If it's a song, sing whether you're good at it or not. If it's a charm, speak it into existence. Birth it into the world around you without judgment. If the dreamlike images seem confusing, don't fret. Write them or draw them to help yourself remember. Not all visions are meaningful, but they're all a part of the process. Sometimes an image that pops up one day will be explained when the time is right, like a wildflower seed lying dormant underground until the conditions are perfect for it to finally grow.

When you're finished with your meditation, come back into your physical body gently, then open your eyes. Take this method as a training exercise. You might not see results immediately, but the more you sit with your own mind, the easier it will get, trust me. Charmers often say they float in this gentle current all the time, even while going about their day-to-day lives. This comes with practice, although no doubt some of you will pick it up quickly. Once you've gotten the hang of the eyes-closed meditation, try going with the flow while out and about in the world.

For daily life, think about your thoughts outside the meditation in the same way you think about them on the *inside*. Let your thoughts rise and fall naturally, without grasping for the good ones or pushing away the bad ones. Let them all swirl into that river of magical inspiration inside of you. When you're able to do this, you'll realize that the thoughts are the river. Your mind is the river. What makes you *you*—your *youness*—is the river as well. Then your river flows into your neighbor's river, your mother's, father's, sister's, brother's, best friend's, and even your enemy's river too. You will begin to see that it's all the same river. Then you will see that all minds and everything else across time and space are the river as well. And in the end, there is only the river.

MAKING THE PATH YOUR OWN

Traditionally, the Charming Way is a solitary path until the practitioner reaches the point where they'd like to pass down some of their methods and words to another; this doesn't have to happen, however. Charmers often work for their own needs as well as for the needs of the community around them; this, too, is optional. I've met many gifted individuals who only work on themselves, or those who limit their practice to helping out friends and family alone. You get to choose how you work and who you work for.

Many of the charming rituals in this book are focused on a solitary practice but can be adapted to one additional person or even group usage. When charming for another, I recommend reciting the verbal charm silently— meaning moving your lips and tongue with the words but not actually producing sound—or reciting it quietly into the palm of your right hand. Both of these are traditional measures for maintaining the secrecy of your verbal charms. This is a good practice, even though the charms contained within this book aren't considered of the secret variety. I especially recommend keeping some level of secrecy when you are working with your own spirit-led charms.

We're living in a time where everything we do is expected to be highly curated and displayed for the entire world to view. This has become a growing

trend in the magical community and while I fully support practitioners practicing as they want to practice, I do know from personal experience that this
constant curating process can lead to serious magical and spiritual burnout. As
a remedy to those experiencing this, I recommend a simple ritual: *keep something secret for yourself*. Not everything we do has to be turned into consumable
media—sometimes we can keep things just for ourselves. Verbal charms are
a great way to connect to this remedy. Maybe this involves keeping a written
journal, black book, Book of Shadows, grimoire, practice book—whatever
you want to call it—but keeping it secret, just for yourself and your work.
Some rituals might be great candidates for curating and displaying through
social media, but keep other rituals to yourself, just for you to look at and use.
You might be surprised by how therapeutic this simple remedy can be. It strips
away all need for curating—the magic flows as it needs to flow, in whatever
form it wants to take, without judgment or criticism.

As you continue to engage with this charming path, you will no doubt
want to incorporate aspects from your own practice, religious or cultural
traditions, etc. Several of the verbal charms in this book have a Christian
basis. This is very common in the Ozarks, as charms were created and passed
through a culture that had a Protestant Christian foundation. Many invoke
biblical figures as part of the charm story, like the charms that name the disciples of Jesus. Others use Christian cultural imagery; for example, charms
that invoke the power of angels or saints. Remember that, traditionally, the
term *angel* has been used in the Ozarks to include many different types of
spirits, including fairies.

My take on religious imagery in verbal charms is a very nontraditional
one. The basis of charming magic is the charmer's own intention, inspiration, and cunning. For this reason, the words of the verbal charm are simply
there to aid the charmer in focusing this power. Or, to use an image used
earlier in this chapter: the magical power is the raw wool, the verbal charm
is the spinning wheel, and the cunning is the motion created by the charmer
to take the wool from chaos to an orderly length of yarn. I tell my charming
students that where their own words would work better, use them. You are
welcome to substitute the Christian characters used in the verbal charm with
deities, saints, or other figures from your own path. This is easier with certain charms than with others. For example, the "Easter Blessing" in chapter
2, which specifically links the death and resurrection of Jesus to the rebirth

of the land in springtime. But, with your cunningness, I have no doubt you'll be able to figure out an alternative if needed.

My approach to verbal charms has been criticized by both outsiders and Ozarkers alike. Some say that changing the words of the charm destroys the power contained within the words. To that I usually respond with a question: "How do you know these words were the words the first charmer used?" Of course we can't know that for sure. Passing down verbal charms is often like the telephone game—what you end up with after hundreds of years of passing is sometimes very different to what was first created. This is especially true when we look at verbal charms that are being passed across different languages and even different religions. Verbal charms have power because we as charmers *give* them power. Making this path your own will allow you to connect to your inborn power in a deeper way than trying to squeeze yourself into a specific box.

EMPOWERING YOUR WORK

Oftentimes a charmer's power manifests through spontaneity, as with Pauline, who was able to craft that beautiful blessing-curse. Her inspiration took the latent, chaotic power inside her and made it manifest into something with a real presence. As it was taught to me, a charmer can take this in-the-moment, raw magic of nature and turn it into something focused, relevant, and with form.

While the Charming Way is by-and-large a path of reactionary magic, many traditional verbal charms are aligned with very specific sets of circumstances. For example, throwing a pinch of salt in an open flame while reciting "Owl, go!" three times as a way of countering the cuss (or curse) associated with hearing an owl hoot. Or charming for prosperity by reciting "Money by the end of the week" whenever you see a redbird (cardinal) land on a branch. It's believed that if you can recite the phrase three times before the bird flies away, the wish will come true. Verbal charms used in divination tend to have specific circumstances required for the spell to work properly, as with love divinations that require the charmer to go outside and gaze at the full moon while reciting a specific verbal charm, or the love ritual in chapter 5 that requires reciting a specific verbal charm only when you hear a dove cooing while also looking at the full moon. In cases such as these, the verbal charms are naturally empowered by the specific circumstances that are fulfilled as part of the ritual process.

We can empower our work in other ways too. The most common method in traditional Ozark folk magic is working within the celestial cycles. This means utilizing the latent power contained in the moon's phases, planetary signs by way of the days of the week, or the zodiac moon signs. All of this information can still be found in most farmer's almanacs. (For many traditional Ozarkers, the almanac has been considered as important as the Bible at times.) That said, magical timings are just suggestions. Again, at its core, the charming path is about connecting to the latent power inside oneself by way of spontaneous magic. But, like I said earlier on, if we want to go downriver quicker, or work against nature's current, we can build ourselves a boat using ritual and auspicious magical timings. Timing suggestions are listed for each of the charm entries in this book.

Formulating the specific timing for a spell can become very complicated very quickly. I recommend working with simpler timings, like days of the week, times of day, and lunar phases—especially for beginners.

Day of the Week	Planet	Associations
Sunday	Sun	Wealth; prosperity; protection
Monday	Moon	Dreaming; divination; emotions; astral travel; subconscious
Tuesday	Mars	Wrath; vengeance; physical energy; strength; will; drive; vitality; competition
Wednesday	Mercury	Healing; communication; connection to others; trickery; deception; illusion
Thursday	Jupiter	Politics; law; faith; optimism; opportunity; knowledge; enlargement; expansion
Friday	Venus	Love; healing/forming relationships; harmony; physical pleasures
Saturday	Saturn	Relationship to authority; organization; self-discipline; boundaries; limitations; restrictions

Time	Associations	Example Work
Dawn	Veil thin with otherworld; peace; tranquility; healing; purification; rebirth	Washing away a curse in a river or burying an illness at a crossroad
Daytime	Time of humankind; day-to-day life; work for illumination	Regular healing/magical work
Dusk	Veil thin with otherworld; diagnosis; introspection; letting go and breaking bonds	Releasing a painful memory into a river or letting a spirit fade into the otherworld
Nighttime	Divination; mysteries; trance; diagnosis; finding answers; calling for aid from the spirit world	Trance journeying to find the source of illness with a client or petitioning the otherworld for aid in work

Lunar Phase	Associations	Example Work
New Moon	New directions; severing or breaking bonds	Removing malign magic; cutting bonds and contracts; severing ties with an enemy
Waxing	Building; increasing; growing	Bringing in new business; looking for love; drawing luck and money to the home; bringing in health after illness
Full Moon	Strength; increasing; growing; protecting	Protection; divination for the diagnosis of an illness
Waning	Decreasing; lessening; removing	Healing illness; healing warts; decreasing power of another

Zodiac House	Zodiac Sign	Planet	Element	Day of the Week	Almanac Association	Area in the Body
1	Aries	Mars	Fire	Tuesday	Head	Eyes; nose; blood pressure; teeth
2	Taurus	Venus	Earth	Friday	Neck	Throat; shoulders; ears; glands
3	Gemini	Mercury	Air	Wednesday	Arms	Shoulders; lungs; nerves; arms; fingers
4	Cancer	Moon	Water	Monday	Breast	Chest; breasts; sides; organs; bile
5	Leo	Sun	Fire	Sunday	Heart	Stomach; spine; upper back; spleen
6	Virgo	Mercury	Earth	Wednesday	Belly/Bowels	Intestines; gallbladder; pancreas; liver
7	Libra	Venus	Air	Friday	Reins	Buttocks; lower back; kidneys
8	Scorpio	Mars	Water	Tuesday	"Secrets"	External/internal genitalia; pelvis; bladder; rectum; ovaries; womb
9	Sagittarius	Jupiter	Fire	Thursday	Thighs	Legs; hips; groin
10	Capricorn	Saturn	Earth	Saturday	Knees	Shins; bones; sinew; nerves
11	Aquarius	Saturn	Air	Saturday	Legs	Ankles; calves; lower blood vessels
12	Pisces	Jupiter	Water	Thursday	Feet	Toes; soles

The zodiac moon days are a bit more complicated to work with. In short, the year is divided first into the twelve zodiac sun signs—when the sun passes through each of the twelve zodiac signs throughout the year. There are also smaller cycles of the twelve zodiac signs, when the moon passes through each of the signs, called the *zodiac moon days*. The moon changes signs every two to three days. Generally speaking, Ozarkers work with the zodiac moon days much more often than the sun days. The moon days are traditionally printed in the farmer's almanac and are used for agricultural purposes as well as household work, healing, and magic. More information about healing with the zodiac moon signs can be found in chapter 4.

Having a working knowledge of the associations for each of the twelve zodiac signs as well as a good almanac on hand will work wonders when it comes to formulating magical timings. With enough practice, it will no doubt become second nature.

CHARM ENTRY STRUCTURE

Each of the chapters in this book are oriented toward a certain category of magical charms, using the blessing charm found in the introduction.

All of the charms in this book have the same basic structure for ease of use. Each charm begins with the specific uses for the charm and its ritual. In some cases, there may be more than one common usage for a charm. After this, information on suggested magical timing is listed. This can include both celestial timing as well as any specific conditions that must be met in order to use the verbal charm and accompanying ritual. Next, the entry lists the specific verbal charm that is to be used, followed by a section listing any ingredients to be used alongside the accompanying ritual. Sometimes specific ingredients to enhance the charm's effectiveness are provided. The suggested ritual procedure is listed after the ingredients.

Ozark verbal charms rarely use any complex or lengthy rituals, but they often do include actions to perform while reciting the charm. Sometimes these actions are simple; for example, reciting the charm a certain number of times (traditionally three, seven, or twelve times, which are all considered sacred numbers in the Ozarks), or reciting the charm while facing a certain direction. Ritual actions might utilize the body with certain hand gestures or motions, often called *passes*. For example, with many healing charms, the practitioner will have their patient face them. Then they will place their two hands on either side of the patient's head, with their palms facing the patient's ears. While reciting the verbal charm, the healer will move their hands in a downward motion from head to foot, usually a few inches away from the skin. This downward motion is made each time the verbal charm is repeated. Another common ritual action includes the breath of the healer, believed to be able to carry the verbal charm directly to their client. A common charm for burns uses this ritual action. After each recitation of the specific verbal charm, the healer will blow across the burn three times. Ritual actions, like magical timing, are meant to enhance—not hinder—your practice; where they can't be utilized effectively, it's perfectly all right to do without them.

The last section of each charm entry highlights any additional notes, factual and folkloric information, or variations on the ritual actions that can be incorporated into the spell. Within the notes section, you will be able to learn a little more about the symbolism behind the images in the charms, many of which are quite complex. Learning more about the significance of these symbols will help you develop charms of your very own. For example, healing charms often use the symbol of the dawn or sunrise; this connects to the idea of renewal, rebirth, newness, etc., which is exactly what a healer might want to invoke as a part of a charming ritual aimed at removing illnesses or hexes.

CHAPTER 2

To Bless You
through the Holy Year ...

Long before folks called her Granny Thornapple, Little Ann was a near-perfect child. Lucy was unable to have any other children, a fact that the local gossips often stoked into fanciful stories. For instance, one that followed Ann and her mother throughout their lives was that Gram Watson had cursed the poor woman's womb the night Little Ann was born. "That's what happens when you have a witch as a midwife!" the gossips would whisper to each other.

But Lucy and Ann just laughed at the silliness of their stories, and Lucy secretly thought to herself that if they'd been present for the real event, they sure would have had a story to tell about witchcraft.

Ann grew wild and tall like pokeweed, as the old-timers in Nelson's Holler liked reminding her of every Sunday at church, or when she had to pick up something from the grocery store. She had coal-black hair, not like her mother, but like her grandmother and namesake, Ann Ganter. She had a little birthmark on her left elbow, supposedly also just like her granny, but she could never get her mother to confirm this as a fact. Lucy was hesitant to confirm any tokens that might set her daughter apart from the rest of the community, and with good reason. She'd grown up watching how people treated other "gifted" individuals like her own mother and Gram Watson. She remembered something her mother always liked to tell her: "Folks in town will run to you for a cure on Saturday and curse your name as a witch on Sunday."

Lucy took this warning to heart and vowed if she ever had the power herself, or if any of her children did, that she'd fight tooth and nail for them against any lying gossips. But this magic often skips generations, as the old-timers once knew, and Lucy grew up as a normal member of the community. It wasn't until Little Ann *started showing more and more tokens of being born different from others that Lucy remembered her late mother's words again.*

Ann cared not about anyone's opinion, save for her mother's and perhaps Gram Watson, whom she liked to visit on Sunday afternoons after church. Gram's cabin was out on the edge of town, down a long and twisting dirt road on the mountainside. It was a good hike from where Ann lived, but she didn't mind. She liked picking wildflowers along the way in the springtime, and blackberries in the summer. She liked cooling her feet in Nelson's Creek, which crossed Gram's property, and watching rabbits go in and out of their burrows over in the old Watson family graveyard. Gram certainly liked the young lady's visits, as she hardly ever saw anyone who didn't want something from her. Every Sunday, she'd bake biscuits or orange rolls for Ann's visits and brew up a pot of herbal tea made from wild plants she gathered on the mountain.

Ann loved Gram's kitchen, which was crammed full of all sorts of interesting things. There were bundles of fragrant herbs drying in the rafters and bees buzzing around vases of fresh flowers set on Gram's little dining table. In the wintertime, the kitchen was the warmest spot in the cabin. Gram would always have a pomander made from orange peel and clove buds simmering on the stove to sweeten the cold air. Ann would sit listening to Gram's stories for hours on end until the sun began to set, and Gram would shuffle her out of the cabin and back on the trail. "Don't tarry, child, but go straight home!" she'd say.

And Ann would listen, for the most part. In the summertime, when the days were longer, she'd linger down by the creek or recline back into the meadow and watch clouds pass up in the sky. On full moon nights, she'd stalk through the woods and watch deer, rabbits, groundhogs, and sometimes even a wild pig forage for food in the underbrush. Once, she swore she saw Gram Watson out on one of these nights, but when she got closer to investigate, all she spied was a big coyote splashing through the creek on its way up the mountain.

From the time Ann was first able to hike out to Gram Watson's house on her own, the old woman would occasionally ask if she was still wearing the little chunk of wood around her neck. Ann would nod and pull out the string to show her. Nothing more was ever said about the amulet until Ann's twelfth birthday, which fell on a Sunday. Ann only had a little time to spend with Gram before her folks were expecting her back home for a big celebratory dinner. Gram put aside all the small talk and got straight down to business. "I reckon it's time you learned about that piece of wood you're wearing," she said, pouring the girl a cup of herbal tea. "What all has your mother said to you about it?"

"Nothin' at all, hardly," Ann answered, shaking her head. "Just that it was somethin' to remember my birth by is all. I just figured it was some special wood or somethin' like that. Just an old superstition maybe."

"There's nothin' superstitious about that amulet," Gram answered, frustrated by Lucy's hesitation to share anything "odd" with her own child. "You're special, Ann. By that I mean you're different from other folks in Nelson's Holler."

"Different how?"

"Well, you're more like how your granny was, or how I am. You've got the gift in you, and it's high time you started using it."

"I've heard some awful things in town about Granny and you, but I never believed them."

"Learn this lesson well, Ann. People will always come a-runnin' to you for help on Saturday and call you a dirty witch on Sunday."

A chill ran up Ann's spine at the old woman's words. She'd heard them only once before, from her mother, when she was a little child. It was an awakened memory, and she figured to herself that if Gram Watson was repeating something her own mother had said, it must be something important.

"But that's a part of all of this," Gram continued, taking Ann's hands into her own. "It's a burden to bear, yes, but it's also a power to behold. You will do great things for people, Little Ann."

Ann wasn't sure she was ready for such great and terrible magic to be a part of her life. She had other plans in mind—college, a family, a house of her own even—and helping the people of Nelson's Holler didn't figure into those plans. But something inside of her reached back toward the day she was born. Something burned like a smoldering ember in her heart every time she held that little chunk of charred and shellacked wood that hung around her neck. She knew that if she wanted answers, she'd have to follow Gram Watson's lead and set aside any fear or apprehension she might have about the hidden things that stalk in the woods at night or about the secret power growing within herself.

Ann nodded silently and Gram began her tale. "My child, you were born on May Day, just after midnight, during the biggest storm Nelson's Holler had seen in years. At the very moment of your birth, of which I know plenty because these hands pulled you from your mother's belly, your granny, Ann Ganter, left this world ..."

THE CHARMS OF EVERYDAY LIFE

Because of their reactionary nature, verbal charms are often employed to address anything that the charmer might come across in their day-to-day lives. This includes work geared toward daily routines, like charming while cooking or washing the dishes, as well as yearly blessings on holidays and during shifting seasons. Charming was once intimately linked to the flow of life itself. Magic was seen as being inseparable from the very cycles that form the framework of our lives. From dawn to dusk, from springtime to winter and back again, verbal charms and prayers were a way for folks to remain connected to this flow of magic in nature as well as inside the home. We can revive this spirit in our lives today.

Looking through the collections of Ozark folklorists like Vance Randolph and Mary Celestia Parler, we see many examples of what we might today call "charms of everyday life." These are, by-and-large, reactionary verbal charms and prayers that address all of the tasks and occurrences that perhaps we modern folk tend to overlook. Pauline used to tell me, "Don't wait to work. Work with whatever you've got on hand." This traditional mindset is sometimes lost on us modern practitioners, as we tend to plan our practices more than work in the moment. At least, this is what I've found within my own work.

The charms of everyday life often ritualize tasks and processes that aren't normally ritualized. This is deeply connected to the Ozark idea of repurposing the stuff of our lives for magic and healing. For example, naming dirty dishes for those in our lives who might need healing, then washing them clean. Or saying a simple prayer over a meal, that as we are fed, so too will all the visible and invisible beings around us be nourished. Or reciting a blessing over a pot of soup that will be given to someone who is sick. The power of these charms is in the cunningness of the charmer. This cunningness is to see every moment of our lives, no matter how mundane, as symbolically rich and able to be utilized as a magical act.

WORKING WITHIN THE CYCLES OF NATURE

Our daily lives and routines all fit into bigger and bigger cycles that spiral out into the universe around us. Our Ozark ancestors would have had a much deeper connection to nature and the cycles of the year than we do today, as having this bond meant survival for the family and community. Verbal charms were used to address all needs on the homestead, including preparing the land in the springtime, planting seeds, praying for rain, praying for rain to go away, harvest blessings and prayers, as well as words to offer when enjoying the bounties of the land. Traditionally, Ozark hillfolk would have only ever had seasonal or holiday celebrations when there was plenty of food to offer; these celebrations weren't frivolous affairs, but ways for hardworking families to give thanks for what the land had provided them. While today we often don't share the same concerns as our ancestors, verbal charms can be used to connect to the wellsprings of latent power that open up during these auspicious cycles, thereby heightening the power of the spell.

One example of this is May Day, which has long been held as an auspicious time of the year. Children born on May Day (like Granny Thornapple) are said to naturally possess many magical powers. Ozarkers of the past often celebrated May Day in very similar ways to their European ancestors, but today the holiday has fallen by the wayside except for healers and magical practitioners. For these folks, May Day is a time to pick magical and medicinal herbs from the fields, forests, and gardens. The power of these plants is especially potent when you pick them at dawn. Harvesting charms were once very common, but I was only gifted a few examples by my own teachers. These charms help to weave the latent magic springing up from within the plants of the field into amulets and other useful manifestations. It's said that the plants you gather and charm at this time are extra potent and should be used in cases of dire need. You can also do what many of our old-timers used to do and braid them into herbal bundles, which can then be hung inside the home for protection against all evil and sickness.

Aside from the seasons, there are celestial cycles that Ozarkers have traditionally utilized in order to empower their work. Determining the most auspicious time to heal or enact some ritual activity relies on matching the correspondences of our work to the correspondences associated with the lunar phases, planetary signs for the days of the week, and the zodiac moon signs for each day. Ozarkers have long had a mild obsession with these cycles of celestial bodies. Nearly everything in one's life can be oriented to these processes, and still to this day, Ozarkers find their best days for all sorts of life's tasks in the farmer's almanac. These auspicious days are determined based on the moon's phases and daily zodiac moon signs.

HONORING THE OTHERWORLD

The seasonal cycles have a deep connection to rituals that honor the invisible entities who surround us throughout the year. Because so many of our seasonal rites are intimately connected to the growing and harvesting cycles, spirits of the land and home naturally find a place alongside rituals for blessing the ground and seeds as well as the harvest. Seasons in and of themselves have an auspicious quality, especially when it comes to the solstices and equinoxes. These times are unusual compared to all the other days of the year. They are liminal times, halfway between two different seasons. In these in-between spaces and times, the veil of the otherworld opens. Likewise, the holidays that make up our traditional lives (like Christmas Eve, May Day, and Halloween) can be auspicious points in this yearly cycle. All of these are times when the veil that separates our world from the otherworld of spirits is thin, allowing for entities to pass through much easier than other times of the year.

This thinness allows us the opportunity to interact with the invisible world in a much deeper way. As one of my teachers said when referring to times when the veil is thin: "When you call, they can *really* hear you." These times are then perfect for leaving out offerings and reciting prayers of thanksgiving. This might seem very strange given the conservative nature of Ozark traditional people, but these ritual actions are in no way seen as being separate from rituals of ordinary, daily life.

Of course the land is alive, and of course there's an invisible cloud of witnesses surrounding us at all times. One farmer I spoke with still left a small portion of his yearly crops for the Little People. He put it to me in a good way: "We can't see germs or microbes either, but we do a lot to build up or get rid of these invisible things too." For many in the Ozarks, even to this day, the Little People and the many other spirit entities in the world are just as much a part of nature as any ordinary creature. Leaving seasonal offerings to these entities is seen as just as natural a process as fertilizing in springtime or burning the fields after the last autumn harvest.

We might be living in a house, but that house is still a part of nature, and we derive our survival from having a good relationship to the land. For many, leaving offerings for their "invisible roommates," as I like to call them, is still a vital part of their yearly—and even daily—cycles. In the old days, charmers were often called out on certain holidays or times of the year to deliver prayers or blessings that would honor both the visible and invisible inhabitants of the land. Farmers who weren't connected to their own innate poetic power would bring charmers to their land to offer blessings, particularly in the springtime. To ease the process, it wasn't uncommon for families to raise a member as a charmer so that one would always be available when needed. The importance put upon maintaining charmers within a bloodline has fallen out of fashion in the past seventy years or so.

The cycles of life are, in the end, yours to connect with and yours to create. Many of our ancient ancestors didn't have calendars but were still able to connect to those deep wellsprings of power that flood the world at certain times of the year. How were they able to do that? They felt that stream deep in their bones. They felt the changing of the world around them. They knew when the last of their crops were ripening, it was time to celebrate the harvest. They knew when the ground began to warm and the snow to melt, it was time to bless the land with fertility and growing charms. I speak, of course, using the voice of my Northern European ancestors, fully recognizing the fact that these growing cycles aren't the same all over the world. This is exactly why each of us need to connect to the cycles of the world by *feeling* those cycles.

THE CHARMS

I'll begin with the charms that ritualize everyday tasks and processes that are often overlooked.

☆ FIRE BUILDING CHARM ☆

Fire was once so important to our ancestors that it was considered almost as a member of the family itself. Fires are often fed, as with this verbal charm, granting them a personality through our use of language. Traditional charms have been used to build, feed, and keep fires in the home for centuries, with many different types held by charmers. When fires were used to heat the home, they would often be "put to bed" at night by sweeping a layer of ash over the live coals. These would then be "woken up" the next morning when fresh wood was added. The waking-up process often involved burning a small amount of dried red cedar (*Juniperus virginiana*) foliage on the coals to create a cleansing smoke that would then be wafted through the house using a hand fan or the breath.

Today, many people don't have the same relationship to fire that our ancestors did. Personally, I don't have a fireplace in my home, although I do have a gas stove—so there's still a bit of a connection there. I have a firepit in my backyard, and if I'm building a fire, it's almost certainly for some magical ritual or purpose. Many of the Neotraditionalist practitioners I've met hold very special relationships to fire; because it's not a part of our daily lives, fires are approached in a sacred way. I can attest to this. Verbal charms can become an important part of this relationship, then. What blessings would *you* give to the flames? What food might *you* offer as gratitude for the fire assisting in your work? This "food" could be physical food items, plants, or incenses, but it could also be the breath or other vital energies. Even our words can transform into a feast to feed the flames.

This verbal charm is specifically used while building a fire, either in a fireplace or outdoors, and it can be any fire, ritual or mundane. This charm can also be used as a blessing upon ritual fires that are lit at the beginning of a ceremony or festival, or even as a reactionary measure that utilizes the lighting of a fire as a means to convey a specific blessing. In the Ozarks, the second form is the most common. This is a good example of a reciprocal charm whereby both the fire itself as well as the charmer (and the family, in this case) receive the blessings from the ritual process.

This charm was given to me in a spontaneous moment of magic when one of my teachers was building a fire in a large stone-ringed pit in his backyard. He told me that he didn't make fires outside anymore unless people were over at his house, but whenever he did, he would recite this charm as a blessing on everyone present.

MAGICAL TIMING

For everyday fires or for bonfires on auspicious holidays. Moon days in Aries (Mars, Tuesday, fire) or Leo (Sun, Sunday, fire)—both fire signs—are good for kindling sacred fires.

CHARM

Feed the fire, [name],
[Name], feed the fire.
Puff, puff, puff! *(Blow three times)*
First you blow it gently,
Then you blow it rough.
Three sparks—
One for me,
One for you,
One for everything in between.

RITUAL INGREDIENTS

Fire-making materials: kindling, wood, matches or lighter, etc.
Red cedar foliage

RITUAL ACTIONS

Begin by lighting a fire using whatever method you would like. Traditionally, a bit of fresh or dried red cedar foliage is given to the fire as its first food; my teacher who gave me this charm always followed this procedure. Once the fire begins to grow, you will begin the verbal charm, which is normally said in a whisper, close to the flames, but not so close that you risk burning yourself.

The name in the brackets should be your own name, as you are the one charming the fire. After the line "Puff, puff, puff!" you will blow three times into the fire. Following the words that come after this action in the charm, you will start with a gentle blowing action, then get stronger. This is seen as feeding the flames with your own vital breath as the sacrifice—a common magical ritual amongst many Ozark healers and practitioners.

The ritual ends with observing the "tokens" or omens of the fire. Specifically, you will count three sparks that fly up out of the fire as you recite the last lines. It's believed that the more sparks that are sent out of the flames, the more blessings will fall upon yourself as the charmer and the others you are charming for. It should be noted that in this verbal charm, everything that is between you and the fire is *everything*, meaning everything around you is blessed because everything is made of the essential flame of life, divinity, what-ever you want to call it. Nothing is outside the reach of the all-encompassing flame.

☆ SEWING CHARM ☆

There are a number of magical uses for this charm, which is based on a tra-ditional Mother Goose rhyme. For practical purposes, reciting this charm before beginning sewing will prevent the needle from breaking in a sewing machine. If you're hand-sewing, it will protect your fingers from getting poked by the needle.

Many people today have lost touch with sewing as an art and necessity. I still enjoy saving scraps of fabric from worn-out clothes or collecting lit-tle bits I find discounted at the local crafting store. I can't help but feel con-nected to my grandmother and ancestors even farther back who had stacks of spare fabric just waiting for a project. I save the fabric mostly for use in charming rituals. I find my intentional connection to the magical objects I make deepens when I'm able to have a hands-on experience making the object.

A common amulet found throughout the Ozarks is a blessing or charm-ing patch. These are small pieces of fabric, usually scraps that are kept around to be used as patches. Using patches as amulets was common in the old days, when folks had to patch their clothes rather than wear new ones. Patches sewn today have lost all practical value and often only have use as an amulet. I don't see this as an issue, but as a connection to tradition, and I encourage magical practitioners of all kinds to develop their sewing skills, not just for blessing patches but amulet crafting in general. Sewing requires time and effort; it allows us to slow down and focus on the work at hand. When I am sewing, I can really work out what my intention with a ritual is and bring some order to my chaotic thoughts.

The individual who gifted me this charm said she recited it to bless her quilting work. This piqued my interest and I had to ask her what she meant by "bless." She just laughed and said that she was taught to recite this verbal charm while working so that her prayers and blessings could be sealed into her quilts and then transferred to whoever would receive the object. When-ever our meetings took place in winter, she would wrap my shoulders in one of her quilts, bringing to my mind a ritual of being wrapped in all of the prayers she spoke into the blanket.

MAGICAL TIMING

Before beginning a sewing project; ritual sewing for amulets.

CHARM

Old Mother Witchett had one eye,
And a tail which she let fly;
Every time she went through a gap,
A bit of her tail she left in a trap.

RITUAL INGREDIENTS

Cloth patch, any fabric, any color (see table)
Red thread, spool
Sewing needles
Thimble (if needed)

RITUAL ACTIONS

Begin this ritual by gathering your red thread, needles, and a patch. Red thread is used in this ritual because, symbolically, red connects to vitality, the blood, and life—all of which are bolstered by the blessings carried by this patch.

Choose any cloth you'd like to make your patch. I like to choose a small patch, usually a three- or four-inch square, but you can use other shapes; for example, hearts are used for love, diamonds for good luck, leaf shapes for growth and growing, etc.

The color of your patch is also something to consider. Red can be used for love, health, strength, and vitality, but there are other colors you could use as well:

Color	Uses
Red	Vitality; health; strength; protection; love
Yellow	Prosperity; favor; "gold" in your pockets
Green	Good luck; luck in games and gambling
Blue	Protection
White	All-purpose; health; protection from fairy magic; cleansing
Black	"Mourning" patch to remember the dead; protection from hexes

Next, you'll want to choose the piece of clothing that will bear your blessing patch. I like to use items that have a pocket: shirts, coats, pants even. This will allow you to sew through the innermost layer of fabric behind the pocket and won't show a stitch on the outside of the clothing item. You can sew your patch so that it is hidden on the inside of your clothing item, or you can display it on the outside.

Once you've gathered the items, recite the verbal charm, then begin sewing. Keep your intention in mind while you sew, and work in a clockwise direction, which is the direction of blessings in the Ozarks. Maybe this patch is going to be a protecting amulet for the wearer, or maybe you want to seal in love, luck, or blessings in general. Whatever you choose, keep it in mind. Visualize these images flowing through the thread and into the patch.

When you're finished sewing, knot the thread close to the patch. In some cases, I've seen individuals then write or embroider the full name and birthdate of the one who will wear the item of clothing onto the patch, but this isn't required.

If you aren't interested in hand-sewing your patch, you can use a machine. Just make sure you recite the charm first, work in a clockwise direction, and keep your intention in mind.

NOTES

The original Mother Goose rhyme that this charm comes from references "Mother Twitchett" rather than "Mother Witchett." It's interesting to see how passing down verbal charms can sometimes be like the telephone game. What a person says and what the other person *hears* are often different things. The informant who gave me this charm said it was an "old witch saying" that had been passed to her, leading me to believe the name Mother Witchett might have been a more intentional transformation than simply a mishearing of the phrase.

☆ SOUP CHARM FOR HEALING ☆

Use this charm when making a healing soup, a common practice amongst many Ozark healers. The idea is that the verbal charm will imbue the soup with its magical power, which will then be transferred to the person who is sick as they eat. This charm isn't for soup alone, but can be applied to preparing other foods as well.

Ozarkers are often very serious when it comes to cooking taboos, especially if healing work is involved. For instance, one healer I worked with swore that using a spoon made from anything other than wood (or bamboo) would ruin whatever was being cooked. Others have taken this belief a step further and say that it's specifically metal that shouldn't be used, even when it comes to cookpots. Many of these believers use glass or stoneware pots and wooden spoons in their work.

Wooden spoons are useful tools for Ozark healers and magical practitioners. Oftentimes individuals will have special spoons that are used just for healing broths and herbal preparations. Some of these have symbols carved or burned into the wood (usually crosses). Others make spoons from specific woods that are associated with magic, specifically red cedar and sassafras, the idea being that the innate magical quality of the wood will pass into whatever is being stirred.

Food and Ozark healing often go hand-in-hand. Food has such a unique ability to comfort and nourish on its own, so it can naturally be used as a container for healing maladies. Specific herbs and other materia can even be incorporated into food items for healing and magic, especially soups, where the heat will draw out the desired chemical compounds. We've lost touch with this ancient connection to food in our modern world, where we so often see food not as a nourisher, but as an enemy or even contaminant to our bodies. Reestablishing deep relationships with nourishing foods and the associated rituals of cooking allows us to connect deeply to the healing process itself.

MAGICAL TIMING
Use the zodiac sign opposite to where the sickness is located or "rooted." See chapter 4 for more information. Cancer (Moon, Monday, water) is an auspicious time for cleansing, as is Taurus (Venus, Friday, earth).

CHARM
What I stir, I stir for [full name].
Four devils, begone! *(Four clanks)*

I stir in blessings. *(Stir three times)*
I cross to uncross. *(Three crosses)*
Down from the mountain,
Up from the holler,
Out of creek and river,
Out of cave and crevice,
Come blessings, come here! *(Three clanks)*

RITUAL INGREDIENTS
Food item that you are cooking
Wooden spoon

RITUAL ACTIONS
The only ritual items needed for this verbal charm are a pot or dish for cooking and a wooden spoon. This ritual will begin when the soup you're cooking has started to simmer. Repeat the verbal charm with the associated actions that are in italics. At the end of the first line, you will say the full name (first, middle, and last) of the person you're healing, who can also be yourself. Even if you are making this soup for yourself, you should still say your full name.

After reciting the second line, you will hit the rim of the cookpot with the wooden spoon in four places so that it makes a clanking sound. First, hit the top rim, then the bottom, then the left side, and finally the right, forming a cross shape.

Next, at the end of the third line, you will stir the soup clockwise three times.

At the end of the fourth line, you will cross the soup with the end of the spoon three times. The direction of this crossing begins at the top of the pot, making a vertical line down to the bottom, then from the left side horizontally to the right.

End the charm with three more clanks of the wooden spoon against the rim of the cookpot. These three should all be in the same spot, anywhere on the rim that you choose. The soup is then covered and cooked normally, following whichever recipe is used.

The charm and ritual actions can be repeated three times: once while the soup is still cold, again when it's simmering, and a third time right before the soup is served.

✫ WASHING CHARM ✫

This unique ritual utilizes the idea of sympathetic magic to connect a person who needs cleansing from a hex or malady to the act of cleaning dishes. It was taught to me by a healer who only ever worked in this way and usually had a long list of names that needed healing. When I asked her why she used this specific method, she just replied, "Cause the dishes need washin' anyhow!"

This charming ritual is a great example of how Ozark healers and magical practitioners have traditionally been able to repurpose household tasks and tools for their work. This sort of repurposing in its varied forms has served as a foundational practice within the tradition since ancient times. A healer's cunning is often marked by their ability to utilize every situation in life to reach their goal, no matter how mundane it might seem on the outside. As a charmer on this path, examine what kinds of daily tasks and rituals you might be able to repurpose for specific healing or magical goals.

This healing charm can be used for any condition, but it works particularly well against curses associated with the fire element—since water is used in the washing. Despite this charm's simpleness, I find it to be a very nice meditative ritual, and a way for me to deeply connect to those in my heart who might need healing.

MAGICAL TIMING

While hand-washing dishes or even cleaning the house. Moon days in Cancer (Moon, Monday, water) is a great time for this ritual, as it connects to the water element and Cancer's cleansing qualities.

CHARM

Good day to you, [full name]!
I place you here to wash you,
I place you here to cleanse you,
I place you here to bless you,

Until all water dries up
In all the wells across the world!

RITUAL INGREDIENTS

Items/dishes that need washing
Soap for washing
Water

RITUAL ACTIONS

This ritual begins by greeting the person being healed, using their first, middle, and last name. If this is yourself, say aloud your own name. Continue the charm while touching the item that will be cleaned, or you can even touch the sink itself if you're using the entire washing session for one individual. As it was taught to me, if you switch individuals being cleansed, you will repeat the process, making sure to greet them and say their full name as well.

There's a visualization that can accompany this work. The healer who passed this to me said she liked to see in her mind the person she was healing, covered in black "muck," as she called it, or dirt. As the dish was washed clean, so would all this black mud and ichor disappear off the person she was keeping in mind, being released down the drain.

This ritual can be used with other methods of cleaning as well, specifically mopping, as this action also involves water. In this variation, you will repeat the same charm before beginning. Visualize that as you're cleaning the floor, you're cleaning the person who is the target of this healing.

NOTES

This verbal charm ends in what I like to call an *infinity clause statement*, which seals the work that's being started by the charm. An infinity clause is an open-ended statement that is used to magically ensure the duration of the work at hand. In this case, the infinity clause of "Until all water dries up / In all the wells across the world!" isn't actually infinite, but is also not likely to occur in the lifetime of the charmer or their client. Other common infinity clauses used in Ozark verbal charms include: "Until all the stars fall from heaven," "Until all good passes from the world," or "Until the stone foundations of the earth give way."

CHARMS FOR THE SEASONAL CYCLES

This next set of charms address the seasonal needs of the homestead and the celebrations that come with those times.

✱ DAFFODIL BUNDLE CHARM ✱

This short verbal charm is based on a well-known nursery rhyme and is used to accompany making flower bundles with daffodils, often called *jon-quils* (*Narcissus* spp.). Because these are some of the first flowers of the year, they represent resilience and the idea that warmth is just around the corner. Their golden petals symbolize abundance, prosperity, and the sun, while their green stalks connect to good luck. Taken together, these flowers are a welcome sight after the cold, dark winter.

Using bundles of plants and flowers as a magical object is a common tradition in the Ozarks. These plant bundles are usually gathered during specific holidays or other auspicious times of the year. Gathering herbs and flowers on May Day, for example, is an old tradition still performed by healers and magical practitioners, who believe the plants gathered at specific times of the year are extra potent. The individual plants within these bundles might be used in remedies and rituals, but what's more common is seeing the entire bundle hung up in the house as a talismanic ward of good luck and protection. Such bundles are usually kept all year and are burned only when a new bundle is created to replace it.

Daffodils can be gathered into magical bundles on specific dates in the late winter and early spring. For example, daffodils are traditionally gathered on Candlemas (February 2), Saint Patrick's Day (March 17), the spring equinox, Good Friday, or Easter Sunday. Other believers say that you have to gather the *first* daffodils that you see and make them into a bundle, otherwise they won't contain as much power. As a charmer, it's up to you to decide how you'd like to connect to this practice.

CAUTION

All parts of the daffodil are poisonous to dogs, cats, and many other animals we might keep as pets. Keep your daffodil bundle in a safe place, away from all household pets. Even just drinking water from a vase that held daffodils could cause your dog or cat to have very serious health issues. If you're concerned, you can hang your daffodil bundle in a closed closet away from pets, or even in your garage. If you want to use this charm without hanging your bundle, you can keep your seven dried daffodil stalks in a sealed box that might be placed on a mantelpiece or on your home altar.

MAGICAL TIMING

Springtime when daffodils are blooming. Auspicious spring days. Moon days in Taurus (Venus, Friday, earth) are good to use with this charm.

CHARM

Daffy-down-dilly has come to town
In a yellow petticoat and a green gown.
Seven stalks for seven blessings!

RITUAL INGREDIENTS

7 daffodil stalks and flowers
White or red string, 2 feet

RITUAL ACTIONS

Because daffodils are often the first flowers to bloom in the spring, they are our first opportunity to create blessed bundles for the home. This short charm is repeated seven times while picking seven daffodil stalks with flowers attached. Daffodils for this blessing bundle must *never* be snipped or cut, but must be broken from the plant with the hands alone.

Daffodils come in a variety of color combinations, and any of them will work for this ritual. Once the seven flowers are picked, tie them into a bundle using your white or red string. The color red is commonly associated in the Ozarks with vital blood or energy, life force, healing, the warmth of fire, and protection—all associated with springtime as well.

Hang your bundle with the flowers facing up or down, although it's easier to have them facing down. You can hook a nail through the string you used to tie up the bundle. Traditionally, bundles like these are hung up on the inside of the home, near the front or back door, or you can hang them at both! These bundles should naturally dry on their own, but keep an eye out for molding. If you are able to keep them for an entire year, it's believed to be extra fortunate and lucky.

If you need to dispose of your bundle, burn it. When you gather new daffodils, burn the old ones outside on a fire.

NOTES

Daffodils or *jonquils*, as they're sometimes called, are common across the Ozark region and often mark old homestead sites where no other signs remain. Many of the daffodils that naturally pop up across the area are related to those first brought here by white settlers from Appalachia, and these varieties would have accompanied families on their sea voyages from Europe. They really are a welcome sight in the early spring, when their bright yellow and white blooms begin to open, sometimes even while packed underneath a layer of snow. In addition to marking homestead sites, I've encountered the folk belief that patches of daffodils show where angels have walked on the earth. Some people take this as a sign of divine blessings upon their home or land.

☆ EASTER BLESSING ☆

This blessing is aimed toward renewing the land and all beings that might live upon it. It connects to the ancient symbolism of Easter as a time for spiritual and physical healing and rebirth. As springtime holidays go, the Easter season is traditionally when Ozark farmers would bless their fields to ensure fertile crops. Many would use blessings like this one. You can perform this on behalf of yourself and your work, as well as for the benefit of your family, community, or town. This charm will certainly give some added energy to all growing things.

MAGICAL TIMING

Easter Sunday, often before dawn, which is seen as a time of spiritual and physical renewal and rebirth.

CHARM

When Jesus did die,
Four women in white,
Brushed his tomb,
Top to bottom,
Bottom to top,
With three branches.
Glad tidings they heard,
That the man had risen.
One shouted north, *(throw)*
One shouted south, *(throw)*
One shouted east, *(throw)*
One shouted west. *(throw)*
Bless this land and
All who live on it.

RITUAL INGREDIENTS

4 small red cedar (*Juniperus virginiana*) branches, or branches from
    another fragrant evergreen tree, or even four herb stalks with leaves
    and flowers intact
Offering foods and drinks (optional)

RITUAL ACTIONS

Begin by picking four red cedar branches, small enough to fit in your hand with ease. You can also use branches from a pine or other fragrant evergreen tree, or you can use four sprigs of your favorite herb that might be growing at the time of the ritual. If you're using herbs, make sure to include the stalk and choose a fairly large sprig, as you will be throwing it as part of the ritual.

Next, take your branches and find your ritual site. This could be your backyard, garden, or even out in the wild somewhere. Make sure you choose a place where you can be distraction-free and focused. Performing this ritual with members of your family or community is a wonderful alternative; in this case, make sure everyone has four branches or herbal sprigs as well.

Face the north and then begin reciting the verbal charm. After reciting the line "One shouted north," throw one of your branches to the north, then rotate clockwise to face the south. Recite the next line and then throw your branch to the south. Continue clockwise, throw the third branch east. End facing the west and throwing your final branch.

You can leave behind any food offerings you'd like at the ritual spot. You can also incorporate this ritual into a community feast, which can take place at the ritual site.

NOTES

This verbal charm uses an apocryphal story surrounding the death and burial of Jesus that doesn't appear in the Bible. What does appear, in all four gospel accounts, is that the resurrected Jesus showed himself to his women disciples before anyone else. These women had arrived with spices and perfumes in order to cleanse the body of their beloved teacher. At most, however, the Bible names three women, not four. In this version of the story, the four women appear with fragrant evergreen branches—a stand-in for the resins and spices used in the Bible—and they perform a very traditional Ozark cleansing rite involving sweeping or brushing. This action mimics that of the household broom and feather duster so that just as a floor is swept clean of dirt, so too can a body be swept clean of illnesses and evil. In this particular charming ritual, we represent the four women dressed in white, and our own evergreen brooms are able to cleanse away every evil, illness, or curse that might be on us or those we're blessing. These branches are then cast away in the four directions along with everything that was cleansed.

✶ MIDSUMMER HERB GATHERING CHARM ✶

Accounts differ widely about the exact date of midsummer in the Ozarks. Some practitioners use Saint John's Eve (June 23); others align midsummer with the summer solstice in the Northern Hemisphere (June 20–21); a few say midsummer needs to be in the middle of summer and place their festivities around the first week of August.

Picking medicinal herbs, roots, and flowers at this auspicious time has a long history across Europe. In many Western folk cultures, May Day is also used as a time for herb picking. In the Southern United States, medicinal plants are sprouting or flowering at either time, so both are used. At one time, midsummer had many associated community rituals, but as a holiday it has mostly fallen out of fashion, replaced here in the Ozarks by Fourth of July celebrations—many of which have the same associations that were given to much older holidays like midsummer.

There are two primary uses for this verbal charm. The first use is to magically bless the herbs picked at this auspicious time, which are said to have more potent medicinal and magical powers. This verbal charm has also been used to help the picker magically find the herbs that they need to pick. In this way, the charm acts as a divination method to allow the magical practitioner the ability to sense the medicines that they or their client will need at that exact moment.

Traditionally, when making magical bundles (as with the Daffodil Bundle Charm), individual plants and flowers are not cut using metal but are hand-picked or cut using a stone or wooden blade. There's an old Ozark belief that metal should never come into contact with our healing and magical plants. This is very difficult to ensure in most cases, apart from when you are personally gathering the plants.

Plant bundles can be used in a number of ways. You can hang them up in your house as protective wards against illnesses, hexes, and evil. Just make sure the plants you pick are safe for your pets, or else hang them somewhere your pet won't be able to reach. The healers I've met who still practice these bundle-gathering rituals hang them away from their other drying herbs so that they can use them throughout the year in remedies that might need more powerful materia. Additionally, you can dry and crush all of the herbs together and use this powder to enhance any magical work; just add a pinch or two to your other materia.

Bundles should be kept for the entire year, or until they are used up, in the case of practitioners. Any of the plants leftover on the next midsummer should be burned on a fire before another bundle is gathered.

MAGICAL TIMING

Midsummer morning, before dawn (representing renewal, rebirth, and healing).

CHARM

Blessed dawn, blessed morning! *(Raise hands toward the sun)*
Sun rising in the east!
As your fire grows,
So let the fire inside these plants grow!
From east, from sun,
From fire, from earth,
Grow, grow, grow!
Let fire burn away all sickness! *(Clap)*
Let fire burn away all hexes! *(Clap)*
Let fire burn away all evil, *(Clap)*
That roams across this wide world!
Mother Mary seals her power
In the hearts of these plants.
(Repeat three times)

RITUAL INGREDIENTS

None

RITUAL ACTIONS

The charm recitation begins facing the east, toward the rising sun. The charm is usually recited in the field where you are going to be picking the herbs and flowers, and if you move areas, the charm is usually repeated.

With the first line, raise your hands so that your palms are on either side of your head and facing toward the sun. As soon as the initial greeting is made, you can lower your hands. There are no other motions until the three lines that begin, "Let fire burn..." You will clap once, as loudly as you can, at the end of each of these three lines. As the charmer who gave me this charm instructed, visualize that as you clap, light shoots out from your palms in all directions.

This charm is usually repeated three times before beginning to pick your plants.

NOTES

This charm invokes the power of Mother Mary, who figures into a large number of verbal charms in the Ozarks. In other examples, Mary uses her power to heal or bless, but in this charm, she is sealing a bit of her own power into the plants themselves—the idea being that anyone who knows the charm and the proper time to pick the plants can do so, receiving a great deal of power and aid. Mary's power is then latent within the plant and can be used by anyone in need. There are beliefs amongst practitioners that I've met where Mary is seen as the mother of medicinal plants and that by gathering roots, leaves, and flowers, we are gathering power directly from her wellspring.

☆ AUTUMN HARVEST PRAYER ☆

As seasonal correspondences go, autumntime is associated with the harvest and "putting up" time, when Ozarkers would be furiously finishing canning and preserving foods before the first chills of winter. In contrast with the "first fruits" period in springtime, this prayer accompanies offerings of the last crops of the year, primarily to the Little People and the guardians of the home. Offerings of the first and last fruits of the year would traditionally appease these two spirit-troops, allowing for protection of the home and land throughout the entire year. There are many stories about families neglecting such kindly offerings and suffering the consequences. As in one tale, where the stingy family refused to leave out the smallest amount of food and drink in the late autumn and found all their stores spoiled by midwinter.

In my personal practice, I use this prayer whenever I feel like autumn and the harvesttime are well and truly here. Unlike Northern Europe (where many of our traditions were originally forged), here in the Ozarks, the idea of August/September as the season of the last harvest (exemplified in the holiday Lammas) doesn't always apply. Temperatures here can remain very hot even after the equinox. So, instead of performing this charm on a specific day, I like to feel it out, which would have no doubt been the method of our ancient ancestors before calendars were solidified. When the season begins to *feel* right, I will wander outside on a cool night, twist my fingers through the soil, and recite this blessing.

This charm utilizes many symbolic connections between the charmer and the natural cycles of nature. First is bringing in the harvest as a symbolic connection to wealth and prosperity. The gold of the grains (usually maize in the Ozarks) has a very real connection to personal fortune and the prosperity of the family. As one of my teachers told me, "If you can grow food, you'll always prosper." After the harvests, the earth and all the entities that dwell on and in it are symbolically put to bed until springtime. This action is common across many agrarian folk cultures where the earth itself is seen as a living entity that needs to rest as well as be woken up when the time is right.

Inside the home, we often find ourselves entering a sort of hibernation along with the darkness of wintertime. This would have been even more visible to our ancestors, as hard labor in the fields turned to activities within the cabin. Back-breaking labor under the hot sun turned into resting near the warm fireplace. So, in this way, this verbal charm isn't just a prayer of thankfulness, nor is it just to honor the land and spiritual entities—it's a way for us humans to reconnect to the cycles of nature and merge our practices and lives with the changing seasons.

MAGICAL TIMING

Autumnal equinox; harvest time; during the "last fruits" period.

CHARM

Refrain: From dirt, to field, to home. *(Repeated after every line)*

Harvest has come in bushelsful!
Bushelsful of golden grains!
Gold can't be et but this can!
This can we bring from hands to hearth!
Hearth-warming hands and hearts!
Hearts from home to deep earth!
Earth, now rest you well and sleep!
Sleep until the daffodillies wake!

Wake, you Watchers watching!
Watch over this hearth and home!
A home for you with food and drink!
Drink bellies full, et bellies full!
Full from head to tippy toes!
Toes stay warm through Winter's cold!
Winter is come and we're off to bed!

RITUAL INGREDIENTS

Bowl / cup

Water

Drink offerings: water, milk, whiskey, moonshine, mead, beer, wine, sweet or herbal liqueurs, tea, coffee

Food offerings: whole cooked foods, raw oats, raw barley, cornmeal, breads, sweets, honey or molasses

Dishes for serving offering, usually a plate for food and cup for drinks

Whisk made from herb stalks or fresh evergreen branches (optional)

RITUAL ACTIONS

The verbal charm accompanies two different ritual actions. The first is the blessing of the fields; which can apply to your home garden, planters on a balcony, window boxes, or simply on a patch of earth. Repeat the lines of the prayer from "Harvest has come in bushelsful!" through "Sleep until the daffodillies wake!" while sprinkling water onto the ground using the fingers of your right hand. You can also use a blessing whisk, often made from dried herb stalks or fresh red cedar or other evergreen branches.

The second part of the prayer involves leaving out offerings for the spirits of the land and home. These can be combined into a single offering or placed on separate plates, one outside and one inside the home. Offerings can be as simple or complex as you like, but there is traditionally both a food item and a drink.

One easy food offering I like to use is a simple mixture of three traditional grains: whole raw barely, whole raw oats, and raw cornmeal. These three grains have a long history of use in the Ozarks and represent the prosperity that comes from having a bounty of nourishing food available. You can leave out cooked foods as well; it's traditional to take a small portion of every item at a large meal and leave it out for the Little People and house spirits.

As far as drinks go, traditionally, hillfolk who still adhere to these folk beliefs will leave an alcoholic drink (usually beer, whiskey, or moonshine) as well as a soft drink like water, milk, soda, or coffee.

Take your food and drink offerings outside. Leave them at the base of a tree. If you're just placing offerings outside, you can repeat the rest of the prayer there.

If you're doing outside/inside offerings, place your two sets on the dining table or kitchen counter—this represents the center or heart (hearth) of the home. Repeat the rest of the prayer, from "Wake, you Watchers watching!" until the end. Then, leave one set of offerings in the kitchen and take the other set outside, to be placed at the base of a tree. (If you're concerned about animals eating the offerings inside the home, you can leave them inside of the cold oven, which has been described to me by several Ozark kitchen witches as being the "womb" or even the "Holy of Holies" inside the home.)

NOTES

The word *et* in the line "Gold can't be et but this can" isn't a typo. It's an Ozark dialect pronunciation of the word "eat" and has been left in to uphold the flow of the verbal charm. It has a short "e" vowel sound, as in the word "ever" or "elephant." This word remains the same no matter the tense. For example:

"We et all the cake last night."
"The cake was et last night."
"Et your greens, child."
"We'll et the cornbread tomorrow night."

☆ HALLOWEEN FEAST BLESSING ☆

This blessing is intended to accompany a feast welcoming the ancestors and wandering spirits who might need something to eat and drink. We welcome the spirits who can easily pass through the thinning veil between worlds at this time of the year. They are fed, given drinks, and healed of their sorrows.

This is seen as very powerful work for the betterment of these spirit entities. That doesn't, however, mean that you need to welcome *all* spirits into your home. The verbal charm itself offers us a provision to welcome those spirits who are kind (but who might need help), as well as those ancestors who want for our own healing and betterment.

This ritual work can be done alone or as a feast, which welcomes human-kind to the table as well. This can be a great way to build community ties. This charming ritual works on several levels, the first being a community-oriented act, as feasts often are. It's about bringing together our friends and family to share a meal, filling our bellies, and leaving healed and happy. Beyond this, though, we are welcoming in our extended family from the otherworld. We are welcoming spirits who are hungry, thirsty, or lost. We welcome them to the table so that they might receive respite and healing from this act of generosity. While it might seem like a simple ritual—and Ozark folk practices are often deceptively simple—this work holds a deep and powerful intention of connection and kindness; we welcome all entities to the feasting table for their betterment, and for ours.

When it comes to magical timing, Halloween is specifically selected for its associations with the dead and ancestral spirits; this is traditionally seen as a time of the year when the veil between worlds is thin, allowing spirits to pass into our world much easier. But historically, for Ozarkers, Christmas Eve was our magically charged and slightly haunted time of the year. Many hillfolk families used Halloween as a harvest festival celebrating light and warmth before the coming winter. Fireside storytelling about witches, ghosts, and monsters was of course present, but not limited to Halloween alone. People often forget that Christmas was a popular time to tell ghost stories as well—let's not forget Charles Dickens's *A Christmas Carol* is essentially a ghost story.

Amongst the Catholics I've met in rural Ozark communities, many of whom had deep ties in the Ozarks, the consensus seems to be that in the "old days," their families would celebrate specifically the triad of All Hallows' Eve (October 31), All Saints' Day (November 1), and All Souls' Day (November 2) as holy feasts. Only later were these merged with popular versions of Halloween, often delivered by Protestant neighbors; Halloween really only became a popular folk holiday in the first part of the twentieth century, when trick-or-treating in its modern form became more common and Halloween-specific home decorations became cheap, consumable products.

Halloween in all of its traditional forms, including Samhain, has been heavily influenced by modern witchcraft traditions like Wicca as well as neo-pagan and reconstructionist pagan communities. Thus, this is definitely an example of a Neotraditionalist practice, one that was given to me by a healer who had deep roots in the Ozarks but who was also influenced by more modern traditions of witchcraft. This feast need not be limited to Halloween alone and can be included in any work done for healing ancestral spirits and otherworldly entities.

MAGICAL TIMING

Halloween; sometimes Halloween Eve is preferred, or exactly at midnight on Halloween.

CHARM

Refrain: Come you now to the table,
Set wide with food and drink.

Come you down from mountain,
Come you up from lake,
Come you out of hollow,
(Refrain)
Come you through the door,
Come you down the hall,
Come you to this hearth,
(Refrain)
Come you glad of heart,
Come you who wander lost,
Come you well-wishers wise,
(Refrain)
Come you eat your fill,
Come you drink your fill,
Come you rest your fill,
(Refrain)

Come you merrily and kind,
Or else don't come at all!

RITUAL INGREDIENTS

Feasting provisions, or a small meal
Plate setting for the spirits' food and drink items

RITUAL ACTIONS

Begin by setting aside a separate plate, cup, and utensils for the offerings you will make to the gathered spirits. Often this is an empty place at the dinner or feasting table, left for any spirits who might enter, but it can also be left on your home altar or even on the cold stovetop. Offerings can be any food and drink items, but I like to take small portions of every item at the meal and place them on the offering plate. You can also do this with drinks; if there is wine, beer, or coffee served, these will be left in separate cups.

As it was related to me, this verbal charm is recited once the offerings have been placed, before anyone at the table begins eating. The practitioner who gave me this charm said that she would open the front door to the house just a crack to allow the spirits to enter, but she let me know that this wasn't necessary to the work. When I have led a Halloween feast using this verbal charm, I like to have a main speaker while everyone at the table recites the refrain. I like to repeat the entire song three times, as is traditional with many verbal charms. When the spirits have been summoned, the feast can begin.

As with many verbal charms that summon the spirits, there is a provision for keeping out those entities who wish to do us some mischief or harm. The ending words offer us the opportunity to invite only those spirits and ancestors who wish to show us kindness, who wish for our growth and healing as well as their own. You are *always* able to choose who you want to invite to the spirit table, and you should never feel coerced to invite ancestors who you know weren't good people, or to invite spirits who you feel uncomfortable around. Your ancestors who want the best for you *will* come forward when needed, and they can even act as a gatekeeper against spirits who aren't so kind.

There is another offering you can include in this ritual that helps feed those entities who aren't allowed to come to the feasting table. As is traditional in other offering feasts, a portion of the food and drinks can be plated, taken outside the house, and left underneath a tree as an offering to everything else. In this way, we are able to help heal all spirits and ancestors that might be wandering around without actually inviting them into our lives and homes—that is, until they themselves are able to heal and grow.

✷ CHRISTMAS EVE FEAST BLESSING ✷

Traditionally, Christmas Eve has been revered as a highly auspicious time of the year by Ozark healers, magical practitioners, and layfolk alike. Of all the seasons and holidays, Ozarkers of the past loved Christmas Eve the most. All magical work done at this time is considered extra auspicious because of the thin veil between the worlds. This traditional blessing, as with the Autumn Harvest Prayer, enacts a ritual that combines words of thanksgiving, offerings to the invisible entities constantly around us, as well as empowerments to individuals who might be present for the blessing ritual.

There are, of course, many traditional Christmastime prayers, blessings, songs, and verses here in the Ozarks. This verbal charm is only one of them, but one that has warmed my heart ever since I received it years ago. Practitioners and healers might find it useful for empowering magical work done on Christmas Eve. Or, it could be a preface recited before passing down verbal charms, power, and traditional knowledge to students and future holders of the magical gift. It can also certainly accompany rituals of gift-giving, whether they are exchanged between humans or with otherworldly beings.

In addition to the Christmas Eve that we know of, on December 24, Ozarkers sometimes celebrate what is called Old Christmas Eve as well as Old Christmas Day, on January 5 and 6—usually reserved for Epiphany. The division between the two dates came about during the change from the Julian to the Gregorian Calendar. Even though this process began in the sixteenth century, many rural areas throughout the Western world were still using the old calendar well into the nineteenth century, depending on how isolated the people in the area were. The Ozark Mountains was one such isolated area, and some people were still using the old Julian Calendar at the time of the Civil War. Once the majority of people made the switch, however, some households retained both the new date of Christmas as well as the old one. Many people celebrated the Twelve Days of Christmas as beginning on the new Christmas Day and ending on Old Christmas. Others merged their celebrations of Epiphany, also called Three Kings' Day or Kings' Day. This holiday honors and recounts the biblical story of the three magi who visited the infant Jesus with gifts of gold, frankincense, and myrrh. Old Christmas Eve is seen as just as powerful as the new date, and it is often used by healers and magical practitioners as an additional auspicious day for work.

Today, many Neotraditionalists prefer to use Yule instead of Christmas, which is on the winter solstice. This charming ritual can easily be used for either celebration.

MAGICAL TIMING

Christmas Eve; Yule; Old Christmas Eve (January 5).

CHARM

A light is raised inside this home,
On the darkest night,
On the darkest night!

A fire behind the grate,
A candle in the window,
On the darkest night!

Welcome all, welcome all!
With joy and happy hearts,
Come in from the cold!

Eat your fill!
Drink your fill!
And leave a happy lot.

Come back in the spring,
When the apples bloom,
And the sun is rising high!

A blessing from lips to ears,

From ears to hearts,

From hearts to lips again.

RITUAL INGREDIENTS

Branch of red cedar (*Juniperus virginiana*) or another fresh
   evergreen branch

Drink offerings: water, milk, whiskey, moonshine, mead, beer,
   wine, sweet or herbal liqueurs, tea, coffee

Food offerings: whole cooked foods, raw oats, raw barley, cornmeal,
   breads, sweets, honey or molasses

Dishes for serving offerings, usually a plate for food and cup for drinks

RITUAL ACTIONS

As with the Autumn Harvest Prayer, this blessing charm usually accompanies the leaving out of offerings for the land spirits, Little People, and other nonhuman entities. Food and drink items can include many different things; on Christmas Eve, seen as a time of feasting, offerings traditionally include a small amount of everything that is served at the feasting table. You can leave out two different sets of offerings—one inside and one outside—or just a single set inside the home, which is traditional. Offering plates and cups are often placed in the "heart" of the home—the kitchen—usually on the cold stovetop or inside the oven (turned off).

Another traditional Christmas Eve ritual includes blessing the home and everyone in it with an evergreen branch, usually red cedar (*Juniperus virginiana*) or pine. Branches that are green and full of foliage are preferred; these symbolize the abundance, prosperity, and power that continues to thrive even on the darkest, coldest nights. The branch is brought into the house, a blessing charm is recited, and then the branch is carried through every room of the house, brushing lightly across the top of every doorway. After this, the branch is touched to the head of every individual present. This blessing branch is traditionally hung up with seasonal greenery until Epiphany, or Old Christmas, on January 6. On this day, it's taken outside and ritually burned, or it is hung back in the evergreen tree from whence it came.

CHAPTER 3

To Grow You
Like a Green Tree...

After Gram Watson finished her tale, Ann couldn't even speak a word. The piece of coal-black wood hanging around her neck felt hot. She shifted uncomfortably in her chair, cleared her throat, then tried to say something, but nothing would come out. Gram noticed the child grow pale and pulled her into a hug. "Now don't you go thinkin' nothin' about that story. It's all in the past."

But it wasn't all in the past, as Gram had said. Ann had felt different for a while now. She never felt like she quite belonged with the others in town. She felt like an outsider despite all her efforts to fit in. And now, Gram had confirmed that she should be feeling different and that made a knot form in Ann's stomach. "I have to go, Gram" was all she could say before standing, giving Gram another hug, and leaving the cabin.

Ann made the decision not to go visiting the woods for a while. She cleared out all the dried yarbs, sticks, roots, and hole stones that hung around her bedroom, gathered while out on the mountain with Gram. She didn't talk anymore to anyone about remedies, the gift, or any of that nonsense, as Ann found herself calling it all. One day, she almost took off her necklace with the little piece of charred wood, but something stopped her hand. She couldn't bear the thought of taking it off after hav-ing worn the thing for as long as she could remember. It'll be the last piece of the puzzle, *she thought to herself.* I'll take it off when I'm good and ready.

Ann's mother had noticed the changes in her daughter, and it worried her to no end. She remembered the times when her mother had struggled with her gifts. She remembered the times when her mother gave up on those gifts, and those she feared even more. Those were dark days. Her mother would spiral into a deep depression followed by a grave illness. Gram Watson was the only person who could ever bring her back to the light again. Lucy didn't want that for her child.

One day, about three months into Ann's self-transformation, Lucy did something she hadn't done since her daughter was born—she hiked up the mountain to visit Gram Watson. The closer she got to the cabin, the more nervous her stomach became. You're being stupid, *she thought to herself.* She delivered your damn baby!

This was enough to calm the woman down, just as she got to the front porch. Gram was already waiting for her with a percolator of coffee brewing and fresh cinnamon rolls right out of the oven. "C'mon in, Lucy!" Gram yelled through the screen door.

Lucy hesitated, took a deep breath, and entered the cabin. She took a seat in the kitchen, knowing full well that's where they'd end up anyway. Anyone who had any kind of problem ended up at Gram's kitchen table with some coffee and a cinnamon roll. She fidgeted in her seat, wondering if Gram was thinking about her while finishing up washing dishes. Lucy was startled back into her body by the sensation of an old black cat rubbing up against her ankle. She jumped a little, then laughed at herself. She reached down and pet the cat on top of the head as Gram wiped her wet hands on an old tea towel before joining Lucy at the kitchen table. "All right then, so what's all this about?" Gram asked gruffly as she sat down in a rickety chair, the chair moaning as Gram moaned as well.

"Ann ain't well Gram," Lucy answered, pulling at the cinnamon roll in front of her.

"What do you mean? What's happened?"

Lucy shook her head and motioned with her hand to calm Gram down. "No, no, nothin' like that Gram. You haven't seen her in a while, so you don't know how she's changed. I can't put my finger on it, but she's becoming a different person. She's starting to look like she belongs with the kids in that Baptist youth group. You know, the ones who look like they're wearing their Easter best. The ones who are always saying 'yes ma'am' and 'no sir' like they don't have any damn thoughts or feelings of their own. I'm just worried for her, Gram, and I know how she used to like comin' out here, so I'm wonderin' if maybe something happened that turned her in this direction?"

Gram cackled to herself and took a big sip of her coffee. "Lucy, do you remember that one summer when your mother found religion again?"

Lucy rolled her eyes. "Oh yes, don't remind me. I doubt I'll ever get all that time we spent at church back."

"Well, you know why she did it, right? She wanted to feel normal for a change. And for people like us, feelin' normal ain't something that's normal. Can you really blame a person who might want to just fit in with the community rather than standin' out all the time? Especially with Ann, she's just now coming into herself, and it's hard at that age, when you got so much change, and then somebody like me comes along and plops a lot more on you. We've all had our moments of rebellion—you can trust me on that."

"But she'll come back to us, Gram, right?"

Gram just shrugged her shoulders and took another sip of her coffee. "Child, I hope so. There's a lot of people in this world that need her gift. But I'll tell you one thing, the seeds have been planted inside of her. And just like the plants of the field, the seeds need the conditions to be just right for them to pop up through the soil. It's our job to make sure the seeds grow, but we can't control those conditions."

Across town, Ann was playing with her classmates on the playground. She was trying hard not to get her dress dirty when all she really wanted to do was jump right in the biggest mud puddle she could find. Despite her new appearance, Ann was still finding it hard to fit in with the other children. Across the grass, she spied Mrs. Glennwell, the librarian, whom she'd had many long conversations with ever since she was a little girl. Mrs. Glennwell was kind to everyone, but especially to the ones who needed kindness the most. Ann decided that if she couldn't play with the others, she could at least talk with her old friend.

As she approached, some voice inside Ann told her that Mrs. Glennwell was having some real trouble. "Her brother ran off with the last of the inheritance money, and now she's left with nothing but dust," the voice said to her. Ann had no idea how she knew that, or even if what the voice was saying was true.

"Mrs. Glennwell?" Ann asked as she sat down next to the woman at a picnic table.

"Yes, Ann?" Mrs. Glennwell replied with a smile. This had been the start of many interesting conversations in the past.

"Why did your brother take off with all your mama's inheritance money?"

Mrs. Glennwell lost her smile, worried about what some gossip in town might have told the girl. "Ann, how do you know about that?"

"I don't really know," Ann shrugged. "But I think I can help!"

Ann pulled a silver dime out of her pocket that her mother had given her to pay for lunch. She handed it to Mrs. Glennwell with a smile. "All you have to do is spit on that dime three times, then plant it in the roots of an oak tree on the new moon, and everything will be all right!"

Mrs. Glennwell clutched the dime in her hand. "Ann, how do you know that? Is it something Gram Watson passed to you?"

Ann looked confused. She couldn't remember where she'd heard the charm before, but she knew it was in her memory somehow. "I don't know," she answered. "But I know it's true, Mrs. Glennwell."

Her friend smiled, then put the dime into her pocket. "It's all right, Ann. Sometimes wishes just pop up inside of us like seeds sprouting in springtime."

Ann paused and wondered to herself what other seeds might be inside of her, just waiting for the conditions to be right to spring up.

GROWING OUR LUCK AND PROSPERITY

Verbal charms often make use of common cultural symbols and correspondences that can be incorporated into the magical ritual itself. One of these common symbols is of the growing of plants, which our agrarian ancestors would have been very familiar with. Just as the plants of the field grow, so too grows the magic that is birthed by the charmer. This symbolic connection between growing plants and growing magic finds its way into a lot of different Ozark rituals, not just those for growing fortune, prosperity, and good luck. For example, it can be found in healing and cleansing rituals as well. A charmer might say something like "As this tree grows, so too let my health grow, improve, and become stronger." Likewise, for getting rid of a disease or a hex, a charmer might employ an opposite of this image, as in the case of "As the grasses and grains of the field die in the autumn, so let this illness die with it." The growing and dying cycles of nature have long been an important part of our visual culture. Many rural people in the Ozarks today are still able to deeply connect with the seasonal cycles of the forests around them and incorporate these symbolic images into their magic work.

Verbal charms themselves are often looked at as being seeds planted within the heart, spirit, or mind of the charmer, either by some divine hand or perhaps by an elder teacher. These seeds often lay dormant until the conditions are just right for them to arise within the charmer. Several healers

I've met told me that certain charms "grew" inside them or appeared on their tongues when the time was just right; these were charms that they had received at a young age but had forgotten until the moment they arose. This adds another mysterious dimension to the charming tradition—the idea that the charms have a life of their own.

Likewise, just as charms can grow within the spirit of the charmer, if not maintained and taken care of, they can wither and die. Charms need to be nourished or watered like you would water plants in your garden. Many charmers I've met tell the same story about how healers and magical practitioners who didn't use their gift or the verbal charms that they had been given, and because of this neglect, the power itself died within the charmer. That's not to say a person couldn't perhaps gain new powers or verbal charms, but there is this idea that those original seeds, because they were never watered, died in the soil rather than rising up and bearing good fruit.

The image of a plant bearing good fruit is another one that finds its way into the charming tradition in many different examples. This can be a deep symbol for the charmer, who waters the seeds planted within their own spirit in order for good fruit to be born later on. This fruit is, of course, the healing or magical act itself. The fruit is then the magic that you give to the community, the interactions you have with the sick and infirmed, and the good work that you do in the world around you. Traditionally, this has heavy biblical connections to the symbol of the tree bearing good fruit and the good works of the Holy Spirit in the world, but also connected to this symbolism is the idea of personal prosperity and fortune being the good fruit produced and, by association, fruits of the magical act as well.

PROSPERITY IN THE MODERN WORLD

Good luck, fortune, opportunity, and personal prosperity are still subjects that are on our minds today. People have to work at jobs for money, so sometimes a person might want to ensure a good job, or perhaps change the conditions within their current job to be better for them. Sometimes we seek to amend our own place in the world through gambling, which historically was a very important way for the poorest of the poor to suddenly find themselves in a much better position and with opportunities they might never have had. Or perhaps prosperity takes on a different meaning, one that goes beyond the material world and points toward personal success and growth in areas of creativity, family, or other pursuits like magic itself, where the fruit that is born isn't necessarily a material good, but something much deeper. Verbal charms have a place within these fields as well. There are verbal charms to help at the gambling tables. There are charms to help boost our confidence for job interviews and charms that can even help heal a relationship with a bad boss. There are charms to help fix our luck, which in and of itself can be a cleansing act, especially if we are suffering from a hex or a curse that might affect our luck as a part of its malign action.

In all these cases, we can still identify the same symbol of bearing good fruit. And as one of my teachers taught me, "If you can heal the root, you can heal the fruit." This means that our verbal charms can address the root of a problem and help amend it within our own bodies and spirits as a way of ensuring the fruit that's birthed later on is of the choicest quality. In this way, verbal charms for good luck and fortune take on a different life and meaning. They become healing acts and, in the end, all Ozark magic aims at maintaining an equilibrium within ourselves and in the world around us.

Success, prosperity, and fortune can be very subjective, depending on the individual, so auspicious timings for these works are quite diverse depending upon what you are specifically wanting to bless. This type of work is generally connected to the planet Jupiter, who rules over all fortune and success. Jupiter's day of the week is Thursday. Jupiter in the fire element yields the zodiac sign Sagittarius, which is an auspicious sign for extroverted success amongst the people—and a very good timing for works related to extroverted jobs or fortune pursuits that rely heavily on charisma. Generally, Virgo is an excellent sign for personal success; Capricorn is best used for charming related to work, employment, enterprise, and money; and Taurus is a beneficial sign for growing the success of hearth and home—or the successes of life that don't have a monetary or materialistic aspect. Aries is a sign that can be used in luck or success related to competition, specifically sports that rely on physical strength and agility. So, you can see how a cunning charmer can interpret almost all of the zodiac signs to fit whatever need they might have.

Sign	Planet	Element	Day	Use
Aries	Mars	Fire	Tuesday	Luck with competitions; courage that leads to prosperity; prosperity above others
Taurus	Venus	Earth	Friday	Success for the hearth and home; familial prosperity; success in farming, gardening, and working with the land
Gemini	Mercury	Air	Wednesday	Augmenting luck; gambling and acquiring quick money
Virgo	Mercury	Earth	Wednesday	Personal success; organization that leads to success; concentration
Libra	Venus	Air	Friday	Legal matters that affect our success and prosperity; business contracts and partnerships; all contract work
Sagittarius	Jupiter	Fire	Thursday	Success out in the world; charisma-based prosperity; jobs that work face-to-face with the public
Capricorn	Saturn	Earth	Saturday	Success with employment, enterprise, and careers; great for work with small businesses

Zodiac Signs for Prosperity

As individuals on the Charming Way, we are gardeners of our magic. We tend to the seeds of power within our own spirits. We water them when they need watering, and we prune them when they need pruning. We watch them grow, watch their flowers bloom, and watch as they produce good fruit. While we might use our verbal charms to grow prosperity and fortune in the world around us, we must always remember that these charms are growing seeds within our own spirits at the same time. As our magic grows from these seeds, so too does our spirit grow.

What seeds are in you that need watering? What seeds of magic can you tend to today and help grow? What does the fruit of this magic look like in your own life and the lives of the community around you? How can you share this fruit with those who are truly in need and help maintain that equilibrium in the world?

However you choose to answer these questions is up to you and you alone. But know that there are seeds already planted inside of you—some of which have been there since your birth. All seeds will grow when the conditions are just right. There's no need to rush anything; the seeds are there, waiting to sprout. Water the seeds inside of you with kindness, with patience, curiosity, and tenderness.

THE CHARMS

The following charms all relate to prosperity of the home and family, or general prosperity work (growing your prosperity). Taurus (Venus, Friday, earth) is a great sign to use. Virgo (Mercury, Wednesday, earth), Libra (Venus, Friday, air), and Capricorn (Saturn, Saturday, earth) are great for business, employment, and money-related prosperity. Libra is especially good for business contracts and legal matters. I like to use Virgo for new business or job ventures and Capricorn for growing established businesses or careers. Gambling work or rituals to augment personal luck are associated with Gemini (Mercury, Wednesday, air).

✲ "BOSS BE GOOD" CHARM ✲

This verbal charm is used to gain favor with an authority figure, especially an employer or supervisor. This favor can take on many different forms. It could be general luck when it comes to your relationship with your boss, or it could be giving yourself authority over a tyrannical figure. It can also lend a certain amount of invisibility when dealing with your boss. This doesn't mean that you might go unnoticed altogether, but rather this ritual work will make it so that your boss will have no reason to watch or criticize you. This work is especially good with micromanagers.

This charm and associated ritual can be used with general authority figures as well, or anyone you want to gain power over. Additionally, you could use this charm if you want someone to see you in a better light. The individual who gave me this charming ritual said that it's "good for bosses, bureaucrats, and bad politicians." Empowerment rituals like this one have been a part of our folk magic for as long as we've had to deal with those in power.

This charm uses another infinity clause: "Until roots grow up, / And branches down," the idea being that this work will continue until the roots of all the trees grow up into the sky like branches and until the branches grow down into the earth like roots.

MAGICAL TIMING

When you are in physical or close contact with your boss, supervisor, or someone with perceived authority over you (may be symbolic). Moon days in Libra (Venus, Friday, air) or Capricorn (Saturn, Saturday, earth) are good for blessing the oil used in the ritual.

CHARM

Be good, be good,
Nose down and follow.

Look over me,
Look under me,
Look across me,
But never at me.

Be good, be good,
We all want good things.

Your eyes see gold in me,
Or else see nothing at all.

Until roots grow up,
And branches down.

RITUAL INGREDIENTS

Bowl
Olive oil

RITUAL ACTIONS

Begin by blessing your olive oil. Pour some olive oil into a bowl. You can use however much you'd like. Recite the verbal charm three times, and after each recitation, blow across the surface of the oil. Bottle this oil to save for future use.

Whenever you are going to be in close physical contact with the person you're charming, rub some of the blessed oil into your hands while reciting the verbal charm again. Contact with the person will activate the action of the verbal charm. Physical contact could include a handshake, a hug, or even passing documents or an object to them.

NOTES

Reciting verbal charms over oil and then anointing the body is common in Ozark folk magic and healing work. There are many oils that can be used, and plant materia can even be added to the oil to empower its purpose. In the oil-based charming rituals I've collected, olive oil is the preferred carrier, but I've had personal success with other oil types.

✶ BUSINESS BLESSING ✶

This traditional charm for growing personal good luck and magnetizing prosperity has been repurposed for blessing a business.

MAGICAL TIMING

Most auspicious when you first open your business. Nighttime. Full moon in Taurus (Venus, Friday, earth) or Capricorn (Saturn, Saturday, earth).

CHARM

What I plant, please let grow.
Silver above and silver below.
From window to door,
From ceiling to floor,
And everything in between.
(Repeat three times)

RITUAL INGREDIENTS

Shovel or spade
Silver item: ring, silver coin, chain, etc.
Potted plant (optional)

RITUAL ACTIONS

Begin by digging a small hole in the ground right outside the front door to your business—as close to the door as you can get. Hold your silver item in your right hand. Repeat the verbal charm three times, blowing into the hole once after every recitation. Then, drop your silver item into the hole and bury with dirt.

While this is a simple ritual, there are several considerations to keep in mind. First is what silver item you would like to use. Note that this will be buried, so don't use a family heirloom or something particularly valuable. Yes, the item must be made of silver, but you can use items that have a certain percentage of silver in them, like old dimes. In the US, dimes were made from 90 percent silver until 1964, so any dime made before that will work for the purposes of this charming ritual. Post-1965, US dimes are usually around 75 percent copper and 25 percent nickel alloy, containing no silver.[6] In addition to silver coins, you could also use necklaces, chains, spoons, or items that are either made of silver or have silver plating (an easier to find and less

---

6. "What Coins Are Silver?"

expensive alternative). One of my teachers said that he used liquid colloidal silver with much success; this can easily be found in many pharmacies and natural health stores.

Another consideration is the burying ritual itself. If you're able to bury the silver item in the ground near the front door of the business, this is best, but isn't always possible. If you don't have access to the ground, you can bury the silver item in a potted plant (or even a full planter) next to the front door. If you run your business from home and don't have a physical location, bury your silver in a potted plant and keep it in your office or near the area where you do most of your work. One woodworker I knew had a charm like this for his business that he kept near the front door of his workshop. The item itself was a glass canning jar filled with dirt and a buried silver item, then sealed. The silver item and dirt combination is what is important—it connects to the idea of planting a seed of success and wealth that will grow for you. If you're like me and kill most house plants unintentionally, then you might want to create a canning jar and dirt container for your silver.

The last consideration is how to maintain your silver charm once it has been planted. To recharge your charm, I recommend repeating the verbal charm three times every full moon while touching the spot where the silver item was buried. Also, make sure your silver item doesn't get dug up. In the event you close your business, you can dig up the silver item again.

NOTES

Charms for prosperity and good luck often connect the full moon and silver. For this reason, it's common to find charmers who use silver dimes in such work as representatives of the moon's radiant light. In this verbal charm, the "Silver above and silver below" of the second line specifically refers to the silver of the full moon and the silver of the item in the charmer's hand. By planting the silver item in the ground, the charmer is planting a seed that contains the fullness of the moon's prosperous power.

✶ CARD GAMES CHARM ✶

As with the "Boss Be Good" Charm, this ritual is used to bless oil that will then be rubbed into the hands before gambling with cards. This verbal charm is very specific in its use for making the charmer extra lucky while playing card games. As it was taught to me, the more power the charmer has, the luckier they will be. In addition, this charm can be used to bless card readings (especially those that use playing cards) for the purpose of divining sources or routes of fortune for the charmer or another person.

MAGICAL TIMING

Before playing cards. Waxing moon, from new to full, is the traditional time period for blessing the oil used in the ritual—begin on the new moon in Gemini (Mercury, Wednesday, air) for added auspiciousness.

CHARM

Four angels,
From four directions,
Light on four fingers,
And say four prayers.

A diamond prayer,
A heart prayer,
A club prayer,
A spade prayer.

Gold in my pockets,
For as long as I live.

RITUAL INGREDIENTS

Ace cards, all four suits
Bowl
Olive oil

RITUAL ACTIONS

Begin by pulling all four aces from a brand-new pack of playing cards. The newness of the cards does matter in this ritual.

Place the aces on a flat surface in the order of diamond, heart, club, and spade. Next, place the bowl on the table, above the cards. Have the olive oil ready, but don't put it in the bowl yet. Recite the verbal charm. When you get to the line "A diamond prayer," place the forefinger of your left hand on the diamond ace. With the next line, place your left thumb on the heart. Then, with the next line, place your right thumb on the club. Finally, place your right forefinger on the spade. Finish the verbal charm, then pick up the four aces in a stack that keeps the same left-to-right order of the cards. Place your stack of aces in the bowl, then pour olive oil over the top of the cards.

Let this oil remain on the playing cards from the new moon to the full. On the full moon, you can remove the playing cards and bottle the oil. Recite the verbal charm again whenever you anoint your hands with the oil.

NOTES

The individual who gave me this charm said there's another version that uses "devils" instead of "angels." I've seen similar gambling charms that invoke a certain number of devils to each sit inside one of the charmer's fingers so that everything they touch (as far as the gambling goes) can be influenced by their infernal power. This charm, involving magic from a more heavenly source, works on a similar principle: the angels are believed to reside in the oil then inside the charmer's hands.

☆ DIME CHARM FOR GOOD LUCK ☆

There are many versions of this verbal charm found throughout the Ozark region. All of them involve looking at the full moon, reciting the charm, and then manipulating a silver object in a specific way. In the case of this charm, that silver is represented by a dime. It's believed that by reciting this charm and following the ritual actions, the charmer will be assured good luck until the next full moon.

MAGICAL TIMING

Full moon in Gemini (Mercury, Wednesday, air) or any full moon.

CHARM

Full moon I see,
Full pockets I see,
Full of silver,
Full of gold,
Until I look on you again!

RITUAL INGREDIENTS

Dime coin

Silver item: ring, bracelet, coin, chain, charm, etc. (optional)

RITUAL ACTIONS

Traditionally, this charming ritual is paired with a dime, but you can use an alternative silver item. Begin by going outside on a full moon night. For this ritual, you should be able to look directly at the full moon. If there is cloud cover, do your best to find where the moon is. If you can't see the moon at all, you will have to wait until the next full moon.

The actual ritual procedure is quite simple. While looking at the full moon, repeat the verbal charm three times, and while you are repeating the charm, turn the silver dime or silver object over in your right pocket using your right hand. Continue to turn the object over and over in your pocket for the full duration of the charm recitation. It's traditional to end this charming ritual by turning your back on the moon and returning indoors.

✳ FINDING A LUCKY OBJECT ✳

This is a divination method that allows the charmer to be able to find a lucky object or "token," as they are sometimes called by Ozarkers. Mountain healers and magical practitioners have traditionally valued natural objects of heightened auspiciousness for use in their work. Auspicious objects are things that are strange, unusual, or rare. Objects that have naturally occurring holes, for example, are somewhat rare and therefore valued as containing more auspiciousness than other objects one might find in nature. A hole stone, also called a hag stone, is one such example. Natural objects that are shaped like animals or common tools are also highly prized as auspicious. One healer I met had a large collection of what he called his "snake sticks," all of which had twisting, serpentine shapes. He used these auspicious items to "snake out" curses from inside his clients.

Such auspicious objects are often difficult to find, but it is believed that those with the second sight can locate them easily. Are you a person who is constantly finding four-leaf clovers? You might have the second sight, particularly for auspicious objects and tools. Don't worry, there are ways for folks who don't have the second sight to locate their own lucky amulets. This verbal charm and ritual is one such way.

Rituals to find lucky or auspicious objects and tools are often very simple. This is because from an Ozark folk perspective, finding such objects relies on the intuition of the practitioner themselves rather than any outward magical work. As in this ritual, where the charmer relies on their own feeling during the ritual, post-charming, as the means to locate the specific object they are seeking. For added help, using tools like pendulums and dowsing rods is a common addition to these rituals.

MAGICAL TIMING

Nighttime. New moon. Zodiac moon days in Gemini (Mercury, Wednesday, air) are good for uncovering hidden things.

CHARM

Pray the Moon—
Good luck be found,
In spring or solid ground.
(Repeat three times)

RITUAL INGREDIENTS

Flashlight or lantern
Dowsing tools: pendulum, dowsing rods, etc. (optional)

RITUAL ACTIONS

This ritual will take place at night, so make sure you have a flashlight or lantern with you to be able to hunt for your summoned lucky object. Go outside at night when the new moon is in the sky. Repeat the verbal charm three times while looking at the moon, if you're able to see it.

After reciting the charm, close your eyes and let yourself be pulled in a certain direction. You might feel like there are multiple directions that are calling to you, but choose one at a time. Follow this deep pulling until it leads you to your object. Once you find the object, sit with it and see how it feels. Examine how the object looks. Are there any auspicious features? Ozarkers traditionally look for signs that the object they found is indeed auspicious: Maybe it's shaped like an animal or household tool. Maybe it's a natural object, like a seedpod that's far away from its host tree (finding a pinecone in a spot where there aren't any pine trees, for example). Auspiciousness can take many different forms, so let your own spirit guide you in this interpretation. If you feel like the object you're holding isn't the correct one, put it down and try again.

NOTES

Some practitioners pair this charm with a pendulum or dowsing object as a way to better locate what they're looking for. Pendulums can come in a variety of shapes, sizes, and materials. For this ritual, you can use a purchased pendulum of your choice, or you can use a traditional Ozark one made from a string tied through a hole stone, or a string tied around the handle of a small knife.

Before you start the ritual, make sure to tell your pendulum what you're looking for. There are many different ways you can use your pendulum, and they are all based on your own practice. Establish, for instance, a counterclockwise spinning direction means "go left" and a clockwise spin means "go right." You can use yes and no answers for the spinning direction as well. After reciting the verbal charm three times, hold your pendulum up and observe the motions it makes. Based on the meanings you established before the ritual, you will then proceed.

This ritual can last from the new moon to the full moon, depending on 1) whether you've located an object that you believe is auspicious, or 2) whether you want to try and locate multiple objects. You will repeat the same ritual each night. Finding auspicious objects like these is traditionally done in the "light of the moon," or during its waxing phase.

☆ GAMBLING BLESSING ☆

This is a quick verbal charm that intends to give you some extra good luck before placing a bet, playing cards, or engaging in other forms of gambling. There is an additional ritual procedure to create a good luck item and blessing oil, which can heighten the effectiveness of the work by adding auspiciousness in the form of lucky materia.

This verbal charm engages with the idea of fast luck for now, but not necessarily luck that will last forever. As one of my teachers taught me, luck for life takes a lot of hard work and sacrifice on the part of the charmer because you're "playing with the Fates," as he said. More often, charmers will choose to do quick work for in-the-moment luck and fortune. Maybe it's winning some cash in the lottery or seeing a bet you placed be successful. Whatever the work is for, the amount won will likely be small, but still more money than you started with. This work for the "small fortune" is often said to bypass the gaze of God, the Fates, and whoever else holds the universe in balance. As my teacher said, "If you work for small goals, but more often, you can walk right underneath Jesus's own nose—if you're good enough."

MAGICAL TIMING

Before you gamble. Oil and nutmeg nut in charming ritual can be blessed on a zodiac moon day in Gemini (Mercury, Wednesday, air). Can begin on the new moon and charge the amulet until the following full moon (especially a full moon in Gemini).

CHARM

Good luck, for now, I call.
For now, I call in good luck.
Not for later,
Nor for tomorrow,
But for now, I call, I call.
Five fingers around money,
I grab it up tight.
Pockets full of gold,
Good luck, for now, I call.
(Repeat three times)

RITUAL INGREDIENTS

Five-finger grass ("cinquefoil," *Potentilla* spp.)
Nutmeg nut
Olive oil
Silver item: ring, bracelet, coin, chain, charm, etc.

RITUAL ACTIONS

On its own, you can repeat the verbal charm three times before you engage in any gambling activity. After each charm recitation, blow across your hands three times.

If you choose to craft a lucky amulet, begin by pouring some olive oil into a small glass canning jar or bottle. Add some fresh or dried five-finger grass (*Potentilla* spp.) to the jar. Let this sit in a silver bowl, or touching a silver item like a ring, necklace, spoon, etc., for three nights or from the new to the full moon.

On the third night, or on the full moon, rub some of the oil onto your whole nutmeg nut while reciting the verbal charm three times. After each recitation, blow onto the nut three times. Rub the nutmeg nut until it is no longer oily; you can even wipe off any excess oil that the nut didn't absorb. Keep this in your pocket and rub it between the forefinger and thumb of your right hand before engaging in any gambling. Anoint with more of your oil on the new and full moon to recharge.

✦ NEW JOB CHARM ✦

This verbal charm can be used in two rituals: one to find or open the doorway to a new job, or to secure yourself favor while in your new position.

Blessing the doorway as a part of the first charming ritual procedure holds the symbolic value of "opening the door," or creating for yourself the opportunity for something new to come along. When you step through to the other side, you become a new person. This simple ritual action can profoundly change how we feel about our situation at hand.

The blessed oil in the second ritual works through physical contact with another person. The magic held on the skin by way of the blessed oil is then transferred to the target that is being charmed as part of the work. Physical contact isn't necessary for this charming ritual.

MAGICAL TIMING

Waxing moon. Zodiac moon days in Taurus (Venus, Friday, earth), Virgo (Mercury, Wednesday, earth), or Capricorn (Saturn, Saturday, earth).

CHARM

I step through the door
And I am here,
Blessed and prosperous.
No foes will come against me,
No lightning will strike me,
No misfortune will find me,
Until the moon stays forever dark.
(Repeat three times)

RITUAL INGREDIENTS

To Find a New Job:
Bowl
Taper candle, white (or beeswax yellow), 10–12 inches, with holder
Matches or lighter
Olive oil

For Favor at a New Job:
Canning jar, glass, with lid
Olive oil
Silver item: ring, silver coin, chain, etc.

RITUAL ACTIONS

The first charming ritual for use with this verbal charm is to find a new job or magically open the doorway for new employment or a new career to find you. Pour some olive oil into a bowl. Go to one of the doors that exits your house. You will begin on the inside of the house.

Open the door fully. Recite the verbal charm three times, blowing across the surface of the olive oil three times after each recitation. Once you're finished with the recitation, take your right forefinger and dip it into the olive oil. Starting at the bottom left corner of the doorframe, trace the entire frame with your finger: from the bottom left corner up to the top left, then right across the top of the doorframe to the top right corner, then down to the bottom right corner, and finish by going left across the floor back to the bottom left corner.

Carrying the candle and bowl, step through the doorway. While outside, rub some of the oil into your hands and feet, then place a small dot over your heart. Rub some onto the taper candle, then go back inside.

Light the taper candle and burn as often as you like in order to shine a light in the darkness so that new work will find you. You can save the oil to anoint additional candles.

★ ★ ★

The second charming ritual is for use after you have already found a new job. This ritual will bring you favor from your new boss and coworkers.

Pour some olive oil into a glass canning jar. Add a silver item to the oil. This can be anything that is pure silver or even silver plated. Repeat the verbal charm three times, blowing into the jar three times after each recitation. Close the lid and let this sit from the new moon to the following full moon.

On the full moon, open the jar and repeat the verbal charm another three times, blowing into the jar three times after each recitation. Remove the silver item. You can now leave this oil in the jar or bottle it for ease of use. Whenever you go to work, rub some of this oil into your hands—especially if you are having a meeting with your boss or other important coworkers, supervisors, or clients.

★ TREE BLESSING FOR PROSPERITY ★

There are two different layers to this traditional verbal charm. The outer layer pertains to the physical prosperity of a fruit tree; you can use this charm in the springtime to bless your fruit trees to be prosperous during the year. This would have been of greater importance to our ancestors, of course, where a bountiful harvest meant survival and perhaps even some money to spare.

Hidden within this outer layer is an inner purpose as well, which pertains to individual prosperity as well as the prosperity of the family, both likened to a tree bearing good and plentiful fruit. With this in mind, you can magically connect your own prosperity, or the prosperity of your home, to the growth of a fruit tree (or any strong, living tree) so that as the tree grows strong, tall, and fruitful, so too will you and all those you're charming for.

The symbolism of the fruitful tree in part comes from the spiritual heritage of Ozark hillfolk, specifically Psalm 1:3 in the Bible ("They are like trees planted by streams of water, which yield their fruit in its season, and their leaves do not wither. In all that they do, they prosper") as well as Isaiah 27:6 ("In days to come Jacob shall take root; Israel shall blossom and put forth shoots and fill the whole world with fruit"), both of which would have been culturally familiar to Ozark people. When we think about the agrarian lives of our ancestors, it's no wonder so much of our magic for prosperity, fortune, and good luck relies on the image of growing plants, specifically those that yield food for families and communities.

A couple curious words are found in the second line of the verbal charm: *youling sop*. According to J. Rendel Harris, the tradition of youling was once very popular throughout southern England and was connected to medieval wassailing practices. It's speculated that youling refers to Yule—a time deeply connected to the wassailing traditions. *Sop* is another word for *sapling*. During Yule, communities would gather in apple orchards with hot cider and sweet treats to sing, or wassail, to their trees as a blessing to ensure prosperity the following spring. In a version of the rhyme from Sussex, the line goes "God bring us a howling crop," meaning a large, prosperous bounty.[7]

MAGICAL TIMING

Waxing moon. Taurus (Venus, Friday, earth) for the home or Capricorn (Saturn, Saturday, earth) for work and money. Spring is a good time for tree charming, especially if you are able to go out just as the tree begins to bud with leaves or flowers (whichever comes first). Just like using the waxing moon, connecting to your chosen tree in the springtime symbolically uses the growth cycle to magically empower the growth of your prosperity. You can also bless your trees on Yule, or the winter solstice, alongside other traditional wassailing practices.

CHARM

Stand fast, root; bear well, top;
God send us a youling sop!

---

7. Harris, *Origin and Meaning of Apple Cults*, 13.

Every twig, apple big,
Every bough, apple enow,
Hats full, caps full,
Fill quarter sacks full.

RITUAL INGREDIENTS

Bowl or cup
Water

Optional Variation:
5-inch cloth square, white
Identifying materials: hair, fingernail clippings, spit, etc.
String, white, 3 feet

RITUAL ACTIONS

For blessing a fruit tree, the ritual can be as simple as repeating the verbal charm three, seven, or twelve times while facing the tree. Verbal charms like these are often whispered to the tree so that only the tree can "hear" it; this protects the power of the verbal charm as well as creates a more intimate relationship between the charmer and the tree itself. It's also common to see verbal charms repeated over a bowl/cup of water before the water is poured onto the tree. Charms may even be "blown" into water; in this ritual, you will repeat the verbal charm and then blow across the surface of the water. This blowing action is repeated after each recitation.

If you want to magically connect your own prosperity to that of a tree, you will need to use a little sympathetic magic. In this case, begin by choosing your tree. A fruit tree (especially apple) is traditional for this specific verbal charm, but any strong, living tree will work. Let me emphasize—make sure you choose a *strong* and *living* tree. As the belief goes, connecting to a sick or dying tree will only make your prosperity sicken and die. This applies to any species of tree.

Once you have your tree picked out, cut out a small square of white cloth. It doesn't have to be very big—a five-inch square would be perfect. Place a few strands of your own hair as well as three fingernail clippings in the center of the cloth square. Bring in the corners of the cloth so that a small bundle is made. Tie the bundle closed with some ordinary white string, then cut a longer length of string that will be used to tie the bundle to your tree. Make sure the string is long enough to go around the trunk.

Take your cloth bundle and extra string out to your chosen tree. Tie the bundle to the tree trunk at eye level. Once tied, repeat the verbal charm three, seven, or twelve times. Eventually, your bundle will fade away, in which case you can make another one. If your bundle happens to fall off the tree, you can repeat the charming process and reattach it to the trunk.

There's a simplified version of this ritual as well, which involves marking the bark of your chosen tree with your own blood, spit, or semen, after which you will recite the verbal charm three, seven, or twelve times.

CHAPTER 4

To Tie Your Ills upon a Stone ...

Three days after Ann's thirteenth birthday, she fell gravely ill. It started with a pain in her chest, then quickly turned into a fever that wouldn't break. Ann's mother tried ice baths, herbal teas, and even some fever pills the pharmacist recommended, but nothing would lower the temperature. Lucy even thought about calling the local doctor in but shook her head at the notion; "Only in dire circumstances," she said under her breath. While the folks of Nelson's Holler appreciated old Doc Winthrop for all the good he brought to the community, there was still some deep paranoia that made people like Lucy and Gram Watson certain that you only went to the doctor's office if you were ready to die. Lucy wasn't ready for Ann to die.

While her mother and the neighbors swarmed busily through the house like little bees, Ann dreamed, completely unaware of her sickness. She dreamed so deep that her dream-body wondered if she was ever going to wake up again. Strange, twisting visions carried her through a pastel-colored sky, then down through rock into the dark bowels of the earth. She flew through Nelson's Holler, spying on her classmates struggling to keep awake in the schoolhouse. She flew through the mercantile and giggled while listening to three old ladies gossip over the barrel of dry oats. She flew to Gram Watson's house and watched her stand at the sink, scraping dried gravy from a cast-iron skillet. As a trick, Ann tugged at one of Gram's long braids. She was shocked when Gram stopped her scrubbing, smiled, and said aloud, "Child, unless you want to help me with my chores, you best be on your way!" Ann always listened to Gram, even in her dreams, so she flew back into the vibrant, formless darkness and lost herself in dreaming once more.

It had been three days since the fever had started, and nothing was helping. Lucy thought she'd call on Gram, but all of a sudden the old woman showed up early one morning. "How'd you know to come, Gram?" Lucy asked, hugging the woman tightly.

"I was washing up dishes the other night and something just told me to come over," Gram answered with a grin.

The old woman began her diagnosis, observing both the physical signs on Ann's body as well as casting divinations using some dried beans that she threw onto an old kitchen towel. She took note of her findings in a tattered little diary she pulled from her pocket. While she worked, she had Lucy brew up a strong herbal tonic in an old clay beanpot on the stove. "How is she, Gram?" Lucy asked, stirring the broth.

Gram shook her head. "This ain't any normal fever," she said, placing a wrinkled hand on the girl's chest. "She'll be okay, when she wants to be."

Lucy rushed to the bedside and grabbed Gram's arm. "Help her, Gram. You have to help her."

"Calm down—the fever won't take her. I had one of these too, when I was about her age. She'll be fine, but she's got to choose to come back."

Lucy began to cry for the third time that morning. Gram comforted her while repeating an old charm inside her mind: In fever see, by the power of the Three, come back to me.

Ann was beginning to find this whole dreaming nonsense a little troublesome. She was pushed and pulled from here to there without any warning whatsoever. The constant turmoil and chaos made her stomach roll and ache. At times, she knew she was dreaming but had absolutely no notion as to what to do about that. Sometimes she felt like she must be dying, and this frightened her even more than the dreaming. In a moment of terror, she hid in an overgrown hedge, hoping the dream wouldn't find her there. As she shook amongst the leaves and branches, she heard a woman singing nearby. Somehow the singing comforted Ann, so much so that she crawled from out of the hedge to find the singer.

On the other side of the hedgerow sat a little cabin. Smoke spiraled up from a chimney in the roof, and Ann could smell beans and ham hocks simmering some-

where inside the house. A woman stood in the garden holding a rake. She sang to herself as she weeded around pepper and squash plants. Ann thought she looked a lot like her mother. I wonder if she's a relation? Ann thought.

Some unseen force pulled the young girl to the garden. She had no idea why, but she even found herself asking the woman if she needed any help. The woman stopped and smiled at Ann. "Sure, looks like you've got good hands," she said, returning to her work.

"Gram always has me working in her garden," Ann replied as she quickly started yanking out weeds from around a squash mound.

"What's your name, child?" the woman asked.

"It's Ann Ganter, ma'am."

"What a coincidence! That's my name too."

As Ann stood confused, the woman pulled her close to her chest in a tight hug.

"Wait a second," Ann said, piecing the puzzle together in her mind. "Are you Granny Ganter?"

The woman smiled and nodded. "Although I don't much look like a Granny, do I?"

Ann laughed, then hugged the woman tight around the waist again. "I always wished I could meet you, Granny."

"I always wished I could meet you too, Ann. But we don't have time right now." She pulled the girl away from her and looked Ann directly in the eyes. "Ann, you have to wake up now, sweetheart."

Ann was reminded that she was dreaming. "Oh, Mama will wake me up soon. It's got to be morning by now."

"No, Ann, this isn't a normal sleep. If you don't wake up, you're going to die."

Ann knew there had been something very strange about this dream, but she wasn't able to think about it too much before everything shifted again. She suddenly grew pale and scared. "I don't know how," she said in a shaky voice, holding back tears.

Granny Ganter just nodded. "It's all right now, Ann, I want you to walk straight through that door into the kitchen. Do you see it?"

Ann turned and saw the open doorway across the verdant garden. "Yes, I see it."

"All right, now don't go off nowhere else. Think to yourself that you're walkin' right through that doorway. You've got to get something out of that kitchen, Ann."

Ann felt a hand push her forward. She thought about turning around to say good-bye to Granny Ganter but remembered her command to walk straight ahead. She walked through the rows of corn. Through the arch of morning glory and clematis vines. Through the kitchen door and felt herself jump awake. She was in her bed, wet from the fever breaking. Next to her, Lucy was shocked awake. Gram rushed into the room and handed the girl a cup of water. As Ann's breathing began to calm once again, she told her caretakers about the dreams she'd had.

✻ ✻ ✻

In the days to follow, Ann didn't have any more of the strange dreams. In fact, she didn't dream at all. But one peculiarity began to arise, noticed only by Ann herself and Gram Watson. It started with a friend and classmate of Ann's, Thomas Grider, who fell ill one day. Ann visited him with some oatmeal cakes her mother had made, and overnight the boy was completely recovered. Within a week, Ann and Gram visited a kind old woman from the church, Miss Edna, who had broken her ankle and was bedridden while it healed. Ann sat at the bedside quietly while Gram and the woman gossiped. Something came over the girl, and she reached out and touched the broken ankle gently. "Careful now," Gram barked.

Ann nodded and softly caressed the ankle for only a moment before returning her hand to her lap. Gram and Miss Edna stayed silent for a moment before returning to their conversation. Overnight, the ankle stopped hurting, and Miss Edna was able to start moving it again, ever so slightly.

As happens with many of the old-timers, no one ever acknowledged these strange occurrences, not even to each other. This was intentional. Everyone knows that to talk too much about miraculous things risks the Fates taking them away. Whenever Ann began questioning the occurrences, Gram would stop her and say, "Let the miracles rest, Ann. There will be time enough to talk about them later."

HEALING THE SEEN AND UNSEEN

In the old days, Ozark healers often worked to address problems of the body and spirit (or mind) together, at the same time. Today, people tend to separate these areas into two distinct fields that the individual can choose between; if you're having trouble with anxiety, you can visit a psychiatrist or medical doctor, or both, or neither. Amongst more traditional healers, the patient doesn't always have the choice. The medicines formulated are aimed at rebalancing these areas simultaneously. A perfect example of this can be seen in the traditional way of administering Ozark herbal preparations, which often also involve a large dose of accompanying verbal charms and prayers. If not prayers, then the healer might sit with their patient and talk. This form of talking isn't just idle chatter; as I observed with one herbal healer, they were able to glean all kinds of pertinent information from a simple friendly conversation. For example, how the client felt about their illness, how their family was assisting in the healing process, what was left undone around the house that needed attention, lifestyle and dietary habits, history of illness in the family, recent travel or exposure to contagion, overall stress that might be in the family, and many more useful details.

Along similar lines, traditional healers often worked with both physical and magical methods of healing—neither of which would have been individual, separated categories. What we might consider a physical illness today, like a fever, was just as likely to be cured by verbal charms, prayers, and ritual as it was to be treated by herbal preparations—depending on the healer, of course. Likewise, hexes and magical illnesses might be cured using very physical methods, such as purging using strong herbal emetics and laxatives, or drinking an herbal tonic to elementally counter a specific hex in the body. All of these methods of addressing both the seen and unseen illnesses would have been considered healing work, with very little separations into individual groups.

Another example of this can be seen with blood stoppers, very traditional specialized healers in the Ozarks who are hard to find these days. Most of the blood stoppers I've met have some magical method of curing (although they will rarely ever call this "magic"), usually a specific verbal charm or prayer. Often, most of them have a physical remedy to pair with their ritual cure—like bandaging or field-dressing methods, or even knowing when a wound needs stitches or additional medical care.

Within this chapter, you will find charms for many magical as well as physical illnesses, presented in a very traditional way—that is, mixed together with little to no distinction between the two areas. Any of these charms can be paired with modern medical care, and I often recommend to my clients that they seek such aid *first* before coming to me for additional work. While our ancestors might not have separated these two areas of the healing process, we modern folk do, and Ozark healers have adjusted their work to meet these changing times. As with the healer I met who prayed over the medications doctors had prescribed to her clients: in talking with her, she expressed contentment in being able to pray for and bless people in a traditional way while knowing that her clients—many of whom were members of her family or close community—were also receiving the best possible medical care.

MAGICAL DIAGNOSTICS

Traditional methods of diagnosis in the Ozarks are often deceptively simple, as with many areas of folk magic practice here. These methods often use techniques of divination, many of which wouldn't even be seen by the patient themselves. The most common procedure I've observed (and the one I use in my own work) begins with the healer collecting useful information through conversation with their patient. These friendly chats are hardly ever formalized, which works to the healer's advantage, as they are able to collect intimate details about their patient that might not be shared in a formal setting. At this point, the healer is already formulating a remedy just based upon these lifestyle questions.

From here, the healer might know exactly what needs to be done. In my own practice, I follow this initial conversation with a divination session. The entire goal of the traditional diagnosis process is uncovering the correspondences of the illness or hex inside the body. These correspondences—which can include elemental, planetary, and zodiac figures—are derived from the nature of the symptoms that are manifesting as well as the location where the illness or hex is rooted, or sitting, within the body. This location is traditionally discovered through divination and might not necessarily be the location where the symptoms are present. For example, the root of a congested chest might not be just in the chest and lungs.

Once the location of the illness or hex is discovered, the healer will determine the preset correspondences for that location—based on the Man of Signs or Zodiac Man figure. When the correspondences are known, the healer knows how to counter them with ritual and ingredients that utilize opposing elemental and zodiac forces.

Once everything is figured, the remedy is formulated and administered. Traditional healers tend to observe their patients closely in the coming days to see if there are any signs of worsening or lessening symptoms. Additional divination sessions are employed as needed. In most cases, if a situation gets better, the remedy is taken as a success. If not, increasingly complex or powerful methods might be brought out to address the issue until it's finally fixed.

WORKING WITH THE SIGNS

The figure of the Man of Signs or Zodiac Man serves as a foundational guide for most traditions of Ozark healing and magic. This figure was often committed to memory but could be easily found in the home almanac (and is still printed in major farmer's almanacs today). In Ozark healing theory, the primary effect of illnesses (physical or magical) is that they force the twelve houses of the body and their associated signs out of balance. This creates disharmony and manifests as bodily symptoms. Bringing the body back to equilibrium is therefore the first goal of the traditional healer. The main tools in their satchel are divinatory methods aimed at finding the exact location (zodiac house) where the illness or hex is rooted in the body. Knowing this then provides a plethora of correspondences that can be countered or opposed as part of the healing process.

There are far too many divinatory methods to mention in this book, especially since our main focus is on charming. I will say, at this point you can use any divinatory methods to examine the current state of the twelve houses, either for a client or for yourself. Many Ozark healers work with a simple system of determining whether a house is auspicious or inauspicious—or, in simpler terms, balanced or out-of-balance. Pendulums and dowsing methods are commonly used, as these can produce a quick answer binary—*yes* or *no, auspicious* or *inauspicious*. Tarot or oracle cards can be pulled for each of the houses, their interpreted meaning offering a glimpse into the current state of that house.

All divinatory methods point toward the same goal: discovering if a house is balanced or out-of-balance. Once that is discovered, most healers use countering methods to bring the house back into balance. For example, let's say an illness or hex is located in the first house of Aries. In order to counter this imbalance, opposing elemental correspondences would be used—in this case, water, since Aries is a fire sign. In addition, this produces an auspicious time to perform healing or cleansing rituals for this illness: a zodiac moon day in Libra, the sign opposite Aries on the zodiac wheel. Additionally, planetary signs can be used to determine herbal ingredients for use in remedies and rituals. For example, in this case, Venus-oriented plants associated with Libra (like rose, blackberry, or mugwort) would be used to counter the Mars planetary influence from Aries.

Generally, healers will counter elemental correspondences with opposing elements, but sometimes the element is taken from the opposite zodiac sign instead. So, in the above example, you could use the air element from Libra as part of the countering ritual instead of the water element.

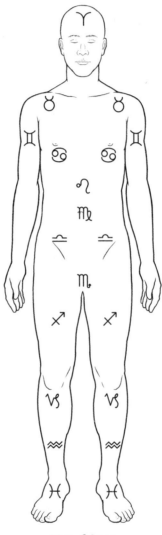

Man of Signs

Zodiac House	Zodiac Sign	Planet	Element	Day of the Week	Opposing Zodiac House	Opposing Zodiac Sign	Opposing Planet	Opposing Element	Opposing Day of the Week
1	Aries	Mars	Fire	Tuesday	7	Libra	Venus	Air	Friday
2	Taurus	Venus	Earth	Friday	8	Scorpio	Mars	Water	Tuesday
3	Gemini	Mercury	Air	Wednesday	9	Sagittarius	Jupiter	Fire	Thursday
4	Cancer	Moon	Water	Monday	10	Capricorn	Saturn	Earth	Saturday
5	Leo	Sun	Fire	Sunday	11	Aquarius	Saturn	Air	Saturday
6	Virgo	Mercury	Earth	Wednesday	12	Pisces	Jupiter	Water	Thursday
7	Libra	Venus	Air	Friday	1	Aries	Mars	Fire	Tuesday
8	Scorpio	Mars	Water	Tuesday	2	Taurus	Venus	Earth	Friday
9	Sagittarius	Jupiter	Fire	Thursday	3	Gemini	Mercury	Air	Wednesday
10	Capricorn	Saturn	Earth	Saturday	4	Cancer	Moon	Water	Monday
11	Aquarius	Saturn	Air	Saturday	5	Leo	Sun	Fire	Sunday
12	Pisces	Jupiter	Water	Thursday	6	Virgo	Mercury	Earth	Wednesday

Zodiac Signs and Opposites

THE CHARMS

The following charms cover many forms of healing. Unlike other areas, auspicious timing for healing rituals are traditionally determined by the countering zodiac and elemental correspondences that are found during the diagnosis process. Zodiac moon days in Cancer (Moon, Monday, water) are good for use with general cleansing or healing charms; Cancer has long been associated with the cleansing process, especially when using the water element.

☆ BLEEDING AND PAIN CHARM ☆

This is a very traditional Ozark verbal charm for stopping pains in the body or a bleeding wound. Of course, these days most of us have modern medical care close by, which I recommend consulting first when facing a serious illness or injury. There are many other blood-stopping charms, including the famous Bible verse, Ezekiel 16:6: "I passed by you and saw you flailing about in your blood. As you lay in your blood, I said to you, 'Live!'" I've found many family Bibles across the region that had this specific verse underlined or marked for quick reference. This verbal charm can be used for any pain or wound, and according to folk belief, the amount of healing is limited solely to the faith the client has in the charmer and the faith the charmer has in their own connection to the Divine or their innate power.

MAGICAL TIMING

Whenever bleeding or pain occurs. Waning moon for chronic pain or to continue healing a stubborn wound.

CHARM

Upon this grave
Three roses grew,
Stop, blood, stop!
From wound to wound

The pain [he/she/they] drew,
Stop, blood, stop!
(Repeat three times)

RITUAL INGREDIENTS
Bowl
Olive oil

RITUAL ACTIONS
The verbal charm can be used on its own without any ritual tools or ingredients. In this case, repeat the verbal charm three times silently, or behind your hand, if you are charming for another person. After each recitation, blow across the wound or the pain area three times, for a grand total of nine breaths.

One of the main uses of this charm goes hand-in-hand with creating a blessing oil. In this ritual, pour a small amount of olive oil into a bowl. Recite the verbal charm three times, blowing across the surface of the oil three times after each recitation. End the ritual by applying the oil to the pain center or wound. This oil can be saved in a bottle and continually applied to the pain or wound. A traditional cycle for healing chronic pain is to bless this oil on the full moon and apply to the painful area three times a day until the new moon.

NOTES
In variations of this charm, the charmer symbolically plucks three roses, which represent the blood and pain, as a part of the charming ritual. Often words to indicate this action are worked into the verbal charm itself, as in this variation I collected:

On a lonely grave
Three roses grew,
Stop!
From wound and blood
The pain [he/she/they] drew,
Stop!
Three roses, three,

Three pains, three,
One away!
Two away!
Three away, all!

In the ritual action I observed, the charmer pantomimed pulling something off the patient from the location of the wound or pain, which he then threw to the west. This was repeated a total of three times.

✭ DOG CHARMING TO CARRY AWAY EVIL ✭

This old verbal charm makes use of humankind's long-abiding friend: the domesticated dog. Specifically, this charm uses a dog to carry away illnesses and hexes, which have been bound to a length of ordinary string. The dog, in this case, isn't affected by the evils it carries, but becomes a magical partner in the ritual act.

Using a live animal as a container for illnesses, hexes, and evil is an ancient practice. Dogs are often favored in the Ozarks, partially because most hillfolk families would have had dogs around them, but also because there's an old folk belief that all canines (including dogs, wolves, coyotes, and even foxes) have the natural ability to carry maladies with them into the woods without taking on the actual illness itself. In some of the folk beliefs, these animals will carry evils away and bury them in places they can't return from.

This charm can be used to carry away all sorts of maladies, hexes, and even unwanted spirits. Whatever can be bound to the string can be carried away by this ritual charming.

MAGICAL TIMING

Waning moon. Cancer (Moon, Monday, water) is a good sign to use for cleansing and healing, or you can use the zodiac sign opposite to where the affliction is rooted in the body.

CHARM

Good dog, wise and well!
Carry this string o'er yonder dell!
Carry this string to field and flower!
Carry it with all your power!

Carry it across seven hills,
Across seven mountains,
Across seven forests!

Let it fall where it belongs!
Let it sprout where its real home is found!

RITUAL INGREDIENTS

String, white or red, 3 feet

RITUAL ACTIONS

This charming procedure begins with binding an illness, hex, or evil to a length of household string, either white or red. This process is traditionally done by spitting three times on the string (or having the one who is ill or cursed spit on the string) while focusing on what is to be removed through this act.

You can use knotting magic here. In this case, start a knot on the left end of the string, but don't close it completely. Blow through the knot while visualizing the evil leaving your body like black smoke, and, while blowing, pull the knot closed. Repeat this for a total of three, seven, or twelve knots. If you are working for someone else, have them blow through the knots.

If you want to remove evil from a place, you can carry the string in a counterclockwise circle around the walls of the room, or through all the rooms in the house. Counterclockwise is considered the direction of removal in the Ozarks. If you're doing this for a house, begin and end at the front door. You can repeat this counterclockwise circle three, seven, or twelve times. When you are finished, take the string completely out of the building, then continue with the charming ritual.

Once you've got your evil string, by whatever means, you're next going to need the other vital part of this charming ritual—a dog. If you're a dog owner, this is an easy feat, but if you aren't, ask a friend or family member if you can borrow their pet for an afternoon. Whether or not you tell them about the ritual is entirely up to your conscience. I will stress that the dog is not harmed in any way by this process. I've found that this ritual is easiest to perform with a dog that loves playing fetch.

Take the dog to an open field or park and begin the ritual by folding the charmed string in half, putting the looped end loosely behind the dog's collar. Don't wrap it around the collar or tie it in place; it should be left very loose. While petting the dog, whisper the verbal charm into its ear. Then, throw a ball or stick and have the dog run after it. This symbolizes these lines in the verbal charm: "Carry it across seven hills, / Across seven mountains, / Across seven forests!" The dog will naturally come back to you. Repeat this running out and returning action until the string falls off or until your dog pulls it off the collar, which might happen. Leave the string wherever it lands and return home.

NOTES

There are many variations that utilize animals taking illnesses away with them. One example uses a fox as the carrier. In this ritual for healing, a person blows three times over a piece of raw meat, repeats the charm below, then throws the meat into the woods to be carried away by a fox:

Red evil,
Red meat,
Red blood,
Red fox,
Carry it away,
Bury it away.

☆ EVIL EYE CHARM ☆

The Evil Eye, or simply *the Eye*, as it's called in the Ozarks, is an often-misunderstood magical illness. Many people believe the Eye is just another way of saying a curse or hex. Actually, the Eye originates in a very specific way. Most who might receive the Eye do so from people who are jealous of them or who have an over-admiration for something about them or their life. This can include anything from admiring a person's appearance to becoming jealous of their wealth or good luck. Unlike most hexes, the Eye can be sent to a person unknowingly. For this reason, in the Ozarks (as well as other cultures that have a strong connection to Evil Eye beliefs) believers don't compliment people very much, lest they inadvertently send them the

Eye. This is especially the case with children, who are seen as being extra vulnerable to receiving the Eye.

This verbal charm is one amongst many that is able to remove the Eye off yourself or another, along with any of the symptoms that might be manifesting as a result of receiving the Eye. This charm requires a specific situation for the charming ritual. In this case, the charmer needs to be touching an elderberry tree (*Sambucus nigra* or *S. canadensis*) or to be grasping some elderberry wood or leaves. Many other charms for the Eye can be used as an immediate counteraction for whenever you might think the Eye is intentionally or inadvertently being put on you. This charm, however, is usually used whenever the effects or symptoms of the Eye begin to manifest.

In some cases, specific divination methods might be used to verify a diagnosis of the Eye, but generally speaking, the Eye manifests in certain discernible symptoms: wasting or withering features, defined by sudden paleness or rashes on the skin, hair falling out, bad luck, losing money or goods, or losing one's talents (e.g., ability to sing). These might seem odd, but when you think about the Eye originating in jealousy or admiration, you can see how the loss of the things in a person's life that might be admired—looks, talents, wealth, etc.—is the perfect symptom for such a curse.

MAGICAL TIMING

Whenever the effects of the Eye have been felt. Moon days in Libra (Venus, Friday, air) are suggested as a counter for the Eye, traditionally placed in the head and therefore ruled by Aries.

CHARM

I've got two eyes,
I've got two feet,
Evil eye—
Go into my feet!
Go from my feet,
Go into the elder!
Go from the elder
Go into the west!
(Repeat three times)

RITUAL INGREDIENTS

Elderberry tree (*Sambucus nigra* or *S. canadensis*)
Elderberry twig, leaves, dried berries, or flowers (optional)
Bowl (optional)

RITUAL ACTIONS

The most difficult part about this charming ritual is finding an elderberry tree, also called *elder*. (There is a workaround to this that we'll look at in the next paragraph.) Begin by locating your elderberry tree. Facing the west, stand close to the tree and grab one of the branches with your right hand, or have the person you're charming grab onto the tree. Repeat the verbal charm three times. After this, let go of the branch and return home.

A variation on this charm uses parts from the elderberry tree when an actual tree cannot be found. Begin by collecting an elderberry branch, leaves, berries, or flowers. Dried berries can be ordered through many different herb retailers online and are probably the easiest to acquire for this ritual. Pour some berries into a bowl and take it outside. Face the west, then begin the verbal charm. At the end of each recitation, throw some of the elderberries into the west. By the end of the third recitation, all your berries should be thrown.

NOTES

Evil Eye beliefs have created some interesting taboos in the Ozarks. One healer I met told me about how in the old days, mothers and their newborn babies were kept inside the cabin for the first forty days before going out into the world. Only their immediate family would be able to see the child during this time; sometimes even the family would be kept away. When the mother did take her child out to meet extended family members or the community, she would often put anti-Eye amulets on the baby (a buckeye nut is common) or speak verbal charms over them as protective measures. People who were overly complimentary of the baby—especially their appearance—were often chided by mothers for giving their child the Eye.

✵ WATER CHARM FOR THE EVIL EYE ✵

This is another traditional charm to remove the Eye from yourself or another person. This verbal charm could be included with others of the reducing or diminishing categories, wherein an illness, hex, or condition like the Evil Eye is reduced piece by piece during the ritual until nothing is left at the end. These charming rituals are paired with physical objects like beans, corn kernels, bread, or even lit matches, which are reduced until all of the assembled objects have been thrown away or destroyed.

MAGICAL TIMING

Waning or new moon. Zodiac moon days in Libra (Venus, Friday, air) to counter the Eye.

CHARM

Eyes that look and looker too!
I throw you back into the water!
From head, from throat,
From chest, from arms,
From hands, from belly,
From legs, from feet!
Back into the water,
May it carry you away!
Carry away the look and looker too!
(Repeat three times)

RITUAL INGREDIENTS

24 dried beans or dried corn kernels; you can also use bread or even
    paper

RITUAL ACTIONS

This charming ritual will require water, preferably moving water like a river or creek, but you can also use a lake, pond, wetland, etc. If you don't have any of these, you can use a toilet that is flushed at the end of the ritual.

Go to your ritual location, taking with you twenty-four dried beans or corn kernels. In some versions of this charm, a small roll, bun, or loaf of bread is used instead.

Once at the water, begin reciting the charm. When you reach the line that begins "From head," touch a single bean, corn kernel, or piece of bread to the corresponding body location before throwing it into the water. Repeat the charm and ritual two more times for a total of three recitations—eight beans, corn kernels, or pieces of bread each time.

When you're finished, turn your back on the water and return home. The Eye and all of its effects will wane and finally disappear on the next new moon.

You can also perform this ritual in your home using your toilet as the source for moving water. This method is just about as traditional as going out to a creek. If you'd like to use this method, I suggest choosing a material that will be gentle on your plumbing. What I've seen used most is toilet paper, torn into twenty-four small pieces, then thrown into the toilet as part of the charming ritual. Other items include flower petals or even small bits of bread torn from a larger bun or loaf. While dried beans and corn kernels are small enough, they are nonetheless dried objects and can get caught in old pipes.

✰ GRAVEYARD CHARM ✰

This verbal charm aims to create a sympathetic connection between the symbol of dying (waning moon) and the cleansing or removal of an illness or hex. Anything can be removed from yourself or another using this charming ritual. It might seem odd to heal an illness or hex in a graveyard, but if you think about the symbolism here, this is a place where things are laid to rest. This is exactly the symbolism we want to use in this cleansing process. What is removed is put into the ground, sealed away there, and laid to rest so that it won't return to us.

The difference between a graveyard and cemetery is often debated in magical circles. In the Ozarks, these words are used interchangeably. Technically speaking, a graveyard is commonly connected to a religious building or structure whereas a cemetery is any ground where the dead are buried. For the purposes of this charm, I will be using the word *graveyard*, but know that you can use a cemetery in this working as well.

MAGICAL TIMING

Waning moon. Moon days in Cancer (Moon, Monday, water) are good for magical cleansing.

CHARM

They are ringing the funeral bell,
What I now grasp will soon be well,
What ill I have do take away
Like [name] in the grave does lay.

RITUAL INGREDIENTS

Offering items: coins, food, drinks, flowers, loose tobacco, dried beans
    or corn kernels, etc. (optional)

RITUAL ACTIONS

This charming ritual does require you to be in a graveyard. This can be any that you choose, but often charmers will go to graveyards where they have family members buried. It's believed that the ancestral spirits will aid in the charming process if they are able.

Begin by going to your chosen graveyard, then find a grave. Any will work for the purposes of this ritual, but again, you can choose a loved one or ancestor. Kneel or sit on the ground while facing the headstone. You can face west, or even find a headstone that will allow you to look toward the west.

Recite the first line of the charm. On the second line, "What I now grasp will soon be well," you will grasp the front of your shirt over your sternum. Recite the third line. On the final line, "Like [name] in the grave does lay," you will place your left hand, palm down, on the ground in front of the headstone. The blank spot in this line will be filled with the first name of whoever is buried beneath you. When you're finished with the charm, stand and leave the graveyard without looking back at the grave. As you leave, so too will you leave behind the sickness or curse.

Some charmers will leave behind a small token of appreciation on the grave as gratitude to the spirit who resides there. This can take the form of three or seven coins (dimes are preferred), a small pile of loose tobacco, a pour of water over the headstone, flowers, or even food items. I highly recommend choosing offering items that won't pollute the land; biodegradable is best. Instead of leaving a pile of coins on top of the headstone, I prefer to leave items like dried beans or corn kernels, which symbolize wealth and prosperity and will biodegrade or be eaten by local wildlife.

NOTES

Using locations, tools, or materia that have touched death as a part of the healing process is a common feature within Ozark folk practice. Coming into contact with death often creates auspicious items or locations. For example, coffin nails—defined as nails that have come into physical contact with a coffin that holds a dead body—are used not only for work related to the spirit world or death, but as auspicious tools in general. The same applies to graveyards, which are seen as auspicious locations.

The graveyard as a power place is a preferred location for many charmers—not just those who work with spirits. Graveyards are places where the veil is thin, as with other auspicious locations. But graveyards often have the added benefit of being closer to town—a useful factor especially for elderly healers who can't get out to the deep woods anymore. These spots can be repositories for our ancestors—not just blood relatives, but ancestors of the work, or those healers who have come before us. By working in graveyards, these spirits are able to add their power to our own.

If you're a worker who is uncomfortable working with spirits, you can still utilize the power of the graveyard and the materia it produces no matter the type of work you do. I often perform certain healing rites in my local graveyards because they are easily accessible places of power and auspiciousness. When I do work there, I make sure to still honor the spirits of the place, even though my ritual might not involve spirits or spirit-influences at all.

✯ MEAT GIVING FOR THE LAND SPIRITS ✯

This verbal charm works on a couple foundational principles. The first is that an illness, hex, or evil spirit can be bound to a physical object through ritual procedure. The second is that there are non-human spirit entities in the world who can consume the things that make us sick or even die without being affected themselves. Binding illnesses and hexes to a physical object that is then destroyed is a key feature of Ozark folk magic practice. It pops up in countless different forms with different containers used, depending on availability and the specific work that's being done. In this case, we're using raw meat as the container for the evil we're wanting to remove. What can be contained is limited only by your imagination.

Land spirits feature heavily in Ozark folk magic practice. These are the animistic entities of the landscape itself. Unlike spirits such as the Little People (Ozark fairies), land spirits are less inclined to be tricksters and are generally neutral in their temperaments, like nature itself is neutral. Land spirits are just as likely to provide gifts of food, healing plants, and secret auspicious locations as they are to, say, flood your home, burn your barn down, or block your road with a landslide.

Because of their neutrality and gentler temperaments, land spirits are much easier to work with for beginners on the Charming Way. Their neutrality mirrors the emotions and intentions that are offered, good or bad. If you give them gifts, they will give equally back. Likewise, if you harm their groves, springs, caves, and pools, they will give equal amounts of harm back to you. Feeding land spirits is the most common way to get them on your side. As with this ritual, food is offered alongside a request to take away some illness, hex, or evil. If offered with sincerity, the charmer is bound to receive a sincere gift in return.

MAGICAL TIMING

Waning moon. Cancer (Moon, Monday, water) is a good sign to use for cleansing and healing, or you can use the zodiac sign opposite to where the affliction is rooted in the body.

CHARM

Lucky ones, eat your meat!
Eat blood and this hex too!
Take it back into the west!
Take it back into the mountains!

Take it back into the forests!
Take it back where it belongs!
Far away from me!
(Repeat seven times)

RITUAL INGREDIENTS

Meat, any kind, cut into 7 pieces
Bowl, large enough to hold the meat

Optional Variation:
Bowl
Bread, cut into 7 pieces (or 7 dinner rolls / American-style biscuits)
Red wine

RITUAL ACTIONS

As with most charming procedures, this ritual is a simple one. First, take seven pieces of raw meat and place them in a bowl. How big the pieces are and what type of meat you use is entirely up to you. Traditionally, pork has been used in the Ozarks because of availability, but you can use any meat as long as it can be cut or divided into seven pieces. For vegetarians and vegans, there is a variation on this practice that uses seven pieces of bread (or even seven dinner rolls, buns, or American-style biscuits) that are dipped into red wine and then placed into a bowl.

Next, you're going to blow seven times across your meat or wine-dipped bread, visualizing each time that black smoke is leaving your body and entering the meat. With each breath, that thing you're wanting to get rid of reduces bit by bit until it's all gone. If you're working for someone else, have them blow onto the meat.

If you're using this ritual to clear out a space or house, carry the bowl in a counterclockwise circle through the entire space while visualizing clouds of thick, black smoke being sucked from the room and into the meat chunks. Repeat this three times. If you're cleansing an entire house, begin and end at the front door. Either way, make sure that at the end of the ritual, you carry the meat completely out of the building.

Once you're finished, go out to the woods or a wooded area. This can be your backyard if you have plenty of space, or if you live in an apartment, you might need to travel to a local park or trail. If you're in a highly urban area, find a secluded spot in an alleyway, park, riverside, warehouse, construction site, or wherever is safe and away from gazing eyes. You're going to be throwing pieces of meat, after all.

Once you're in a safe spot, repeat the verbal charm seven times. At the end of each recitation, throw a piece of meat or bread into the woods. End the ritual by turning your back on the work and returning home without looking back.

NOTES

This charm makes use of a very specific idea that is common to Ozark charming, which is that illnesses, hexes, and evil in general don't belong here in our world. Their presence signifies that something is out of balance. The healing process is then seeking to return to equilibrium—meaning the illness or hex is no longer present. In Ozark cosmology, west is considered the direction of evil and contagion. The lands in the west, which don't actually exist on our physical plane but are a part of the otherworld, are the home of all evil and sickness. This is the place where these evil things are from and the place that they are returned to in order to bring equilibrium to the body and spirit. The other directions also have specific correspondences that can be used as part of many different charming rituals.

Direction	Color	Associations
East	White/Red	Land of Blessings; dawn; rebirth and renewal; rising sun
South	White/Yellow	Land of Plenty; fortune; prosperity; good luck; gold and riches
West	Black/Brown	Land of Evil; sickness and disease; evil spirits; hexes; monsters
North	Blue	Land of Cold; "cold" illnesses; hunger and thirst; cold animals (reptiles and amphibians) who cause cold illnesses

Direction Associations

✱ PREGNANCY BLESSING ✱

This traditional verbal charm is used to bless a pregnancy. It can be performed each full moon throughout the entire term, but especially if there is a full moon in Taurus or Cancer. You can perform this ritual for yourself or for another.

MAGICAL TIMING

Full moon. Moons in Taurus (Venus, Friday, earth) or Cancer (Moon, Monday, water) are good for this ritual.

CHARM

The egg is round,
Belly is round,
Moon is round!
I tie a round string
Into seven round knots,
For baby and bearer's health!
(Repeat three times)

RITUAL INGREDIENTS

1 egg
String, white, 2 feet

RITUAL ACTIONS

Begin by having the pregnant person lie down on their back. Place the egg in their navel so that it will balance in place; it can be against bare skin or on top of clothing. Repeat the verbal charm three times silently or in a whisper while facing your head away from the person you're working on.

After repeating the charm, take one end of the string in each hand. Starting on the left end of the string, begin to tie a knot but don't close it completely yet. Repeat the phrase, "For baby and bearer's health!" then blow through the knot. While you're blowing, pull the knot closed. Continue in this same manner from left to right on the string for a total of seven knots. When you're finished, you can have the pregnant person wear this string tied around their right wrist.

Take the egg outside and smash it against a tree or throw it into running water. The belief is that through the charming process, the egg will absorb any illnesses or hexes that need to be removed from the body. Destroying the egg afterward then dispels whatever was collected.

If you do this ritual again during the pregnancy, you can replace the string that is currently worn with a new one and burn the old one. Whenever the string breaks and falls off, burn it. If it is still intact when the baby is born, you can remove the knotted string and tie it on the crib where the baby can't reach it.

NOTES

There are many Ozark charms and rituals surrounding fertility, pregnancy, and birth. This area of magic would have been the specialty of granny women in the past. Sadly, over the years, we've lost much of our magical connection to the birth process, but I'm beginning to see it make a comeback. The art of the midwives and granny women was just that: *an art*.

☆ SEPARATION CHARM ☆

Here is a traditional tongue twister repurposed as a separation ritual. This verbal charm has many uses with regard to removing illnesses, hexes, evil entities, etc., from yourself or another. It can be used as a way of separating yourself from another person and forming a strong, magical boundary between the two (or more) of you. Anything that can be separated can be the target of this charming ritual.

MAGICAL TIMING

During the waning moon or on a new moon. Zodiac moon days in Cancer (Moon, Monday, water) are good for general cleansing, and Capricorn (Saturn, Saturday, earth) is a good time for working with boundaries and separation.

CHARM

Int-ery, mint-ery, cut-ery, corn,
Apple seed, and apple thorn;
Wine, brier, limber lock,

Three geese in a flock,
One flew east, one flew west,
And one flew over the goose's nest.

RITUAL INGREDIENTS

3 small bread rolls, boules, buns, biscuits, or other throwable bread
   items
Food coloring, black or red (optional)
Paintbrush (optional)

RITUAL ACTIONS

You can work this charming ritual in a couple different ways. The easiest is to take your three small buns or bread items outside to a field or open area where you will be able to throw each of them without any issues. While holding the three buns, imagine that the thing you wish to be separated from—whether it's an illness, hex, or entity—moves from inside your body into your breath. Then, blow three times over the buns, imagining that black smoke pours out of your body and into the buns. After the third breath, all of the smoke will be out of your body.

Recite the verbal charm while facing east. When you come to the words "One flew east," throw one of the buns into the east. Then turn counterclockwise to face the west, and with the words "One flew west," throw a bun in that direction. Turn counterclockwise to face the south. Say the final line: "And one flew over the goose's nest." Then throw the last remaining bun in that direction.

The second option for this ritual is geared toward separating yourself from a person or group of people. In this ritual, begin by writing the name of the person you want to be separated from on each of the three buns, using black or red food coloring and a thin paintbrush. If you're targeting a group of people, you can separate the names onto the three buns; they don't all have to appear on each unless you're only targeting one individual. Complete the rest of the ritual as it appears above.

NOTES

Disposable food items are commonly used in Ozark folk magic and healing as containers for illnesses, hexes, and even entities. These items are readily available in the home and rot away relatively quickly. This allows the charmer to connect the symbolism of waning or cleansing to the disintegration process. Popular food containers include small buns or other bread items, apples, onions, potatoes, pieces of meat, and I've even seen popped popcorn used as containers. There's a deeper layer to using these items as a part of cleansing work—they're edible. This means that these food items will be consumed by animals, fungi, microbes, and even otherworldly entities, thereby breaking apart, separating, and further cleansing whatever was sealed within the items.

✴ TOOTHACHE CHARM ✴

This is a very old and traditional charm for relieving the pain caused by a toothache. This charm can be repeated when the pain happens, or some charmers who align with more specific magical or auspicious timings will wait until the moon is in Libra; the teeth are in the head, which, according to the Man of Signs, is ruled by Aries, and is therefore countered by the opposing sign of Libra.

MAGICAL TIMING

When the tooth begins to ache. Zodiac moon days in Libra (Venus, Friday, air).

CHARM

Peter was sitting on a boulder stone,
When Jesus he passed by.
Peter said, "My Lord, my God,
How my tooth doth ache!"
Jesus said, "Peter thou art whole!
And whosoever keeps these words for My sake
Shall never have another dreaded toothache."
(Repeat three times)

RITUAL INGREDIENTS

Cup of water (optional)

RITUAL ACTIONS

As a stand-alone verbal charm, there aren't any ritual actions to perform besides reciting the charm three times. I've also seen charmers recite the charm three times, and after each time, they blow across a cup of water. At the end of the charming, they then swish the water around in their mouth before spitting it out onto dirt, a moving body of water, or even in a toilet.

NOTES

This charm invokes an apocryphal story from the Bible wherein Jesus meets Peter on the road and Peter complains about his toothache. This doesn't actually occur in the biblical narrative. There are many verbal charms that follow this pattern of creating a story with famous biblical characters and putting them in situations that are similar to what is currently being healed. There are examples of characters like Moses, Peter, Paul, and even Jesus himself experiencing maladies like burns, toothaches, bleeding wounds, hexes, etc., who are then miraculously healed as a part of the charm story. By reciting the tale in the form of a verbal charm, the charmer is then able to grab hold of the same power that healed these individuals in the past and bring it through time to the present. Charming stories like these aren't seen as sacrilegious at all, and historically, it was common for Ozarkers to believe these stories were actually found in the Bible. Many biblical legends were passed down orally rather than read, so you can imagine how different sorts of tales and legends might easily pop up.

☆ TYING ILLNESSES AND HEXES TO A STONE ☆

This charm ritually ties or binds a targeted malady to a stone that is then disposed of alongside whatever has been sealed inside. Anything can be bound to the stone, even the power of an enemy or evil entity.

Binding or sealing maladies into natural containers is a common feature of Ozark folk healing and magical practice. Variations use items like onions, apples, or potatoes, all of which will rot away along with whatever might be sealed within the object. The water in this ritual represents both cleansing and sealing. In some cases, a charmer might prefer flowing water (like in a river or creek) as a way of symbolizing cleansing that removes and carries away sickness and evil. Others prefer stagnant water, as with one charmer who preferred a pond, or even better, a wetland area, which will seal away whatever was carried with the container deep down in the mud.

MAGICAL TIMING
Waning moon. Zodiac moon days in Cancer (Moon, Monday, water) are good for cleansing.

CHARM
You there! Evil one!
Go from flesh to string!
Go from string to stone!
Go from stone to water!
And begone to the west,
Where all sickness and evil lives!

RITUAL INGREDIENTS
1 stone, small
String, white, 3 feet

RITUAL ACTIONS
Begin by locating your source of water. This can be any natural body of water, including a pond, swamp, river, creek, lake, ocean, or wetland—as long as there is a good amount of water present. Take your stone and string with you to the water. (You can also wait and find a stone near wherever you have picked as your ritual spot.) You will need to face both the water and the west, so move yourself around until you find the perfect spot.

Hold the string in your dominant hand and the stone in your other hand. Recite the first two lines, and when you say "string," hold up the string in your hand. Recite the third line, then wrap the string around the stone in a counterclockwise direction until you reach the end. Tie the two loose ends together in three knots.

Recite the fourth line, then throw the stone into the body of water as far as you can. Finish the charming ritual with the final two lines. Then, turn around and return home without looking back at the water.

☆ WART CHARM ☆

This simple charming ritual is used to eliminate pesky warts from the body. In the old days, warts were very common amongst Ozark hillfolk, so much so that I've personally collected at least a hundred charms and rituals for healing this malady. Today they aren't as much of an issue for folks, but I did want to include a couple wart charms to honor my hillfolk ancestors.

Many wart charms use the sympathetic connection between the shrinking of the moon's light and the shrinking of the wart. The waning moon is a natural time to connect to the power that banishes, cleanses, separates, and removes. This is the traditional time to perform any acts of healing.

MAGICAL TIMING
Waning moon. Zodiac moon sign opposite to where the wart is located.

CHARM
What I see increase,
What I rub decrease,
By dark moon above,
And dark moon below.

RITUAL INGREDIENTS
None

RITUAL ACTIONS
While outside, begin the charming ritual by reciting the first and second line, then make three counterclockwise circles around each wart with the thumb of your right hand. Your thumb doesn't need to touch the skin. When you're finished, recite the rest of the charm. It's believed that the warts charmed in this way will decrease in size until they disappear completely on or around the next new moon.

✫ WART CHARM: ANOTHER VERSION ✫

Here is a second version of the previous charm. Offering a ribbon in this variation is an old practice symbolizing a sacrifice given for healing work. One charmer told me that red ribbons represent blood and hearken back to ancient sacrifices offered as payment for miraculous healing. I'm not sure how true this might be, but what I do know is that ribbons of all colors as well as strips of cloth are the preferred sacrifice in many Ozark rituals. This is especially true for those involving trees, where the ribbons or cloth strips are often tied into the branches of the tree used during the healing ritual, or even tied around the trunk.

MAGICAL TIMING

Waning moon. Zodiac moon days in Cancer (Moon, Monday, water) are good for cleansing.

CHARM

Stump water, stump water,
Take these [number] warts!
And I shall give you
A pretty red ribbon
For your long-matted hair.

RITUAL INGREDIENTS

Ribbon, red, 1 foot
Spoon
Stump water (still in the stump)

RITUAL ACTIONS

This wart charming ritual requires a very specialized magical ingredient called *stump water*, which is water that has collected inside a stump or in recessed areas at the base of trees. For this ritual you will need a spoon to collect the water from the stump. I recommend using a small dessert spoon of any material, or you could use a teaspoon measurer. There are some charmers who swear against using metal to collect auspicious waters, so if you'd like, you can use a plastic or wooden spoon for this ritual, but it isn't required.

Once you have your spoon, you will also need a one-foot length of red ribbon. Width of the ribbon doesn't matter so much, but try to keep it under an inch. Take these outside and start hunting for stump water. The best time is right after it rains, but in the cooler months, the early morning dew can collect into these hidden pools. Trees that have been cut to stumps are a great place to look—especially older ones that are beginning to form holes and bowls on the top of the trunk. I've found stump water at the base of living trees when bowls form in exposed roots. You don't need very much water for this ritual.

When you've located a source for stump water, begin your charm recitation with the first two lines. The blank corresponds to how many warts you want to get rid of. After this line, take your spoon and collect some of the stump water. Pour this over each of your warts. You might need to collect more from the source depending on how many warts you're charming. When you've wet all your warts with the stump water, finish the charm. Then, tie the red ribbon to the stump, or if you're using a living tree, you can tie it in the branches.

NOTES

Stump water is an interesting ingredient in Ozark folk healing and magic. Because this water hasn't technically touched the ground yet, it is considered highly auspicious for healing purposes. Sometimes it's called *flying water* because it's said to hang between the heavens and the earth. I don't advise drinking stump water, although there are several Ozark remedies that say to do this.

CHAPTER 5

To Bring You Love, If It Be True ...

At fifteen years old, Ann had grown in confidence and kindness. She was well-loved by everyone in Nelson's Holler, even her enemies. Rumors still occasionally surfaced about her strange gifts, but they never stuck around for very long. Ann had many allies in the community who were quick to come to her defense. One such individual was Ann's schoolmate Thomas Grider, who could have spread all kinds of gossip, as he'd experienced her healing powers firsthand. But he didn't, recognizing that gifts like Ann's shouldn't ever be shamed.

Ann and Thomas were about as close of friends as you can get. In fact, a lot of people in Nelson's Holler thought they might somehow be kin, as they always seemed to be together. At school they sat in desks positioned right next to each other, which meant they could partner up for class assignments. In church, they sat in the same pew, but of course still near enough to Thomas's mother so she could keep an eye on them. For Ann, Thomas's heart was a mystery that even her gifts could never pierce. She never assumed anything more about their relationship than what she received at face value, and this seemed to suit Thomas just fine.

One day during the winter holiday, Ann and Thomas were sledding down Bobcat Slope out near Paul Landry's mill. They'd been at it so long that their faces were bright red and foreheads sweating. Their knees and hips ached from continuously walking back up to the top of the hill. As they struggled to catch their breath, both lying spread out on their backs in the snow, Ann reached over and punched Thomas hard in the shoulder. "Ouch!" he cried, rubbing the spot with his gloved hand. "What the hell was that for?"

"Do you love me?" Ann asked without a second thought.

The boy didn't say anything. Ann sat up and threw some snow in his face.
"Well?" she shouted.

"Stop, Ann," Thomas answered, wiping the snow out of his eyes and mouth.

"Usually when a girl asks if you love her, you're supposed to say yes."

"Usually?"

Ann paused, clarifying in her own mind what she meant. "I mean, that's what they say."

"Who are they?"

Ann threw more snow at Thomas. "Are you just gonna ask me stupid questions or give me an answer?"

"I can't give you the answer you want right now."

In silence, Ann stood and started walking back home, leaving Thomas in the snow behind her. He shouted after her, but Ann didn't turn around to look.

Ann thought she'd walk home but ended up on Nelson's Creek, headed to Gram's cabin. She held back tears, thinking to herself that she should be angry, not sad. When she got to the house, a lazy black cat greeted her on the front porch with a yawn. Ann reached down and scratched behind his ears before going inside. There was a big fire warming the front room and Ann could hear Gram working in the kitchen. She started to announce herself when she heard Gram's voice call out, "C'mon in, Ann!"

How does she know these things? Ann thought to herself with a smile. After all these years, it still never ceased to amaze her.

The kitchen table was topped with dried fruits, candied cherries, sugared ginger, and cups of spices. Ann breathed in the scented air as she sat down. Gram stood at the countertop furiously stirring something in a big ceramic bowl. "Is it fruitcake time already?" Ann asked excitedly.

Gram sat down in a chair across from the girl. She dropped the bowl on table with a thud and wiped sweat and flour off her forehead with her apron. "It's fruitcake time already," she answered, massaging her mixing arm with her calloused hand. "Do an old woman a favor and mix for a while."

Ann happily grabbed the bowl and wooden spoon and began stirring the thick batter.

"What made you grace my table this morning, Ann?" Gram asked, tossing a handful of raisins into the bowl.

"I want a love spell, Gram," Ann asked firmly. She'd figured there was no use beating around the bush—Gram would see right through that.

"Oh, you do?" Gram laughed.

"This is serious, Gram. I want to make someone love me."

Gram sat back in her chair with a sigh, "That sounds very familiar," she said with a grin. "How about a story while you stir?"

Lucy Ganter was what the town's folk called hell on wheels. Even at fifteen, she was an unstoppable force in Nelson's Holler. She lied, stole, drank moonshine, partied, drove too fast in cars that didn't belong to her, and did all the things that made her mother stay up worrying all night. When asked why she did the things she did, Lucy would just laugh and say, "Got to give them church gossips something to gossip about!" Lucy was the source of most of the gossip in Nelson's Holler since she was thirteen.

Lucy had one point of weakness in her armored shell, and his name was Harry Talbot. They'd been friends since they were in diapers, and if there was any balancing force in the universe to Lucy's chaos, it was Harry. It was Harry who paid for everything Lucy stole (behind her back, of course). It was Harry who watered down her moonshine so she didn't drink so much. It was Harry who always suggested stopping off at the swimming hole when Lucy was driving too recklessly. Harry was a constant companion, but Lucy never really noticed him until one night, under a bright, full autumn moon, when a glimmer in his eye sent a shiver down her spine that she was sure she'd never recover from. Maybe it was the moonshine talking, but mid-conversation Lucy all of a sudden interrupted with, "Do you love me, Harry?"

The boy stopped talking. His voice cracked as he tried to process what he'd just heard. "I, uh, um. Lucy? I, uh ..." but nothing intelligent would come out.

Lucy nodded, turned away from the swimming hole, walked back to the car, and drove off, leaving poor Harry behind her in the shadows.

The next morning, Lucy rushed out to Nelson's Creek to see Gram Watson. She'd spent all night devising a plan and gathering her courage. She knew that old witch had some tricks up her sleeve, or at least that's what everyone in Nelson's Holler liked to say. The cabin was a hike up the mountain from the main road, up what *very few people would actually call a path; it was more like an old, dried-up creek bed. Lucy followed the trail through spiderwebs, greenbrier walls that blocked the path, and too many strange noises to count. She never once stopped, though, know-ing her quest was too important.*

When Lucy finally did reach the cabin, she saw a woman sitting in a rocking chair out on the front porch. She was about the same age as Lucy's mother, or so Lucy reckoned. Her hair was braided into two long plaits that were then twisted around the crown of her head. She wore an old black dress with a dirty, patchwork apron on top. As she sat smoking her briar pipe, Lucy sat down on a porch step to catch her breath. "You Gram Watson?" she asked.

The woman blew out a spiraling river of tobacco smoke. "I'm Gram Watson."

"You don't look old enough to be a granny."

"And how old do you reckon I am?" the woman laughed.

Lucy didn't answer, knowing she was likely to offend the woman by naming any age. "I need some help," she said, changing subjects.

"Why do you think I'm out on the front porch? What do you want?"

Lucy hesitated for a moment, then blurted out her request, "I want someone to love me."

Gram smiled and took another puff on her pipe. "Now that's a big request."

"I don't have much money, but I can work for you to pay it off."

"And what makes you think I'll answer this request?"

"I've heard what folks say about you. I'm not afraid."

Gram fished around in the front pocket of her apron and pulled out a wrinkled notecard. "Write their name on that," she handed the card and a pencil to Lucy. "Then put what money you brought on the step and go home."

"And this'll work? He'll really love me?"

"It'll work. I guarantee it'll work."

Lucy furiously wrote "Harold Linus Talbot" on the notecard, then handed it back to Gram. "Make it fast," Lucy said aloud before she could catch herself.

Gram laughed and put the notecard back into her apron pocket. "Go home," she said sternly, returning to her tobacco pipe.

Matters of the heart can make for complicated magic, made even more complex when dealing with the misguided tendencies of youth. Gram Watson's magic always

worked, and it always worked fast. Within the week, Lucy started noticing Harry noticing her a little more than before. He couldn't seem to keep away from her. They'd practically been inseparable even before the spell, but this felt different. It was everything Lucy thought she wanted.

The spell really ramped up after a month, when Harry asked Lucy on an official date. "Not as friends, right?" Lucy asked.

Harry laughed. "No, not as friends," he answered in a whisper, blushing.

That night they drove thirty minutes to the drive-in movie theater. Harry decided it would be best if he drove them. Lucy just gave him a grin and said, "All right, have at it. Just this once, though."

After that they spent even more time with each other, if that was possible. Folks around town saw them holding hands and started making up all sorts of stories. Neither of the two denied the rumors, but they also didn't give out more information than they needed to. They were as close as a couple could get. At one point, about three months into the relationship, Lucy was sure that Harry was going to propose to her. He'd planned out a fancy dinner, which he cooked himself. That was another thing to love about Harry; he really knew how to cook a meal. Lucy, on the other hand, could burn ice cream.

Lucy spent the entire evening waiting for Harry to pull out a ring, but it never happened. Despite having a lovely evening, Lucy went home crying. She swore up and down, mostly at Gram, that the spell hadn't worked. The next morning, she went straight to Harry's house. He was surprised to see her since she had left in such a huff the night before. She refused his offer of coming inside and stayed behind on the porch, choosing instead to talk to him through the screen door. "You either show me you love me or I'm gone, Harold Talbot," was the first thing she said, then crossed her arms and waited for a reply.

Harry stood staring at her through the door. He thought they'd been having a good time, and more than anything in the world, he never wanted to rush Lucy. "Well then, I guess we best get married," he said, more than halfway unsure of himself.

Lucy smiled and pulled open the screen door. She jumped forward and gave him a big hug. By the end of the day, they'd set the date, told the families, and Harry even went out and bought a little gold engagement ring for his future wife. Harry's heart told him this was a bad idea—he'd been feeling it for a while now. But despite all of *that, the words that were coming out of his mouth, which didn't feel like his own, had another plan in mind.*

★   ★   ★

Love stories always have a happy ending, don't they? But that's not really how life works. "Matters of the heart are tricky," Gram said while checking on the fruitcake baking in the oven. "It's best to leave all of that alone, unless there's a lesson to teach."

Ann had never heard the story of her mother and Harry Talbot before. She wondered why anyone would have kept that from her. Gram sat back down and sighed. "Matters of the heart are tricky …" she whispered to herself.

Sometimes love—or obsession with love—turns into commitment, brings in contracts, and causes two very different and chaotic forces to collide and then burn up like a dead star. A happy ending would have meant Lucy and Harry got married and lived the rest of their lives just as in love with each other as they were in the beginning. But Ann knew the future, or rather the present. Harry was nowhere to be found. Ann had heard his name before, as he was well liked in the community. But folks said something strange came over him one morning and he just up and ran off in a hurry. They said that he left town for some big city up north. They said that he left behind a wife and a daughter to survive on their own, but never said who they were.

LOVE MAGIC AND CONSENT

Love magic is just as controversial today as it ever has been. Love magic was once seen as just as important of a focus as healing work or practices for augmenting luck and fortune. This accounts for the vast number of love spells and divination methods collected by folklorists and practitioners across the centuries. That said, we also find a great many cautionary tales relating to love divinations and magic in the Ozarks. Love magic is one area that can go so wrong, so quickly. These cautionary tales warn against playing with matters of the heart. But cautionary tales are just that: cautions. I don't consider love magic to be a taboo subject, but I do believe that precautions and safety measures need to be in place before working with the heart. At the very foundation of this work, we can find good ethics. The same ethics that we put into place with any magical work that we do.

I talk about consent and love magic a great deal in my first book, *Ozark Folk Magic: Plants, Prayers & Healing*, but there are some simple considerations that are worth repeating. In my own practice, I try to hold the intention that whatever work I'm doing will build upon what is naturally present. If there's no natural love present, then no love will grow. It's a simple yet powerful idea that will maintain a healthy balance between the client you are working with and the potential target of the work. This idea can also extend to healing work in general. If the person you're working with doesn't want to be healed, then no healing will happen.

There are always at least two sides to the magical process—the deepest relationship being that of the magical practitioner and their client. In my own work, I often find that I grow when my client grows. I heal when my client heals. I'm cleansed when my client is cleansed. Likewise, I often suffer when my client suffers. Recognizing this powerful relationship can help maintain a good balance between both parties so that neither of you are pulling the other down. In my experience, a healthy exchange of energy between practitioner and client is a foundational consideration for all magical practices.

We often establish firm consent with our clients before proceeding with any magical work, but do we consider the consent of third parties? Let's say my client asks me to make a charm to soften their spouse's feelings toward them; do I consider the spouse's feelings? Every story has an array of different angles—different viewpoints. Remembering this will help you when considering the types of work you will do. None of this is to say that love work should never be done—I do it in my own practice. With all forms of magic, you must consider what you know about the situation as well as what you *don't* know. It's by looking at the areas we don't know about that we are able to create healthy boundaries with our work and our clients. And in creating these healthy boundaries, we're able to prevent suffering.

DIVINATIONS AND PARTY GAMES

Many of the traditional love divinations and verbal charms we have as part of the Ozark folk record were originally considered to be party games. Many of these love games are based on much older systems of magical ritual, however. In the Ozarks, the term *party game* itself was a way to hide practices that would otherwise be condemned by the community. This is especially true with divinatory systems. As with one storyteller I met, who said she and her sister "knew all kinds of love charms" that they would perform as children under the guise of games. For her, these love divinations were a fun game to be played on a lazy, rainy afternoon. Under the surface, though, they held a tinge of seriousness in that the outcome of the divination could possibly come to fruition.

Probably the most famous example of this in the Ozarks is the dumb supper tradition, which was detailed by Vance Randolph in his *Ozark Magic and Folklore* in the first part of the twentieth century. The dumb supper has been transformed over the years to be a way of contacting the dead, or in some cases I've seen, it's now used as an ancestral feast, usually enacted around Halloween. In the Ozarks, though, the dumb supper was traditionally a love divination ritual, a "party game," to identify one's future spouse.

The process itself is a lengthy ritual usually held at night, in some cases at midnight. The participants all gather in one person's home, entering backward through the back door of the house. From here, all the preparations are done while walking backward and, if able, done in reverse order. There are many interpretations for this action, with the most likely being a sort of reordering of nature—working against the flow of time as a way to open the veil for divination. As these dumb suppers were commonly performed by children or teenagers, the meal that is set out at the dinner table is usually something simple, like buttered toast or cheese and crackers.

All participants then sit at the table, leaving an empty chair beside them. Food is distributed, and each person makes sure to place some at the empty setting next to them. All the lights are turned off and a single candle is lit in the center of the table. One participant will crack a window in the dining room, then return to their seat. At this point, sometimes there is an accompanying verbal charm that everyone recites; other times, the participants simply sit in silence. It's said that within the hour, each participant will see a shadowy representation of their future spouse enter the room and sit in the empty chair next to them. If no spouse appears, this is taken as a grave omen that the individual will forever be a spinster or that the timing for such a divination just isn't right.

The dumb supper is just one example of a love divination being used as entertainment. There are many more out there. Nursery rhymes are sometimes used as love divination charms or even ritual processes, as with the popular counting charm "He/she/they love(s) me, he/she/they love(s) me not," usually paired with plucking single petals from a flower. Are these games? Well, yes, they are. But these are also ways of divining knowledge.

Still to this day, there are mixed feelings about such seemingly innocent rhymes and games. In 2013 I attended a rural church service with an informant of mine, and the preacher staunchly condemned similar games as being "evil witchcraft." Vance Randolph himself approached them as silly superstitions without, in my opinion, truly asking his informants how *they* actually viewed these practices.

We see this pop up a lot within the charming tradition—charms become games, games become charms. Where's the line? Is there even a line at all? Perhaps it's all about intention; I believe it is. As we've seen elsewhere, a charmer with a focused intention can make powerful magic happen from even the simplest, silliest ingredients.

THE CHARMS

The following charms will all assist with love work, which is generally associated with Taurus (Venus, Friday, earth) for relationships without contractual obligations or Libra (Venus, Friday, air) for marriages and relationships that have a verbal commitment. For inviting in new love affairs, or for drawing true love to you, I like to use the grounding earth element of Taurus; or Virgo (Mercury, Wednesday, earth) for pleasant, romantic love; or the fiery nature of Sagittarius (Jupiter, Saturday, fire) for one-night stands or temporary passions. For working with boundaries related to love and relationships—either creating or destroying them—Capricorn (Saturn, Saturday, earth) is traditionally used. For divination rituals related to love, use Pisces (Jupiter, Thursday, water) for general divinations and Aquarius (Saturn, Saturday, air) for divinations relating to your personal love interest.

☆ APPLE SEED DIVINATION ☆

This is an old charm traditionally used to determine if someone loves or hates you. There are many similar divinations in the Ozarks; love and marriage divinations were once as common as wart cures in the Ozarks! In the old days, marriage was seen as a vital part of survival in the hills. This verbal charm and accompanying ritual could also be used to determine if someone is your enemy by changing the intention behind the love from that of romance to something more like platonic friendship or affection.

MAGICAL TIMING

Full moon. Zodiac moon days in Gemini (Mercury, Wednesday, air) or Pisces (Jupiter, Thursday, water) are good for divination work.

CHARM

[Full name of the person]
If you love me, pop and fly;
If you hate me, lay and die.

RITUAL INGREDIENTS

Apple seeds
Charcoal
Heatproof container
Lighter or matches

RITUAL ACTIONS

For this ritual, you will need dried apple seeds. Traditionally, the apple seeds used are collected from three different apples. This can create another divination ritual within the main one, though it isn't necessary: Cut three apples in half so that the star shape around the apple core is showing; this is done by slicing the apple across the core rather than through the stem. Seeds that are sliced by the knife are discarded, and whole seeds are placed to the side. When all the seeds from the three apples have been collected, you can count how many you have. An even number is auspicious, signifying good luck with regard to the entire ritual. An odd number is inauspicious, and in some cases, the charmer won't proceed with the rest of the ritual until they are able to take seeds from three more apples.

Whether you perform the extra divination or not, once you have some seeds, proceed with the main ritual. This ritual can easily be done indoors, but you will be producing smoke. Begin by lighting your charcoal. The easiest way to perform this charming ritual is to use an incense charcoal and burner; that way you don't have to light any charcoal briquettes.

The number of seeds you have corresponds to the number of times you can divine with this ritual. In some cases, charmers have said that you can only divine once for each name; others say you can divine up to three times per name. Begin by reciting the first, middle, and last name of the person you are divining for. Then, recite the rest of the verbal charm. After you are finished, drop a single apple seed on the coal and listen for a distinct popping or snapping sound as a confirmation of the target's love for you. If the seed is silent or just sizzles and smokes, this is seen as a sign that the person does not love you.

NOTES

The apple has an interesting place in Ozark materia. It is commonly used as a destroyable container for illnesses and hexes. In certain retribution rituals, it's used as a stand-in for the enemy you might be working against. One such apple rite can be found in my *Ozark Mountain Spell Book*. Apples have a long association with love magic, and in some folk beliefs, the fruit itself is said to be an aphrodisiac. Other love spells utilize apple wood, apple blossoms, and sometimes even the leaves, as in one charming ritual where a person slaps their naked body with wet apple leaves while reciting the words "No longer blind, / Apple find! / Apple find, / I'm no longer blind!" seven times. They will then see their true love in the dreams that follow the leaf-slapping.

☆ CALLING LOVE TO YOU FROM AFAR ☆

The purpose of this verbal charm is essentially a road-opening work of sorts, only instead of monetary opportunities or a new job/business, the target is a romantic or sexual relationship. At first glance, this work might appear very frivolous—an assumption that often accompanies love work. This sort of summoning ritual can be a powerful form of healing, though, if that intention is what the charmer is holding. Love can take on many different forms and meanings and doesn't necessarily just correspond to romance and sex. Whether you're seeking someone for the rest of your life, someone just for now, or a love that cannot be embodied in a physical form, this ritual can assist you in opening the door to receive whatever you are calling for.

Two classic Ozark love birds are used in this charm: the redbird and the turtle dove. Both of these are often invoked as spirit helpers in charming rituals for love. In this specific charm, they will carry your call to the four directions. And, as the charmer who taught me this ritual said, they will also bring back signs or tokens of your love before the next full moon, so keep an eye out for doves and redbirds!

MAGICAL TIMING

Full moon or waxing zodiac moon day in Gemini (Mercury, Wednesday, air) for general or quick, uninhibited love affairs, or Virgo (Mercury, Wednesday, earth) for committed relationships and marriages.

CHARM

What I call for, quickly come.
I send my call on the wind's back!
I send my call on the redbird's back!
I send my call on the dove's back!
What I call for, quickly come!
Without haste nor hurry, come.
Come with a smile and warm heart,
Come with care and tenderness,
Or else, don't come at all!
I call from the east and the west,
I call from the north and the south,
What I call for, quickly come!

RITUAL INGREDIENTS

None

RITUAL ACTIONS

This particular charming ritual requires no ingredients at all. Go outside to a place where you can be alone and as secluded as possible. You can perform this ritual indoors, but if you do, make sure you open a window so the work can fly outside.

Begin by facing east. Recite the first line of the charm. After each of the "I send..." lines, blow toward the east three times. Continue with the charm recitation. When you reach the line "I call from the east and the west," you will turn clockwise from east to west. Then, with the following line, turn clockwise to the north and then to the south. You will end the charm facing south.

With the ritual complete, return home. Or, if you are already home, shut the window you left open for this ritual. Your love will come to you before the next full moon, or Mercury will bring a vision of them to you in a dream.

NOTES

This love charm uses a Mercury moon day as opposed to the classic Venus day that is usually associated with love work. Mercury (in the form of Gemini or Virgo) is better able to facilitate the quick-communication aspect of this charm, as he carries your message through the sky and on the back of the wind.

☆ COUNTING DIVINATION ☆

This is a traditional counting divination to determine if there are mutual sentiments of romance and love between yourself and another. There are many variations of these counting charms in the Ozarks, and not all of them are used in love magic. Charms like this one traditionally use small objects that can be counted.

MAGICAL TIMING

Full moon. Zodiac moon days in Gemini (Mercury, Wednesday, air) or Pisces (Jupiter, Thursday, water) are good for divination work.

CHARM

One, he [she/they] loves; two, he loves;
Three, he loves, they say;
Four, he loves with all his heart;
Five, he casts away.
Six, he loves;
Seven, she [he/they] loves;
Eight, they both love.
Nine, he comes; ten, he tarries;
Eleven, he courts; twelve, he marries.

RITUAL INGREDIENTS

Countable objects: flower petals, chunks of bread, dried beans or corn kernels, etc.

RITUAL ACTIONS

Pair this verbal charm with specific objects that can be separated and counted. It's traditional in the Ozarks to use a flower head that has many petals, such as the oxeye daisy (*Leucanthemum vulgare*), black-eyed Susan (*Rudbeckia hirta*), or purple coneflower (*Echinacea* spp.). If using flowers, you will pull a single petal from the head for every number mentioned in the charm. Only pull a single petal at a time. So, in the line "Three, he loves, they say," you will pull off one petal, not three. If you reach the end of the charm and still have petals, start over until all have been pulled off. The number you land on when all petals have been removed is your divinatory answer.

Lines six and seven are a bit different than the others. Line six signifies that the other person loves you, while line seven indicates that you alone are the one who loves in this situation. Line eight then shows that mutual love is present on both sides.

You can use other objects with this charming ritual. Sometimes a small bun, roll, or loaf of bread is torn into numerous pieces that are then put into a large bowl. This bowl is then taken outside and the pieces are thrown one by one while reciting the verbal charm. The number you stop on when you reach the last piece of bread is your divination. As with the petals, if you reach the end of the verbal charm before the pieces are all thrown, you will start the recitation over again.

Dried beans and corn kernels can be used in similar ways. Grab a handful of either, then place them in a bowl. Go outside and toss them one at a time into the grass while reciting the verbal charm.

NOTES

Another counting charm that utilizes plucking flower petals from a single head is the famous "He/she/they love(s) me, he/she/they love(s) me not" that might even be familiar to you, reader. However, people don't often know that counting divinations are used to find out other kinds of information too; see chapter 8 for examples of such divinations.

✫ FULL MOON LOVE DIVINATION ✫

Another popular love divination, this charming ritual involves looking to nature for signs that point to the identity of a person who is in love with the charmer. This ritual was also traditionally used to identify the name of the person the charmer was to marry.

MAGICAL TIMING

When you hear a dove coo while looking at the full moon (in any zodiac sign).

CHARM

Bright moon, clear moon,
Bright and fair,
Lift up your right foot
There'll be a hair.

RITUAL INGREDIENTS

None

RITUAL ACTIONS

This charming ritual has a very specific timing. It's believed that the verbal charm will only work if the correct conditions are met. In this case, those conditions are as follows: First, you must be outside under the full moon, which must be visible. Second, you must repeat the charm and ritual *after* hearing a dove coo. Ozark charmers—and even layfolk who happen to know some love divinations—are very serious about this specific timing. A person might go quite a long time before the exact conditions are met, but in case you want to try, here is the ritual procedure.

Once the ritual stage has been set, you will immediately repeat the verbal charm all the way through. After finishing, lift up your right foot. There will be a hair on the ground in the shape of either a full first name or an initial of the one who loves you. Because this charming ritual is performed at night, it's recommended that you take a flashlight outside with you so you are able to find the hair.

In some variations on this ritual, the charmer will first draw the shape made by the hair or take a photo of it, then carefully remove the hair and take it back inside. As this is believed to be a representation of the person who is in love with or destined to marry the charmer, it can be used in other charming rituals to either strengthen that bond, make the love progress faster, or even break the love and send it away.

NOTES

There are many variations on this love divination, not all of which utilize a very specific verbal charm and magical timing. In one version, a person goes outside and finds a stick. With a knife, they mark one end of the stick as the "arrow" (two lines) and the opposite as the "butt" (one line). After this, they toss the stick into the air and let it land on the ground. They then walk thirty-three steps in a straight line in the direction the arrow end of the stick is pointing. Once they've reached their destination, they will pull up a rock that is at their feet. Under the rock will be a hair or root shaped like the name (or initial) of the one who loves them.

☆ KNIFE CHARM ☆

This is a simple yet powerful verbal charm for keeping a relationship together. By its nature, it can only be performed by the individual(s) in the relationship itself, however many individuals that might be. Love takes on many different dimensions and while this charm has commonly been used in amorous relationships between two people, it can also be employed for polyamorous groups. It can be used to maintain the strength of platonic love as well. You can perform this ritual alone or with the other member(s) of the relationship. I will say, it is a very potent experience to enact this ritual together.

It's worth noting that this verbal charm uses wording that you don't often hear in traditional love charms. Most seek to force the hand of nature or bend another person's will, both of which are extremely problematic approaches today. This charm, however, aligns the speaker with the flow of nature rather than against it. So, there is a possibility that this charming ritual could fail if the other person doesn't, in fact, love you like you love them. This charm can then act as a sort of love divination; if you are suddenly severed from the other person/people encompassed by the ritual, then perhaps this is a sign that it wasn't meant to be.

MAGICAL TIMING

Full moon in Taurus (Venus, Friday, earth) for love and romance without contractual obligations, or full moon in Libra (Venus, Friday, air) for marriages.

CHARM

If you love me as I love you,
No knife shall cut our love in two!
(Repeat three times)

RITUAL INGREDIENTS

Cloth, white (or a tea towel)
Ink pen, black
Knife; can be any kind, but it must be sharp, and you will be hiding the
    knife as part of the ritual, so don't use one you need in daily life
5-inch paper square
String, white, spool
Candle (optional)

RITUAL ACTIONS

As this charming ritual is commonly performed with the other person/people in the relationship, that's where we'll begin. First, write the full name (first, middle, and last) of each person in the relationship on the paper square. To deepen the connection, you can add each person's birthdate.

Have each person add their own identifying materials on top of the paper square. These can be strands of hair, fingernail clippings, spit, blood, etc.—whatever they are comfortable contributing. If you're using items that might fall off the paper, like hair for instance, seal them to the paper using drips of candle wax.

Next, carefully wrap the paper square around the knife blade, with the writing and identifying materials facing inward toward the blade. Tie the paper square to the blade using a small piece of your string. After the paper is held in place, have everyone present repeat the verbal charm together three times.

Then, take turns wrapping the knife blade with string until it is completely covered in a few layers. Cut the string, then knot the loose ends together. Finish the ritual by wrapping the knife in the white cloth, then hiding it in a place where no one else will ever find it.

NOTES

There's a common folk belief in the Ozarks that a knife can magically cut or sever a relationship between two or more people. In one example, passing a knife to another person blade-first signifies the relationship will soon be cut apart unless the proper countermeasures are enacted. Gifting a knife to someone is seen as bad luck for the relationship unless the person receiving the gift is able to pay a little something for it. I've personally seen this folk ritual performed: the gifted knife also came with a penny that the recipient then gave back to the gift-giver as payment. In a way, this verbal charm is a sort of countermeasure for one of these folk instances as well as protection for the relationship from a more outright severing curse.

☆ LEAF DIVINATION ☆

This verbal charm is another common ritual to bring a lover to you quickly, whether that love is romantic, sexual, or long-term (as in invoking a future spouse). As with other love divinations, this charming ritual involves searching the natural landscape for omens or tokens of your love's identity or signs that will point you in their direction.

MAGICAL TIMING

Full moon in Pisces (Jupiter, Thursday, water) for general divination or Aquarius (Saturn, Saturday, air) for divinations relating to your personal love interest.

CHARM

Scattered leaves around I see,
Where can my true lover be?
The white dog barks at last!
And my love comes running fast!

RITUAL INGREDIENTS

None

RITUAL ACTIONS

Go to a secluded area, preferably in a garden or forest. Face the east and lean over so that your hands can touch the ground. Say the first line of the verbal charm. Wipe your hands through the leaves around you as you speak the second line. Then, stand back up and cup your hands behind each ear while you repeat the third line. After this, cross your arms across your chest, right arm over the left, and say the last line.

After you finish the verbal charm, look at the forest floor around you for any signs or omens that might have been summoned during the ritual, specifically amongst fallen leaves. There are many tokens you can look for. Common examples include grass, twigs, and debris shaped like the initial(s) of the one who truly loves you. You may even notice bits of hair that are colored the same as your true love's hair, or even full portraits of your future spouse made in the dirt or on dead leaves.

As a summoning ritual, this verbal charm acts as a way to bring your love to you, which likely won't occur at the exact time the charm is recited. Your love might appear to you in a dream the night of the ritual, or they may suddenly stumble into your life without warning.

This ritual is considered extra auspicious if you hear a dog barking while reciting the verbal charm. It's said that the dog bark will come from the direction where your true love lives. It should not be taken as a sign of failure if no dog barks during the ritual.

NOTES

Another variation on this ritual uses the line "Scattered rocks around I see" instead of using the word *leaves*. This ritual would then be performed on the rocky bank of a creek or lake, or even on a gravel road. In this ritual, the charmer picks up rocks around them, looking underneath for any omens or tokens of their love's identity.

✴ MAY DAY CHARM ✴

This charming ritual utilizes dew blessed by the dawn on May Day to ensure favor and love from all people—or at least until the next May Day. Traditional dew charms like this are often used to beautify the one who washes with the water, or to remove blemishes, moles, and even warts. This specific verbal charm, however, works in such a way that the charmer, no matter their appearance, will be granted a boon of magical attractiveness to all around them.

MAGICAL TIMING

May 1 (May Day) at, or right before, dawn.

CHARM

The one who on the first of May,
Goes to the fields at break of day,
And washes in dew from grass or tree,
Will e'er after beloved be.

RITUAL INGREDIENTS

Cloth, towel, or handkerchief
Bottle or jar (optional)

RITUAL ACTIONS

Arise before dawn and go to a field or an area where there are lots of trees and flowers that have collected dew. Face the rising sun and hold up your cloth or handkerchief by two corners, forming a square or rectangle. Recite the verbal charm. Then, pull your cloth across the flowers, grasses, and tree leaves, collecting the dew. When the cloth is wet, take and wipe it across your face and areas of exposed skin while repeating the verbal charm again.

To make a natural Venusian ritual water, continue collecting the dew using your cloth. Then wring the wet cloth into a jar or bottle and save it for future use.

Be careful what plants you collect this dew from. Avoid plants that you might be allergic to as well as plants that could irritate the skin, like poison ivy.

NOTES

A similar charming ritual takes place on Christmas Eve, another auspicious time to work magical rituals in the Ozarks. For this rite, the charmer goes out just before midnight on Christmas Eve and collects snow, dew, or, in some variations, well/spring water. This is then added to a bath to increase the charmer's beauty and help them gain favor from others.

✳ REDBIRD CHARMING ✳

This verbal charm is spoken in response to seeing a redbird (cardinal) land near you. It's said that if the redbird flies away from its perch at the end of the charm, your wish for love will come true. This charm is used most often as a way of calling love or a lover into your life. Sometimes the name of a specific person is spoken before the charm begins as a way of magically summoning them into your life. In most cases, though, this charm is left open-ended and is intended to quickly summon whatever love nature has in store for you.

MAGICAL TIMING

When you see a redbird (cardinal, *Cardinalis cardinalis*).

CHARM

Fly my bird,
Fly I say;
Bring me my love,
Now fly, fly away!

RITUAL INGREDIENTS

None

RITUAL ACTIONS

The charming ritual begins whenever you see a redbird land somewhere near you, whether it is on a tree branch, the ground, etc. In the Ozarks, redbirds are used as a part of this ritual, but the verbal charm itself doesn't name a specific bird species, so you're welcome to use another. Doves are also associated with love magic.

Once you spot a bird that has perched, repeat the verbal charm while looking at the bird. It's believed that if the bird has listened to you, it will fly away immediately. If not, it will remain in place, and another bird should be chosen and the ritual repeated. If the ritual is successful, your love should appear in your life within three days of the ritual—whether that's a specific person or a little extra love and favor in general.

It's sometimes said that the bird used as a part of the charming ritual will later return with strands of hair that are the same color as your true love's hair, or with string in the shape of your true love's initial(s).

NOTES

Redbirds are a "witch bird" in Ozark folklore. Witch birds are considered to have extra innate magical ability, and it is favorable for humans to use them as familiars and partners in charming rituals. Other examples of witch birds include owls, crows (and sometimes blackbirds in general), woodpeckers (especially the pileated woodpecker), and vultures (called buzzards).

In addition to being used in rituals for love, redbirds are said to bring money and good luck. In one ritual, the practitioner waits for a redbird to land on the ground or perch on a branch, then repeats the verbal charm "Money by the end of the week" three times. If you make it through all three recitations before the bird flies away, you will receive extra money by the end of the week, the idea being that the redbird has the magical ability to bring you wealth and good luck as the result of a successful charming ritual.

CHAPTER 6
To Set a Watch
on House and Home ...

The Dead Winter was the worst one Nelson's Holler had ever known before. It got that name on account of it killing livestock, pets, and old-timers all across town— from Michael Landry's cattle pastures in the north to Nancy Flewitt's chicken houses in the south. It was so cold that Old Man Pickett's pond froze solid for damn near the entirety of January. The local kids would have had a great time skating on the ice had it not been too cold to leave the house. It was the winter Tanner Pickett claimed he saw his dog's pee freeze into a solid stream while outside for a walk. Everyone knew Tanner Pickett was a liar, but they also remembered how cold it was during the Dead Winter, causing much debate over the next few years.

Ann was living with Gram Watson at the time. After graduating from school, she started her official apprenticeship. She mostly just helped out around the house, and whenever Gram was called to deliver a baby, she was right there at the bedside helping in any way she could. Ann's mother wasn't thrilled with this career path, but she never voiced this aloud. She would have preferred Ann get a job at one of the department stores downtown or maybe even continue her schooling. Ann had other plans for herself, though, knowing full well she'd go crazy if she got stuck in some boring office all her life. Working with Gram was far from boring.

As frigid winds descended upon Nelson's Holler, Gram came down sick with a fever and cough. Ann hadn't ever seen Gram get sick before. In all her years, Ann always knew Gram to possess a health and vigor that was surprising for such an old woman. It scared Ann half to death to see her mentor and surrogate grandmother laid out in bed, barely able to pull herself to her feet.

For the first few days, Gram was able to give Ann instructions on brewing up herbal broths for her and how to keep track of her progressing symptoms. After that, though, her fever got worse, and Gram was only able to mumble a few incoherent words. Ann got even more frightened at this point. She was no doctor, no healer, she barely even knew the right herbs to use to try and break Gram's fever. She halfway considered calling old Doc Winthrop in to help but knew that Gram would skin her alive if she did so.

One cold night as Gram slept shivering in her bed, Ann searched through the old woman's house for her black book. It was something she had only ever seen a few times when Gram was in dire need, and she absolutely never had a chance to look through the pages. Gram protected that book with the utmost care. Ann had heard all of the rumors that circulated through town about Gram's book, but of course didn't believe a word of them. The older Gram got, the more she jotted down notes and scribbled drawings in that black book to help with her failing memory.

Ann searched high and low but couldn't find the book. She'd all but given up hope when she noticed Gram had woken from her troubled sleep and was pointing toward the kitchen. Ann followed in the direction her finger pointed and ended up at a tall china cabinet. She searched through the shelves but only found ordinary cookbooks and loose pieces of paper with recipes written on them. She pulled a stool over and carefully stood on top. She stretched her arm until she was able to reach the very top of the cabinet. There she felt a dusty book. Pulling it down off the cabinet, she saw that it was Gram's secret tome. While in form the book was just an old daily planner Gram had bought from the local pharmacy, Ann held it with the care she'd give a prized treasure.

Ann spent the next few hours rummaging through the pages, looking for a cure that would help. There were many strange things written in the book—things Ann didn't yet understand. As she sat close to the firelight, Ann heard something hit the roof above her. It was an odd sound made more troublesome by the fact that it broke through near-complete silence, apart from the crackling of the fireplace. Ann sat motionless with her ear pointed toward the ceiling to try and hear more. After just a moment, she heard what sounded like claws scraping against the shingles, as though some animal was trying to keep its balance on the roof. At first Ann thought it must be a raccoon or possum rummaging around for something to eat, but the way the creature moved made Ann very nervous. Her concentration was broken by the sound of Gram struggling in the bed. Ann rushed over and the old woman clamped down hard on her wrist with her hand. Their eyes met and Ann knew that something was very wrong. Gram shivered but managed to get out a few words, "Soul...sucker...help..." before falling back into her fever dream.

Ann turned to grab the black book and saw the pages turning wildly, as though blown by a gust of wind, but Ann felt no air moving inside the cabin. The pages finally stopped, and the book flung open. Ann grabbed up the tome and looked at the spell written out on the pages. "To Protect the Sick Against Soul Suckers" was the title. She read quickly through the procedure as the clawing noise on the roof grew more frantic toward the chimney. With shaking hands, she grabbed up Gram's briar-wood pipe and stuffed a plug of tobacco into the bowl. She went back to the book and read further. Tobacco smoke was required for Gram's spell.

The creature had reached the chimney and Ann could hear it begin clawing its way down the stones. As she tried lighting the pipe, the book fell closed to the floor. Ann swore under her breath and tried to find the page she'd just been on. The clawing sound was now mixed with a low growling and hissing as the creature descended down the chimney, completely unaffected by the fire beneath it.

Ann's heart was racing in her chest. She couldn't find the right page in the book. As she looked toward the fireplace in fear, something inside of her ignited. She suddenly felt completely calm. The chip of wood that hung around her neck seemed to vibrate against her chest. Ann lit the pipe and took two long puffs, then a third, which she held in her mouth. She wasn't quite sure why she was doing this, but something about it just felt right. It was as though she was acting out some memory she'd long forgotten. She stepped firmly toward the chimney, then stopped and blew a strong line of tobacco smoke right toward the fire. The creature scratched and clawed against the stones as though it was struggling against something, trying to pull back out of the chimney.

"Remember the charm, child!" Gram yelled before falling unconscious again.

"Carry him crow!" Ann yelled toward the fireplace, blowing another trail of tobacco smoke. "Carry him kite!" A third stream of smoke twisted an unnatural line toward the sound of frantic clawing and scratching inside the chimney. "Carry him away 'til the apples are ripe! And when they're ripe and ready to fall, bring him back, apples and all!"

The scratching intensified. It sounded to Ann like whatever demon was inside the chimney was using all its strength to remain there. Then, all of a sudden, the clambering stopped. All she heard now was the popping of embers in the fireplace *and Gram's heavy breathing in the bed. She rushed over and found the woman sweating bullets. Ann reached out a hand and Gram's forehead felt cool to the touch. Her fever had broken.*

Ann watched over her mentor the rest of the night. Occasionally she set a boundary around the outside of the house by walking the perimeter in a clockwise direction while smoking the tobacco pipe. Like the words she'd spoken inside the house, this method came to her as though remembering something lost. Ann didn't know where it came from, but she wasn't about to question the magic.

WORDS AS PROTECTIVE WARDS

In the Ozark charming tradition, protective magic is almost as common to see as healing work. As one of my teachers said, "The best way to heal sickness is to never catch it in the first place." This notion applies to hexes as well, with protective amulets and warding charms often being used as the first line of defense against anything malign or harmful that might enter the home or body. Verbal charms for protection often invoke the aid of divine or otherworldly figures like angels, saints, or even departed loved ones. It's not uncommon to hear charms that invoke the power of the Virgin Mary or saintly figures that aren't normally associated with Protestant Christianity. This hearkens back to the much older origins of many of these verbal charms, passed down through family and practice lineages for centuries. Roman Catholic elements abound in the form of saint veneration, despite the fact that the family might not be Catholic themselves.

The Psalms are highly prized as holding specific power against illnesses and evil. These are traditionally memorized by charmers and, in some cases, are altered with additional verses empowered by spontaneous poetic magic. Guardian angels are often given a martial appearance in these protective charms. Flaming swords and spears are put into their hands as they are sent out by the charmer to watch over home and family. Psalm 23 is a much-beloved charm for general protection.

BUILDING MAGICAL FENCES

Verbal charms are often born from the life experiences of the charmers themselves. Images within the charms aren't too far from what charmers would have encountered on a daily basis. This is exemplified in the "brier fence" category of verbal charms. These protective wards all build upon a common image: that of a hanging barrier made from greenbrier vines (*Smilax rotundifolia*). Greenbrier is a common plant across the Ozark region. When left alone, it can form walls of thorny vines from the ground to the treetops. These areas of thick vine growth are often called *brier hells* by Ozark hillfolk. If you've ever been caught in one while hiking, you'll know why.

Similar images pop up throughout the Ozark charming tradition. Honey locust trees (*Gleditsia triacanthos*), for example, were once traditionally planted as natural fence posts. The trunks and branches of the trees are covered in thick clusters of thorns. I once collected a honey locust thorn that was six inches long! These trees have a beautiful and sinister quality about them. There's no questioning why charmers have used honey locusts as images in fence charms, or why the thorns from such trees are sometimes used in protective rituals.

As with greenbrier vines, blackberry canes are used in fence-building charms to create protective barriers. Blackberry canes have the unique quality of being able to take root at either end of the cane, forming arches. Images of weaving these blackberry arches together into walls and fences often pop up in protective charms.

Many verbal charms take on fewer real-world elements but build upon similar ideas of fence- and wall-making. It's common to encounter charms that invoke "fiery walls," or fences made from the elements themselves: lightning walls, walls of ice, or fences made from stone, sunshine, or holy fire. These images are sometimes mixed with others; for instance, fiery brier walls. As with healing traditions, elemental correspondences are often formulated to counter very specific work, as in the case of one healer I met who determined through divination that an enemy of his was trying to use fire-based charms on him. He countered their fire with a protective ward made from storm clouds and heavy rain.

CONFUSION AS A MAZE

Unlike the more passive forms of warding that involve creating magical fences and walls to keep illnesses and evil away, there are also forms of *active* protection that involve creating illusions in the minds of potential enemies. This category of protective work often involves what I like to call *impossible charms*. These are verbal charms intended to confuse or misguide specific enemies who are targeted as part of protection work or general illnesses and evils that might wander through the land. These impossible charms often make use of strange images that are magically planted in the mind of a target in order to confuse or distract them from their malicious goals. Traditional tongue twisters and rhymes are often used as part of this work, as are verbal charms with seemingly impossible infinity clauses. One example of this is the simple charm "Evil, you shall not come near me until a solid-gold tree grows from an acorn." Verbal charms like these intentionally create impossible situations to contend with.

The impossible charms highlighted in this chapter all aim to create a maze within the mind of the target, the idea being that one of the best forms of protection magic is distracting evil, illnesses, or enemies away from you altogether. There's a sense with many of these impossible charms that the power of the targeted individual (or sometimes even their personal soul) is what is locked away in this maze of words. Until the target is able to free themselves by making the impossible statements possible—or by fulfilling the requirements of the verbal charm—they will find themselves completely unable to work against the charmer in any way.

In one story I heard, a charmer recited one of these impossible charms with the target being a wealthy land developer trying to buy his farm. According to the charmer, the rich man all of a sudden started losing paperwork and forgetting to follow up with the charmer about the purchase. Pretty soon he was so distracted he left the area altogether and started developing properties several hours away. At the time I was told this story, the charmer claimed he hadn't heard a single word from the rich man for almost twenty years.

THE CHARMS

Protection work is generally associated with the two Mars signs of Aries (Mars, Tuesday, fire) and Scorpio (Mars, Tuesday, water) as these are considered the "warrior" signs in the Ozarks. These signs offer two different ways of working elementally: fire with Aries and water with Scorpio. Taurus (Venus, Friday, earth), works to protect the home and family, and Cancer (Moon, Monday, water) for personal or family protection. Leo (Sun, Sunday, fire) is good to use with ritual work for protection against evil influences and entities because of its association with the Sun, illumination, and the element fire.

☆ BOOGER CHARM ☆

This protective verbal charm specifically targets Ozark otherworldly entities known as *boogers* and will ensure that they cannot enter your home or harm the ones inside. The charming ritual can be enacted as often as you need, but I like to repeat it every full moon, as this is believed to be a time when spirits are at their most powerful.

The word *booger* has its origin in the same root as the English *boogie*, as in the mythical evil spirit known as *the boogie man* (*bogey man*) and variations found throughout folklore like *bogle*, *bogart*, and even *bug*, as in the dreaded *bugbear*.

In Ozark folklore, the booger is a shape-shifting creature who appears as an all-black (including the eyes) animal. The animal form depends on what the booger is trying to achieve, with birds and small animals used for spying and vicious creatures like wolves, dogs, and even bears used to attack humans. In some accounts, boogers are actually shape-shifting witches that can take the form of an all-black animal, but in most of the tall tales they are creatures of their own.

Boogers can only be killed with silver (specifically silver bullets), but they can be scared away, harmed, or warded against using verbal charms and ritual. Boogers are often included alongside other entities in charming verses or—as in the case of this ritual—specifically targeted on their own.

MAGICAL TIMING

Nighttime. Use zodiac moon days in Taurus (Venus, Friday, earth) for home protection, Cancer (Moon, Monday, water) for personal or family protection, or Scorpio (Mars, Tuesday, water) and Aries (Mars, Tuesday, fire) for personal protection.

CHARM

Booger, don't you come near me,
Don't you come to the one you see,
Not until you count every root,
Not until you count every fruit,
On every tree and every stack,
From here to Jerusalem and back!
(Repeat three times)

RITUAL INGREDIENTS

Bowl or mug
Red cedar (*Juniperus virginiana*) or juniper berries, lightly crushed
Red cedar branch, small; a small pine branch with needles; or a
    paintbrush
Salt
Water

RITUAL ACTIONS

Begin by filling your bowl or mug with some water. Add three pinches of salt as well as your red cedar or juniper berries that have been lightly crushed. Take this, along with your red cedar or pine branch (or paintbrush), to the front door of your house. This charming ritual will be performed while standing in the doorway.

Traditionally, you should be standing half inside the house and half outside. This is considered to be a liminal space, or a place between this world and the otherworld. You will then begin the verbal charm recitation. At the end of each line, dip your red cedar/pine branch/paintbrush into the bowl and flick some water away from you.

Repeat the entire verbal charm a total of three times. When you're finished, throw the remainder of the water outside, then close the door. You can save your branch for future blessings or hang it above your front door as a protective ward.

NOTES

As a verbal charm for personal protection, you can recite these words three times over water, then use it as a daily ritual bath. You can also recite the charm three times over olive oil that can be saved and used as a protective anointing oil. This will ensure that you are well-protected from boogers both inside and outside the home.

This verbal charm makes use of a certain kind of impossible task language, much like the infinity clause found in other charms (see "Washing Charm" in chapter 2). An impossible task is set as a part of the charming ritual, with the idea being that the entity targeted by the magical work must complete the task before they are able to harm the charmer. In this case, any boogers who want to approach a home (or an individual) must first count every root and every fruit on every tree and stack in the entire world. If the charming ritual is repeated on a regular basis, whatever work the booger has accomplished since the previous ritual is made void.

✯ OWL CHARMING ✯

Some might think this is a very strange verbal charm, but in Ozark folklore, the owl is a carrier of magical power—and not just the good kind. Owls can be servants of all kinds of practitioners, but they are traditionally associated with those who practice malign magic. It's very common, even today, to see Ozarkers become uncomfortable when they hear an owl hoot. This is especially true when the little Eastern screech owl (*Megascops asio*) lets loose its screams. The screech owl is said to scream when someone nearby is receiving a curse. If you're the only one around, that cursed person is you. This verbal charm is one of many variations aimed at countering the hex the owl brings with it. It's traditionally recited whenever an owl call is heard or whenever a charmer sees an owl, day or night—with or without a call.

Because of their associations as hex-bringers, traditional healers are often adamant about watching out for tokens or omens from owls during the healing process. In the old days, healers would sometimes even stay overnight with their patients—especially those with grave illnesses—to listen for owls coming to steal away the sick person's soul or life force, symbolized in the breath. If an owl call was heard or an owl was seen through a window, a charming ritual like this one would be performed immediately as a counter-action before the owl was able to suck out the sick person's final breaths.

MAGICAL TIMING

Whenever you hear an owl hoot, most especially a screech owl, or whenever you see an owl in general.

CHARM

Off the house!
Out of tree!*
Fly back to the west,
Fly back to your master!*
Earth, ash, coal, cinder,
Wood, spark, flame, blaze!*
As fire burns salt,
Fire burn this hex!*

RITUAL INGREDIENTS

Salt
Candle (optional)

RITUAL ACTIONS

In a simple ritual to accompany this verbal charm, pour some ordinary table salt (or whichever kind of salt you have on hand) into your right hand and go to the open front door of your home. Facing outside, repeat the verbal charm. Wherever you see an asterisk (*) at the end of a line, throw a pinch of salt outside using your left hand. When you're finished, close the door behind you. If the owl is still heard, repeat the ritual action.

In a more traditional version of this charming ritual, the salt is thrown into an open flame instead of outside. This flame is usually in the form of a wood-burning stove or fireplace. If you're like me and don't have access to a fireplace, you can light a candle of any size or shape and toss the pinches of salt into this flame. I like to use a taper candle so that I can toss the salt through the flame and it won't remain in the wax, like with a jar candle. You can pair this candle ritual with the first variation: toss the salt through the candle flame and outside the house through the open front door.

If you have a gas stovetop, you can also throw the salt into this flame, but cleanup will likely be a little more difficult.

NOTES

Owls are considered to be witch birds by Ozark hillfolk; they join the ranks of others like redbirds (cardinals), woodpeckers, and blue jays. Specific bird species like these are considered to hold far more innate magic within themselves than other bird varieties, and therefore, they are often viewed with great suspicion. In some cases, folks even believe them to be witches or mountain wizards in disguise. For this reason, many healers and magical practitioners invoke these birds (or often archetypes of these birds as spirits) in their rituals and verbal charms as a way of adding auspiciousness, or power, to their work. According to folk belief, these birds will work for whoever calls and gives them an offering, whether the work is for healing or hexing. As one of my teachers told me, "Even healers should be suspicious of what they bring."

✶ PRAYER BEFORE SLEEPING ✶

This is a very traditional charm based in Christian mythology to protect oneself while sleeping. The belief is that we as human beings are vulnerable to spiritual and magical attacks while sleeping, so protective prayers and verbal charms like this one are a common feature of traditional Ozark folk practice. There are many variations on this verbal charm, most of which invoke specific biblical figures as protectors.

This is a great example of verbal charms that utilize specific archetypal figures as a part of the magical action. Here, it's the four Gospel writers from the Christian Bible. Each of these figures carry with them very specific correspondences that can be invoked as part of a healing or magical act. As a team, they are even more powerful. Each figure represents a cardinal direction as well as a side/post of the bed where the charmer will be sleeping. Because of this correspondence, we're invoking the limitless power of the four directions as a whole. The macrocosm is brought down and merged with the microcosm.

On the cosmic level, the four Gospel writers stand as unshakable pillars of the four directions, holding up the very foundations of the universe. This balance and equilibrium is brought into the microcosm of the bedroom by four angels, each of which serves a specific ritual purpose. The four posts or pillars of the charmer's bed then become like the pillars of the heavens above—just as strong, just as balanced. These four figures aren't just invoked because of their associations with Jesus in the Bible, but because they embody all of the sacred correspondences behind the number four itself. This number is often used in verbal charms that aim at balancing a body that is out of equilibrium or in strengthening as part of a protective ritual. This is especially the case with any charms for the house or household—four being a number that connects to the four walls of a room, four sides to the house, four posts on the bed, etc.

MAGICAL TIMING
Before going to sleep.

CHARM
Matthew, Mark, Luke, and John,
Guard the bed that I lay on!
Four corners to my bed,
Four angels round my head;
One to watch, one to pray,
And two to bear my soul away!
(Repeat three times)

RITUAL INGREDIENTS
Bowl (optional)
Water (optional)

RITUAL ACTIONS
The simplest way of performing this charming ritual is to recite the verbal charm three times while facing east, which is considered the direction of blessing. If you don't want to use the biblical figures in the charm, you can

replace the first line with, "East, South, West, and North," which will invoke the same imagery of bringing in the cosmic directions.

As a variation, you can add a traditional water blessing to the ritual. In this case, fill a small bowl with some water. After each of the three charm recitations, flick some water around your bed using the fingers of your right hand. Then, place the bowl at the head of your bed or underneath your bed, positioned underneath where your head will be. In the morning when you wake up, take and dispose of this water—do not drink it or let your pets drink it. The belief is that the water that was blessed as part of the charming ritual will absorb or trap anything that might try to get to you while you're sleeping. Disposing of the water then banishes whatever evil spirits or sicknesses were trapped. Traditionally, this water is poured onto the trunk of a strong, living tree, like an oak. Or, pour it into a running body of water, down the toilet, or simply down the sink drain.

☆ REVERSING CHARM ☆

This verbal charm is used to magically reverse hexes, illnesses, and even the Evil Eye before they stick onto their intended victim. Think of it as creating the effect many of us remember from our childhoods: "I'm rubber, you're glue. Whatever you say bounces off me and sticks to you!" As this is a warding practice, the primary goal is to destroy evil before it befalls the charmer. The idea is that the water and the verbal charm create a magical barrier around the charmer that will reverse or deflect any evil that might come against them. You can, however, use this charming ritual as a cleansing act as well—in cases where these things have already invaded the body.

Many Ozark reversing charms make use of imagery involving some sort of misdirection, as in this case, where a hunter (the hexer) aims for a pigeon (intended victim) but actually shoots a crow (misdirection). The healer who gave me this charm believed that shooting crows meant terrible bad luck, so not only does the one throwing the hex have their work reversed back to them, but they also have an added curse from killing this symbolic crow.

MAGICAL TIMING

Full moon. As this protection rite uses water, zodiac moon days in Cancer (Moon, Monday, water) are best.

CHARM

All of a row,
Bend the bow,
Shot at a pigeon,
And killed a crow.

RITUAL INGREDIENTS

Bowl
Salt
Water

RITUAL ACTIONS

Begin by filling a bowl with some water. It can be any size and amount, but you will be washing your body, so make sure you don't use too little water. Once filled, add three pinches of salt; any kind will do, but I like to use sea salt. Stir the water with the forefinger of your right hand in a counterclockwise direction until the salt is dissolved—or as close as you can get. Counterclockwise is considered the direction of removal.

Strip off all your clothes and face the east. Wash your entire body from head to toe three times with the salt water; repeat the verbal charm constantly while washing. Unlike Ozark cleansing baths, in this ritual there's no need to have the force of the water flow over your skin, so you can just gather a small amount in your hands and wipe it over your body. You want to make sure all areas of your skin are at least dampened by the water before you end the ritual and all of the water is gone from the bowl.

You can follow this ritual with a regular bath or shower. Repeat this ritual as often as you like to maintain the protective barrier around your body.

☆ SNAIL PROTECTION CHARM ☆

Here is another example of a transformation from nursery rhyme to verbal charm. In particular, this rhyme is used as protection against all magical forces, specifically against enemies or another charmer who might be throwing a curse at you. This is generally considered to be a common countercharm used to quickly reverse all hexes and even the Evil Eye. It's most often recited at the moment of encountering an enemy or when some token or omen leads you to believe that they might be trying to curse you. This reactionary charming is traditionally called *taking the cuss*, or *curse*, off the situation.

MAGICAL TIMING

As a countercharm immediately after seeing your enemy or an inauspicious omen. You can also perform as a separate charming ritual; Aries (Mars, Tuesday, fire) or Scorpio (Mars, Tuesday, water) are good zodiac moon days to use.

CHARM

Four and twenty tailors went to kill a snail,
The best among them would not touch her tail;
She put out her horns like a little Kelly cow—
Run, tailors, run, or she'll kill you all a'now!

RITUAL INGREDIENTS

Snail shell (optional)
String (optional)

RITUAL ACTIONS

As a simple countercharm, there aren't many ritual actions that need to be performed.

In one example that I collected, the charmer crossed her arms across her chest right arm over the left as she recited the first line. This motion is itself a common Ozark countercharm specifically for the Evil Eye, but it works in cases of other hexes as well. With the second line, she put her hands on her backside, one hand on each cheek, to symbolize the snail's tail. On the third line, she moved her hands up to the sides of her head, pointing the forefinger of each hand outward like a horn. This action remained until the very end of the last line, when she brought her hands out in front of her and clapped loudly on the final word of the verbal charm.

This countermeasure would be made while facing your enemy or facing the direction of the one who sent the curse to you. In some cases, I've heard charmers say that your enemy must be in your line of sight in order for the countercharm to work.

Additionally, you can use this verbal charm while creating an amulet for protection. In this simple ritual, a string is tied through a hole in a snail shell—usually one that is large enough to accommodate a string, but I've seen very small snail shells strung using thin wire or fishing line. While facing east, the direction of blessing, recite the verbal charm and then blow across the snail shell three times at the end of the recitation. The idea here is that the wearer of this amulet will have the power of this monstrous snail invoked in the verbal charm that will protect them from all evil and hexes.

NOTES

When I first started collecting charms across the Ozark Mountains, I found this specific one in several different variations, all of which involved a monstrous and seemingly magical snail. Unfortunately, most of my informants were unable to provide me any folkloric significance for why the snail was specifically used as a part of these verbal charms. But in one case, a charmer did tell me that in the old days (however long ago that might have been), people believed that snails contained venom that could be injected into an unknowing victim using a small horn that would extend out of the snail's body. This folk belief seems to have originated with European families who, at one point, were snail gatherers—this being an important source of food for many people across Northern Europe.

Even though snails have, as far as I can tell, never been a part of the Ozark diet, folk beliefs surrounding these mollusks seemed to have remained in some cases. The same informant told me that to see snail or slug trails around the front door of your home indicates that these creatures are trying to protect you from some incoming hex. He said that in his own work, whenever he saw these trails around his own home or the home of the person he was working for, he took this as a token that cleansing would need to be done in order to fully stop the hex from entering. What might be considered a garden pest to some is a powerful protector to others.

✶ THIEF CHARM ✶

This is a traditional charm used to compel a thief to return stolen property to you. This charming ritual works on the principle that the thief will be punished by having their luck taken away until they return what they have stolen. Once returned, the magical effects will stop unless the charmer chooses to continue them.

MAGICAL TIMING

Midnight. To be performed the night after you were robbed (or your house/ vehicle was broken into). Typically, charmers won't wait for the appropriate zodiac moon sign, but it is auspicious to begin this charming ritual at midnight on a Taurus (Venus, Friday, earth), Scorpio (Mars, Tuesday, water), or Capricorn (Saturn, Saturday, earth) moon day.

CHARM

I eat thy luck!*
I drink thy luck!*
When the Sun sees thee,
Come you back to me!*

RITUAL INGREDIENTS

Hammer
3 new nails
1 sheet of paper, white
Pen or marker, red
Scissors

RITUAL ACTIONS

Begin by cutting out a human shape from a white piece of paper. It can be as large as you like, but I usually try to make one as big as I can from a single sheet of US letter-sized paper. It's very important that if the thief left behind any identifying materials (like hair, clothing, or blood) that you attach these with a few drops of candlewax; you could also wipe any liquid materials on the paper doll for added connection. In the case of clothing left behind, attach a small cutout scrap.

If you don't have identifying materials, it's traditional to carry your doll representation of the thief through the rooms of your house where items were stolen—especially places where there is any damage—and *show* the paper doll the crime scene. One of my teachers even suggested saying "Look what you did" to the doll as you walk through the spaces. This will connect the doll directly to the thief who was there.

Once you've done this, draw a large red heart in the chest area of the doll. Then, go outside, taking with you the doll, a hammer, and one new nail. The nail can be from an already-opened package, but it shouldn't have ever been used before. You will need to find a place where you can nail up your doll. This can be a wooden fence post, tree (preferably dead), or even the siding of your house—as long as it's wooden. Black oak trees (*Quercus velutina*) are preferred in the Ozarks for such curses. If you don't have one of these places around you, you can nail the doll to a wall inside your house; using a room that was most affected by the break-in is best. Wherever you are, take the doll and hold it against where it will be nailed. Repeat the verbal charm, and when you see an asterisk (*) at the end of a line, hit your nail into the doll, through the heart you drew. You should hit the nail a total of three times.

You will repeat this same ritual at midnight for two more nights, each time driving an additional nail through the doll's heart. It's believed that by the end of the third ritual (third nail), the thief will return or be caught, or you will learn their identity. You can repeat this charming ritual additional times, beyond just the three, if needed, with another nail added each time. Examine your dreams on these nights, as it's possible the thief will appear to you there instead of in the waking world.

✳ THIEF CHARM: ANOTHER VERSION ✳

Unlike the previous verbal charm, this version holds little hope for any return of property. Instead, it simply aims to magically whip or beat the thief, hopefully so much that they quit their evil ways—or, at the very least, to ensure the thief won't strike the same house twice.

MAGICAL TIMING

Same as the previous charm. Midnight of the evening after you were robbed (or your house/vehicle was broken into). There is no need to wait for the appropriate zodiac moon sign, but you can begin this charming ritual at midnight on a Taurus (Venus, Friday, earth), Scorpio (Mars, Tuesday, water), or Capricorn (Saturn, Saturday, earth) moon day.

CHARM

Tom, Tom, the piper's son,
Stole a pig and away he run!
The pig was eat and Tom was beat,
And he went crying down the street.
(Repeat three times)

RITUAL INGREDIENTS

Cast-iron skillet or shallow cooking pan
1 sheet of paper, white
Scissors
Switch made from a tree branch, or a broom
Water

RITUAL ACTIONS

As with the previous charming ritual, begin by cutting out the figure of the thief who is being targeted. Once finished, place your paper doll into the cast-iron skillet. Add any identifying materials that you have from the thief (if any) directly into the skillet. Now, this ritual will get a little messy, so I recommend taking your skillet outside. Heat some water to boiling and then pour it into the skillet, over the doll. (You can also heat the water and the skillet on the stovetop, if you're performing this ritual inside the house.)

Find yourself a pliable tree-branch switch. Good switches can be made from willow, redbud, witch hazel, and peach trees, but you can use any branch as long as it is very pliable and won't break easily. A broom, preferably one made from natural broomcorn, is a great alternative.

Repeat the verbal charm and after each line, strike the water and paper doll once with your switch or broom. You will repeat the entire verbal charm three times in total, beating the doll twelve times. When you're finished, you can take the doll and whatever water is left and throw them into a creek or river. It's also traditional to bury them at the base of a black oak tree, or any dead/dying tree—the idea being that you are connecting the power of the thief to the waning life force of the dying tree.

NOTES

Magical work against thieves/thieving is as old and varied as wart charms. While we still have to worry about these issues today, our ancestors would have suffered far more dire consequences from being robbed. As with one folk story—similar in content to the rhyme this verbal charm is based on—where a farmer woke up to see his prized pig had been stolen in the night. This was truly a crushing blow, as the farmer was going to sell the fattened pig to buy supplies for the coming winter. Fearing the worst for himself and his family, the farmer went to a local "witch woman" for help. She asked if the thief had left anything behind at the scene of the crime, however small or insignificant it might seem. The farmer handed the woman a small scrap of fabric from the thief's shirt that had been torn off on a nail as he struggled with the pig. The old woman took the scrap cloth and put it in a skillet, then grabbed a bundle of peach tree switches from the corner and began furiously whipping the skillet while muttering some verbal charms. The farmer returned home, and within three days, he saw the pig back in its pen and a stranger standing on his doorstep. It was the thief, covered in cuts and bruises from head to toe. He sincerely apologized to the farmer and told him he was about to turn himself in with the sheriff to atone for his sins and hopefully stop whatever was whipping him all night long as he slept.

Poppet work in the Ozarks can take many different forms. Paper dolls are inexpensive and very easy to make, so they are usually the preferred medium. Older variations include dolls made from corn husks, wax, wood, and even scraps of clothing from the targets of the curse. Many people assume that these sorts of dolls are only used in curse work, but that isn't necessarily the case. In terms of hexes, these poppets are traditionally called *spite dolls* in the Ozarks. Healers use similar dolls as a way of magically working on their clients from afar. In form, they might look exactly like a spite doll and are often filled with identifying materials from the person that is being worked on or made to physically look like the person themselves. But while the two types of dolls might look similar, the work done with them is very different.

✴ **THREE-PRONG BRANCH CHARM** ✴

This is a charming ritual specifically used to bless a three-pronged branch as a protecting ward. This is considered a general-purpose protection charm used against illnesses, hexes, the Evil Eye, and unwanted entities. The verbal charm itself is used as part of the blessing process for the ward but can be repeated anytime protection from the branch might be required.

MAGICAL TIMING

Empowering warding objects to protect the home and family is good to do on Taurus (Venus, Friday, earth) or Cancer (Moon, Monday, water) moon days. General or personal protection is good on Aries (Mars, Tuesday, fire) or Scorpio (Mars, Tuesday, water) moon days.

CHARM

This branch of three,
This branch I see,
Guard me,
Save me,
Good for me and good for thee!
(Repeat four times)

RITUAL INGREDIENTS

Ribbon, red, 1 foot long by 1–2 inches wide (cut one for each branch to
be blessed)
3-pronged red cedar (*Juniperus virginiana*) branch or alternative tree
species

RITUAL ACTIONS

The main component of this charming ritual is the three-pronged branch that will be blessed as your ward. Traditionally, this branch is taken from a red cedar tree, which has a long history of use as a mighty protector against all ills and evils. Other trees can be used if red cedars are not available to you. As our red cedars are actually junipers, not cedar trees, common juniper or other varieties can be used as well. Juniper is the preferred alternative tree. It's also possible to use sassafras (*Sassafras albidum*), spicebush (*Lindera benzoin*), or witch hazel (*Hamamelis virginiana* or *H. vernalis*). The easiest alternative to acquire is a branch from an oak tree, preferably white oak (*Quercus alba*).

Find a branch that has a naturally formed three-pronged end and cut it from the tree. Your branch should be, at most, two inches in diameter—any bigger will be very difficult to work with. It can be as long as you want, but I try to cut my branches down to under three feet long. Trim off any foliage and extra branches, leaving behind a cleaned branch apart from three distinct prongs at one end. The main thing to remember when choosing a branch is that you want one that has a *natural* three-pronged end, not one that is whittled or cut into that shape. If you'd like to drive this ward into the ground as a part of the ritual, go ahead and cut or whittle the non-branching end into a spike.

These branch wards are usually driven into the ground close to the front door of the home. If you don't have access to open ground, you can lean or hang them up outside or inside the home near the front door as well as additional exits. I've seen branch wards like this hung horizontally *above* the door—either inside and outside the home. (If you'd like wards outside of multiple entrances to your home, you can craft additional wards during the same charming ritual.)

Once you have your branch made, begin the charming ritual. Stand outside (or inside, if that is where you're keeping your ward) and face the east. Hold the branch(es) with your right hand, outstretched vertically in front of you. If you're blessing multiple branches, you can use both hands to hold them all. Repeat the entire verbal charm once, then turn clockwise to the south. Repeat the verbal charm, then turn clockwise to the west. Repeat the verbal charm, then turn to the north. Finish with a fourth and final recitation of the charm, then tie the length of red ribbon onto the center prong of every ward you've created. Take your wards and drive them into the ground, hang them up, or use them however you choose.

Personal amulets for protection can be crafted using this same ritual, but with much smaller three-pronged branches that can be carried in a vehicle or physically on a person. You can often find these small branches on younger red cedar trees.

✵ TRAVELING PRAYER ✵

This prayer and accompanying ritual is used as a method of magical protection during travel. It can be used for all forms of travel, including by vehicle or by air. While this charming ritual has specifically been used for long travel, you can use it for short trips or even your daily commute. We can even go deeper and connect to the idea of traveling through one's own life; in this way, you can use the charming ritual as road-opening work to bless your personal path and clear all obstacles ahead of you.

Traveling charms and prayers are a common feature of Ozark folk magic. These go back to the old days, when hillfolk often had to travel great distances by mule to get where they needed to go. If you've ever traveled through the backwoods areas of the Ozarks, you'll know how dangerous even paved roads can be around here. More and more, I find myself giving out this charming ritual to people who have anxieties about air travel. I myself use this verbal charm whenever I'm about to go onto an airplane, and it always calms me down.

This verbal charm uses a comparison between the wheel of the sun and the wheels of the vehicle used to travel, whether that is the wagon wheel of our ancestors or the modern tire. Just as the sun is an unbreakable force, so too is the vehicle strengthened against physical damage. The physical and metaphysical illumination of the sun as a symbol of healing and protection is an important feature of this charm. This light hearkens back to a favored Bible verse of healers and charmers, John 1:5: "The light shines in the darkness, and the darkness did not overtake it."

Mountains are another feature invoked in this verbal charm. Calling down power or powerful entities from distant, mythical mountains is common in many Ozark charms and prayers. Because of their nearness to the heavens, mountains are considered highly auspicious locations and power places for Ozark charmers and layfolk alike. For healers and charmers, these are places that will add power to your own power. For this reason, they are commonly invoked within verbal charms.

MAGICAL TIMING

To be performed before traveling.

CHARM

The golden sun can't be stopped,
My golden wheel can't be stopped!

Imps and devils have tried but
My golden wheel can't be stopped!

Three blessings from three mountains,
One for the road ahead,*
One for the stay,*
One for the road back again.*

Devils may try their worst but
My golden wheel can't be stopped!

Three blessings from three mountains,
One for the storms,*
One for the bandits,*
One rough road ahead.*

Imps may try their hardest but
My golden wheel can't be stopped!

Against sickness, blights, and evil,
My golden wheel rolls onward,
Across three mountains and
Back home safely again.

RITUAL INGREDIENTS

Bowl or mug
3 small branches of red cedar (*Juniperus virginiana*), juniper, or pine—
    with leaves/needles
Water
Olive oil (optional)

RITUAL ACTIONS

The most common version of this ritual is for blessing a vehicle before traveling. Variations will be provided after this procedure.

First, fill your bowl or mug with water. Take this and three red cedar, juniper, or pine branches out to the vehicle you will be using for travel. Stand on the west side of your vehicle so that when you face the vehicle, you are also facing east. Hold your three branches in your right hand and the bowl or mug of water in your left. Repeat the verbal charm, and whenever an asterisk (*) appears at the end of a line, dip the three branches (as a bundle) into the water, then throw some over the vehicle.

When you have finished the verbal charm, take whatever water is left over and pour it as an offering at the base of a tree. Take the three branches you used as part of the blessing and keep them in your vehicle during your trip. When you return home, you can burn these branches as another offering.

If you're wanting to use this verbal charm for other forms of travel, here is what you can do. Begin with a bowl of water or some olive oil. Recite the verbal charm but this time, when you see the asterisk (*), blow across the surface of the water or olive oil. After you've finished, you can wash yourself with the water before you leave home. If you used olive oil, rub a small amount into your hands while at home and then bottle the rest for use while on your trip.

✯ WOODEN POST CHARM ✯

This simple verbal charm is recited over a fence post as a way of creating a magical barrier surrounding the home. The posts or pillars of a front porch or house can also be charmed as protective wards against intruding illnesses, hexes, or entities.

While this verbal charm is quite short and simple, it makes use of a common characteristic of magical charms in the Ozarks: the overpowering clause. Basically, this is a phrase (or multiple phrases) inserted into a verbal charm that will empower the charmer above whatever they are charming against.

MAGICAL TIMING

Full moon. Zodiac moon days in Aries (Mars, Tuesday, fire), Taurus (Venus, Friday, earth), or Leo (Sun, Sunday, fire).

CHARM

Here stands a post!
Who put it there?

One better than you:
Touch it if you dare?

RITUAL INGREDIENTS

Hammer or mallet

Red cedar (*Juniperus virginiana*) branch, a wooden fence post, or the
posts of your front porch

Ribbon, red, 1 foot (or big enough to tie around the post)

RITUAL ACTIONS

There are a couple ways to work this charming ritual. The first way uses an
existing fence post or post on the front porch of the home. In this case, you
will tie the red ribbon around the post and knot three times. Then, you will
repeat the verbal charm while touching the post with your right hand.

The second method uses a branch of red cedar or a red cedar post. The
post can be of other types of wood too, it's just that red cedar has deep associations with protection magic. Alternative woods include oak, elm, sassafras, Osage orange (*Maclura pomifera*), or black locust (*Robinia pseudoacacia*).
Your branch or post can be of any length or thickness, but note that a thin-
ner branch will be easier to drive into the ground with a hammer.

Take your branch and choose your spot. As a ward, this post will protect
against evils that pass by it, so think about the areas of your home that are
trafficked the most. This is usually somewhere near the front door of the
house or the side of the driveway.

Once you have your spot picked out, tie the red ribbon on the top of the
post and seal with three knots. Then, hammer the post into the ground, just
deep enough so that it stays in place. You want to be careful about going
too deep, as you could possibly hit underground water, sewer, or electric
lines. If you're using a larger post, you might need a post-hole digger, a type
of specialized shovel specifically for digging fence post holes. In this case,
be extra careful about digging too deep. You can research where lines are
buried around your house before performing this ritual. When your post is
secure in the ground, recite the verbal charm while touching the post with
your right hand.

Protective posts like these can be fed or recharged like you would an amulet. Full and new moons are traditional times for recharging. Simply pour a small amount of alcohol on the post; beer, wine, mead, whiskey, moonshine, or gin (contains juniper) are common. You can repeat the verbal charm during recharging if you want to.

NOTES

Hand-carved fence posts in the Ozarks are an interesting bit of folk knowledge that is sadly dying out. Traditional woods for fence posts include black locust and Osage orange for their strength and durability, and red cedar, which is naturally pest- and weather-resistant. As with all Ozark folkways, there's another layer underneath this one. Specific types of wood were picked because of their magical protection—although hillfolk would rarely talk about this power using the term *magic*. Red cedar in particular is favored as a protective tree, and all parts feature in rituals throughout Ozark folk magic practice. The black locust, honey locust, and Osage orange have thorns, so there's another symbolic association here between protection work and the use of thorns. Thorns are common materia in Ozark folk practice, used to create magical swords, spears, and fences against evil and sickness.

CHAPTER 7
To Right All Wrongs
that You Might See ...

One hot summer evening, a stranger came to Nelson's Holler. Folks all knew he was a stranger on account of nobody knowing him—and everyone knew everyone in Nelson's Holler. The stranger was first spotted near Marcum's Mercantile down on Main Street. Lily-Kate Marcum stopped her sweeping of the front porch to watch the man saunter all the way from the post office, cross the front of her store, where he smiled and nodded to her, then continue on past to the café two doors down. Later corroborated tales would confirm that others on Main had also seen this smile-and-nod from the stranger, as well as his disappearing into the café. Less than a minute after the incident, Gram Watson's telephone rang. Ann hurried from the kitchen to answer it, wiping off a trail of sweat from her forehead as she ran. "Yes? Hello?" she said, frustrated by the interruption.

"Gram? Is that you?" Lily-Kate Marcum asked on the other end of the line.

Ann recognized Lily-Kate's raspy voice. "No, Lily-Kate, it's Ann Ganter."

"Oh, well you tell Gram to call me back. I just saw a stranger come down Main Street and I thought she should be warned."

Ann rolled her eyes, "All right, Lily-Kate, I'll have her call you as soon as she can." She hung up the telephone just as Lily-Kate began to respond.

Old busybody, Ann said to herself as she returned to her work in the kitchen.

She was too busy to be dealing with local nonsense today. She had to make yarb broths for three different sick folks in town, she had a church lady coming over in an hour for a love potion, and to top it all off, she had to clean up a mess from her thirty-ninth birthday party the night before. Over the past few weeks, Gram's ability to get out of bed had lessened almost every day. She took to napping and reading mostly, as well as ringing a little bell for Ann's assistance—Ann hated that bell with a fiery passion. But, the apprentice turned master was happy to help out. She had no idea how old Gram was, and never dared to ask. Just about every day, though, she wondered if this would be the day Gram finally passed away. While she'd come to terms with the practicality of life and death, emotionally she was still a little girl curled up on Gram's lap listening to old stories.

Ann was up to her elbows washing a big canning pot when there was a knock at the front door. She swore under her breath, closed her eyes briefly to calm her nerves, and headed out of the kitchen. Just as she reached for the doorknob, another loud knock sounded, and Gram yelled from the back bedroom, "Get that door, Ann!"

Ann took another deep breath in, then out. "I'm on it, Gram!" she yelled back.

At the door stood what Ann thought looked like a funeral mourner. The figure was dressed in a large black dress and even wore a wide hat with a black veil hanging down over their face. "Thank you, sweetheart," they said as they pushed into the house.

"Miss Ida Lee?" Ann asked, closing the door behind the figure.

The old woman removed the hat and veil and hung it up on a peg on the wall. "I don't mean no offense, sweetheart, you can't be too careful with folks watchin'. I don't want them to get the wrong idea."

Ann laughed to herself and showed the old gossip to the kitchen.

"Did you hear about the stranger spotted over at the mercantile?" Miss Ida Lee asked, pouring herself a cup of coffee.

"Yes, I heard something about that."

"Lily-Kate said he had strange, dark eyes and coal-black hair. You know Little Freddy Landry who works over at the café?"

Ann nodded while she stirred one of her broths with a long wooden spoon. "Little Freddy," as the town called him, was nearly twenty by now, but Ann guessed he would never get rid of the name.

"Well he said," Miss Ida Lee continued, "that the stranger just walked right into the café, sat down at the counter, and ordered himself the biggest piece of coconut cream pie that they had. He didn't even order any food first!"

"I can't even imagine!" Ann said sarcastically.

"It was real strange too; Little Freddy said he ordered a cup of hot chamomile tea to go with it. He had to rummage through all the cabinets just to find some. You know no one drinks that stuff."

Ann did find this to be a little peculiar. She wondered who this stranger might be and if he was single. As she smiled to herself, she heard the thud of Gram's cane hitting the hardwood floor as she came down the hallway. Ann rushed over to make sure the old woman didn't fall down. Gram was in some kind of hurry. "You need something, Gram?" Ann asked.

The old woman pushed her aside as though she was on a mission. She stepped right over and sat down at the kitchen table. "You said he drank chamomile tea?" Gram asked, dead serious and staring right at Miss Ida Lee.

The poor woman nodded her head nervously. "Yes, Gram, that's what Little Freddy said."

Gram snapped her fingers together like she had some idea appear. "I bet he's still there," she said under her breath. "Ann!" she yelled.

"I'm right here, no need to shout," Ann replied, crouching down next to Gram.

"Good, good. Ann, I need you to hurry down to the café. Now, when I say hurry, I mean hurry, child."

Gram rummaged through the deep pockets of her house dress. She pulled out a small bundle wrapped in black cloth and tied with white kitchen string. "Give this to that stranger, then hurry back as fast as you can."

Ann might have been puzzled by this request if anyone other than Gram had asked. Over her many years apprenticing with the old woman, Ann had fulfilled stranger requests than this one. She took the bundle and started to clean herself up a bit when Gram shouted "Hurry!" behind her. Ann jumped and rushed out of the cabin, apron still tied around her waist.

☆　☆　☆

By the time Ann got down to town, she was huffing and coughing, not used to being in such a rush. Just as she opened the café door, a figure almost stepped right into her. "I'm so sorry!" she said, moving to the side.

"It's no bother," the man replied.

Ann looked up into the man's dark eyes, colored like pits of coal. He had shoulder-length black hair that shimmered like crow feathers. He wore a slate-gray snap-button shirt and blue jeans. Ann stammered as she stared at the stranger smiling back at her. "Say, I, um, I don't recognize you," she finally said.

"Not from around here," the man answered, lighting a cigarette as he sat down on a wooden bench outside the café. "Not for a long time, anyway."

"This might sound odd, but a woman named Gram Watson told me to give you this." Ann pulled the tied bundle out of her pocket and handed it to the stranger.

"Thank you," he answered, as though he was expecting to receive the item.

"What is it? If you don't mind me asking?"

The stranger chuckled to himself. "The tale's too long to tell. Just tell Gram that I'll return the favor."

Before she could ask another question, the stranger stood, nodded to Ann, then headed down Main Street toward the hotel.

Ann hurried back to Gram's house. By the time she got back, Miss Ida Lee had already picked up the love potion she'd requested and headed stealthily back down to town. Gram was sitting on the front porch smoking her briar-wood pipe when Ann walked up. She sat forward, anxious for her apprentice's return. "Did'ya do it?" she asked in a low voice.

Ann nodded. "That fella seemed nice, Gram. He told me to tell you he'd return the favor."

Gram stood up so quickly that Ann rushed forward to grab her in case she toppled over. The old woman slapped her away, then shuffled back into the cabin. Ann followed behind her silently. "What's wrong, Gram?" she asked as the old woman blazed a trail through the front room and right into the kitchen.

Gram didn't answer at first. She pulled out the big cookpot Ann had washed earlier and placed it on the woodstove. She filled it with a pitcher of water, then started throwing in pinches and handfuls of herbs from around the kitchen. Ann tried helping, but the old woman motioned silently for her to sit down at the kitchen table.

"Gram, you're scaring me," Ann said, fidgeting with the strings on her apron. "What's wrong?"

Gram stirred the pot with a long wooden spoon, muttered some words under her breath, then walked over to Ann. "Stand up, child," she said, pulling the woman to her feet. She started poking and prodding over her body like she was looking for something. "It's got to be here somewhere," she whispered to herself.

"Can I help you with somethin'?" Ann asked, confused by the examination.

Gram didn't answer, but just continued her work. When she was at Ann's back, she suddenly stopped with a satisfied grunt. Ann felt her pull something out of her knitted sweater and then return to her front again. "Found it," Gram said with a smile, holding up what looked like a tiny ball of dark-colored wax pressed onto one side of a spiny cocklebur.

"What the hell is that?" Ann asked, leaning forward to try and get a better view of the strange object.

Gram grunted and hurried over to her cookpot, now steaming. "It's a curse!" she cackled as she dropped the object into the boiling water.

"A curse? How'd it get on me?" Ann exclaimed.

While she'd cured her fair share of curses before, from clients around town as well as for herself, she'd never encountered one like this.

"He put it on you!" Gram exclaimed from the cookpot.

"Gram, we never even got close to each other. And besides, why would he do something like that?"

"He's a sly one—and got fast hands! I never guessed he'd be back, but I reckon it had to happen eventually. He's here for me, Ann."

To say that Gram was cagey about her personal life was an understatement. It took Ann until she was almost twenty-three before she learned Gram's first name—Eleanor. Gram liked to keep to herself, and Ann had almost come to rely on this personality trait. "That man you met today is called Otho Green," Gram continued, "and he was once my husband."

Ann sat in silent shock for a moment. "Husband?" she finally managed to gasp. "No, Gram, that man couldn't have been more than thirty-five at the most."

"I swear to you that what I say is true, child. He was always good at changing his looks."

Ann sat in disbelief but motioned for Gram to continue with her tale.

"I won't say much, just that we were in love, married, then we parted ways. He's evil, Ann. About as close to the devil as you can get."

Ann started to speak, but Gram interrupted her. "No more, now. We'll boil the curse away and hopefully he'll move on out of town again."

In the days that followed, there weren't any more reports from Nelson's Holler about their stranger. Rumors still flew around for almost a year after the incident, however. Ann's life went back to normal, or as normal as it could be living with Gram. Then, one day, the rains moved into the holler. The sky clouded up around five in the morning on a Tuesday. By sunrise a torrential downpour fell across the entire range of Nelson's Holler—but only on Nelson's Holler. Local meteorologists called it a freak *occurrence of nature's unpredictability. The community pastor called it a sign of the apocalypse. Gram called it a hex.*

The rains continued for three days without stopping. Fields were flooding. Bridges were breaking as creeks and rivers swelled beyond their natural boundaries. Many people in the lowlands had taken shelter uphill. Luckily, Ann and Gram lived on the mountain, but Nelson's Creek was so high it had washed out the dirt road below them, preventing any escape.

When the rains began, Gram caught a fever. Ann rushed into action making a strong yarb broth for her and reciting some protective verbal charms to ensure her work would be successful. By the third day, the fever was bad as ever. With no sign of the rains stopping, Ann began to worry that this would be Gram's last fever.

Late one night, Ann had finally dozed off in a chair at Gram's bedside. Just as she started to dream of better days, she was shocked awake by Gram grabbing hard onto her arm. Heart racing, Ann leaned forward to hear what the old woman was trying to say. The words were broken, but she managed to make out "It's ... Otho ... I'm ... gone ..." before Gram relaxed back into her bed and breathed her last few breaths.

Lightning struck a tree outside the cabin, making Ann scream and cutting the electricity to the house. Ann breathed hard, shallow breaths as she stared at Gram, lifeless in her bed. She felt her body frozen in place. Thoughts raced through her head, but she couldn't move to take any action. If you don't move, she thought to herself, you'll be next. Anger stoked some fire in her belly. She felt her veins boil and her legs and fingertips tingle with pinpricks. She counted in her head. One ... She moved her fingers and toes. Two ... She tightened her grip on the chair's wooden arms. Three ... She forced herself to stand up.

Panic, fear, sadness no longer defined her current state—she was filled with a fiery anger. She hurried through the dark cabin, her path illuminated only by flashes of lightning outside. She lit a couple candles on the kitchen table, then stoked the woodstove until tongues of flame lapped out of the iron mouth. Another loud clap of thunder shook the cabin. Ann looked out the kitchen window into the night. "Thunder, either help me or stay out of my way!" she yelled as the sky rumbled its reply.

Ann had no idea what to do. She tried calming her thoughts to find some spell, rite, or words that would help, but none came to her. A long, rumbling roll of thunder shook the walls, sending something crashing to the floor behind Ann. She jumped, then rushed over. An old metal picture frame lay shattered on the wood floor.

Ann swore she'd never seen it before. She leaned over and gently swept some of the glass away from an ancient photo of a young man and woman, smiling arm-in-arm together on an ornate couch. She flipped it over to the other side, where in ink "Otho and Eleanor, forever" was written. A tear rolled down Ann's cheek as she stood back up. A spell suddenly came to mind.

Ann first let the fire grow in her stomach again. She took the photo over to the kitchen counter and, with a swift motion of a sharp knife, cut it clean in two, separating Gram and Otho. After this she stuck a fireplace poker into the hot coals of the woodstove and watched as it began to glow red. She grabbed an onion from the kitchen windowsill, took the hot poker, and drove a hole right through the center. She rolled Otho's photograph up into a tight tube and slipped it into the passage through the onion made by the hot poker. To end her ritual, she took the onion to the woodstove and tossed it into the coals. As the flames sputtered and spat around the onion, Ann repeated Isaiah 5:24, a curse from the Bible that Gram had given to her. "Therefore, as the tongue of fire devours the stubble and as dry grass sinks down in the flame, so their root will become rotten, and their blossom go up like dust ..."

After the first recitation, the onion spewed steam into the coals and Ann could swear she saw Otho's grimacing face in the smoke—ancient, wrinkled, with sunken cheeks and coal-black eyes. Ann recited the words again, this time blowing into the coals after speaking. The onion sunk down into itself as its skin began to char. Ann recited the words a third and final time while throwing a handful of red cedar berries onto the fire. The onion split apart into seven sections, all of which instantly caught on fire. With a final hiss of steam, Otho's spectral face disappeared. The coals crackled quietly as what remained of the onion was reduced to ash.

Ann could hear the rain outside slow, then finally stop altogether. Feeling a heavy weight in her chest, Ann stood, returned to Gram's bedroom, and allowed herself to weep at the old woman's bedside.

CURSING WITH MOTHER GOOSE

Whenever I start talking about Ozark verbal charms, it surprises people to hear that many beloved nursery rhymes are consistently repurposed as charming verses. This includes curses as well as blessings. In fact, the number of potential hexing charms I've collected from Mother Goose's rhymes alone often make people rethink sharing them with their own children. For me, this shows how important language is, especially in oral folk cultures.

How much knowledge and power are we able to pass down through these so-called children's verses?

One of my favorite verbal curses comes from a very unsettling nursery rhyme that I remember reading as a child in an old collection of Mother Goose poems. Even back then, I remember thinking to myself, *This is a curse*, and I could imagine a fairytale witch casting it at their enemies during a thunderstorm. The rhyme goes:

> Tell, tale, tit,
> Your tongue shall be split,
> And all the dogs in town,
> Shall have a bit!

This rhyme makes for a fantastic retribution charm against slanderers; the charming ritual might hex the target's tongue to speak no lies about you any longer. Another of my favorites specifically targets liars:

> Liar, liar, lickspit,
> Turn about the candlestick;
> What's good for liars?
> Brimstone and fires!

I tell my students "Charms are empowered by your individual connection to the words and the intention you supply." Lengthy prayers and poems can be very powerful, but from an oral folk culture perspective, being able to recite lines from memory is far more meaningful. This has continued to be a reason for Ozark healers' connection to simple, poetic charms passed down orally through family or practice lineages as well as the consistent repurposing of verses from the Bible, song lyrics, and, yes, Mother Goose's rhymes.

WORKING AS NATURE WORKS

As I've discussed elsewhere, Ozark healers and magical practitioners of the past and present didn't always fit the stereotypical mold of "witch" versus "healer" that has been presented by folklorists and storytellers for centuries now. The old way of thinking was that the healer always healed, and the witch always hurt. This divide has historically been a way to target already-marginalized members of the community. If you're able to target a person's gift as being evil, you can target the person themselves. Our healers often did work against supposed witches, but only as a way of protecting their own practices from suspicions of witchcraft. When talking with healers themselves, you are far more likely to find individuals working in the gray, or neutral, realm of magic. This is absolutely not to say that it's common to find healers throwing curses left and right at anyone who might anger them. The majority of Traditionalists still abide by their Protestant Christian values, which uphold healing rather than harming as the correct path. Cursing does happen, of course, and we should remember that healers and magical practitioners in the Ozarks traditionally don't abide by any common creed or binding set of rules like you find in Wicca, for example, apart from their religious leanings. There is no one way to practice Ozark folk magic and healing. Everyone works in their own way based on a combination of inherited and created practices.

What I mean by the "neutral realm" of magic is that it's very common to see healers and magical practitioners—even those who are more traditional—providing work that would normally be considered taboo if practiced openly. This includes practices like divination, love magic, work for good luck at gambling, and yes, retribution or curse work. The situation is a little different these days, when fewer and fewer of the old taboos are still in place, but there are traditional healers in conservative communities who are still hiding much of the work they do from the community at large. It's interesting to note communities who simultaneously condemn witchcraft while still supporting the role of their traditional healers. This has long been the case in the Ozarks. It's common to hear even healers themselves staunchly defending their magic while simultaneously condemning similar practices from the witchcraft community.

For many Ozark practitioners, this neutral magic works the way nature works. Many healers see their role as an extension of the work of nature itself. Just as nature is neutral, so too is the magic of the healer. Nature gives and nature takes away. If heavy rains flood your home, was it an act of evil? If lightning strikes a tree and it falls on your car, was that evil? Are we even able to apply such a dualistic system to the workings of nature? For myself as well as many folk healers here in the Ozarks, that answer is a resounding no. And returning back to more traditional workers in the Ozarks, if you're still questioning the position of cursing amongst Christian healers, believe me when I tell you that I've met many praying grannies and pious folk who work in this very same way. Many of them quote a line from Job for their justification: "Naked I came from my mother's womb, and naked shall I return there; the Lord gave, and the Lord has taken away."[8] In this way, you can substitute *nature* for *God*, as is often done. The role of the traditional healer then becomes that of an empowered emissary of Heaven, working in all the ways God has worked in the Bible. And let me tell you, there are a whole lot of curses in the Bible.

CURSING AND RETRIBUTION

What do I mean by retribution work, exactly? I discuss this subject in greater detail in *Ozark Folk Magic: Plants, Prayers & Healing*. There is also an entire chapter devoted to retribution spells and rituals in the *Ozark Mountain Spell Book*. In short, what I call retribution work is a method of combined cleansing and protection that aims to return curses and malign work back to its sender, whether or not that is an actual practitioner. I like to call this the "return to sender" work. Retribution work isn't hexing without good reason. It's not even aimed at harming another person. The traditional healers who taught me these methods all had a few common goals in mind: 1) getting rid of a hex, 2) preventing future hexes from befalling themselves or their clients, and 3) getting the hexer to see their wicked ways and change. That last part is particularly important. In most of the retribution-type charms I've seen, there's a way to immediately stop the work—pending, perhaps, the hexer asking for forgiveness or admitting to how cursing without reason can be detrimental to others. In this way, retribution work is actually healing work.

Addressing the second item in that list, many of the retribution charms in this chapter are aimed toward the enemy of the practitioner themselves. This is actually a more traditional way of working than you might suspect. We have many similar verbal charms that have been passed down for centuries—so binding your enemy, or confusing them away from you, isn't a modern form of magic. In the old days, rivalries amongst practitioners were very common in small communities where healers often had to fight for

---

8. Job 1:21.

their livelihood. I myself have collected several stories about healers driving rival practitioners out of town with their magic, or healers fighting to prove themselves against their enemies in town. The basis of this work is to ensure that your enemy no longer thinks about preventing or interfering with your work. There are many methods to achieve this goal, everything from distracting and confusing your enemy, to wiping yourself out of their minds altogether, to even lessening their power so that they don't have the energy to work against you.

CLEANSING AFTER CURSING

A recommendation that I haven't included in the other chapters of this book is cleansing after any of the following retribution rituals. This is a very traditional way of working because cursing of any kind, even for good reason, is still generally seen as something that can contaminate your body and spirit. As one of my teachers taught me, "Cursing can get stuck inside you," meaning this type of work does have the potential to corrupt, especially when you start to see the results of your ritual practice. Power of any kind has this same potential, which is why I recommend a regular cleansing schedule for any practitioner.

Personally, I recommend taking a traditional cleansing bath after any retribution work. Here is an easy bath method. Take a plastic tea pitcher or a big bowl and fill with hot (not boiling) water. Add three pinches of salt as well as any cleansing herbs you might have. Mint, hyssop, rosemary, sassafras leaf, juniper berries, or mugwort are all good to use. I like to put them in a mesh tea ball or cloth bag so they are easy to remove later. Let this sit until the water is cool.

Take out the herbs, then carry the pitcher and a coffee cup or small bowl to your shower or bathtub, or even outside. (You will be bathing naked, so make sure if you're performing this bath outside that it's in a private area.) Place the coffee cup in between your feet. Face the east, then say, "What I wash is removed." Pour some water over your head. Repeat the charm again and pour a second time. Repeat the charm a third time and pour the rest of the water overhead. By the end of the third pour, all the water should be gone. (You can do this seven or twelve times instead of the three, depending on how long you want to spend with the practice.) While pouring the water, visualize a stream of pure white light flowing through your body from head to toe, cleansing you of filth that leaves through the soles of your feet.

If you'd like to work with Bible magic, you can recite Psalm 51:7 instead of the verbal charm: "Purge me with hyssop, and I shall be clean; wash me, and I shall be whiter than snow." This is a very traditional cleansing Psalm in the Ozarks, and you can use just the one verse or the entire Psalm.

When you're finished, dry off and take the coffee cup—which will have some water in it—outside and pour it on the roots of a strong, living tree. Oak or red cedar are best. You can also throw the remaining drops into moving water if you live by a river or creek.

I like to do this cleansing bath weekly, but I certainly recommend doing this *immediately* after any retribution ritual.

THE CHARMS

As with protective charms, Aries (Mars, Tuesday, fire) and Scorpio (Mars, Tuesday, water) are traditionally used as "warrior" signs. Gemini (Mercury, Wednesday, air) is often used when sending magical retribution across distances, or for spells aimed at spying on enemies. For work with binding and boundaries, use Capricorn (Saturn, Saturday, earth). Because retribution work is associated with the darker side of magic, many practitioners traditionally perform these rites at night—midnight in particular—or at dusk. Midnight and twilight are both considered liminal times and have associations with lessening or diminishing rites. Traditionally, the new moon, specifically, or the waning moon, generally, are good times for working against enemies or enacting retribution.

☆ ANNOYING YOUR ENEMY ☆

As an act of retribution magic, this simple verbal charm aims to annoy rather than harm an enemy as a way to convince them to quit or avoid whatever magical actions they might be taking against you. The charmer who gave this to me used it whenever she saw one of her enemies, who often appeared in her dreams. She said she would sometimes wake up in the middle of the night after such a dream and repeat the verbal charm until she was calmed again. While this charm can of course be used for more malign magic, its primary intention is as a distraction so that the target of the charm will have to deal with the spectral buzzing and humming of these spirit-insects rather than focusing on you.

The basis of this charming ritual is the belief in sympathetic magic, specifically the Law of Similarity as coined by James George Frazer in *The Golden Bough*. The charmer is using the actions of flies and bees as a symbol that can then be magically reproduced inside of ritual's target, in a similar way to how animal teeth and claws are commonly used in rituals for magical protection (as well as cursing). This specific curse, or magical retribution, can be considered a much smaller and more benign version of the dreaded "live things" hex wherein insects, reptiles, and even sometimes small mammals are magically grown inside of a victim's body in order to torture them into submission or drive them insane.

MAGICAL TIMING

Whenever you see your enemy—in person or in a dream/vision. Gemini (Mercury, Wednesday, air) zodiac moon days work well for this charm because of Gemini's associations with communication, dreams, and magical sending.

CHARM

Buzz, says the blue-fly,
Hum, says the bee;
Buzz and hum they cry,
And so do we.
(Repeat as many times as needed)

RITUAL INGREDIENTS

Bamboo chopstick or disposable spoon
Beeswax chunk or candle
Bowl
9 dried flies *or* peppercorns
Wax paper
9 dried bees (optional)

Optional Variation:
All of the above ingredients, plus:
Hammer
Nail
Photograph of your enemy, or paper square

RITUAL ACTIONS

As with many verbal charms, there is the simple version of the charming ritual and a more complex one. In this case, the simplest way of using this charm is to recite it as many times as possible, almost as a sort of mantra, while looking at your enemy. Line of sight is considered necessary for the purposes of this charm. Line of sight, I've found out, can include looking at a photograph of the person or even seeing them in a dream. In-person is generally considered more powerful, however.

While reciting the charm under your breath, visualize bees and flies swarming around the person and flying in and out of their ears, nose, and mouth. Charming rituals like this are empowered by holding identifying materials from the person—like hair, clothing scraps, etc.—in your left hand while you are reciting the charm.

While talking with one informant, I learned a cursing ritual that uses dried and crushed flies and bees to magically buzz and fly inside your enemy's skull. In an effort to avoid actually having to kill living creatures, I have formulated alternative ingredients that I assure you are just as powerful when paired with this verbal charm and the proper intention. You can also collect insects that are already dead. While finding dead houseflies is an easy task, finding bees that have naturally died is another story. Please, whatever you do, don't kill bees for the purposes of this charming ritual. They are vital members of our ecosystems, without whom the foods we eat would never grow.

If you'd like to use my alternative ingredients, you will need nine whole peppercorns and a chunk of beeswax for melting. This can be a beeswax candle if you don't have a way of melting the chunks of beeswax. Crush your nine peppercorns (or dried flies) in a mortar and pestle until you have a powder. At this point, if you happen to have nine dried bees, you will add them to the mortar and pestle and grind them into a powder with the flies. If you don't have any dried bees, you can leave them out, as they are symbolized in the beeswax that is going to be used.

Add the powder to a bowl lined with wax paper. Next, add a small amount of melted beeswax to your powder, or you can let a lit beeswax candle drip into the powder. Using a bamboo chopstick or disposable spoon, stir the wax and powder until you are able to form a ball. Add more melted beeswax as needed. Once the ball is slightly cool, you can even pick it up in the wax paper and form it into a ball with your hands. Let this ball dry on the wax paper until it is completely hard.

Take your wax ball to your enemy's house. Face the house so that the west is at your back. Recite the verbal charm nine times, then throw the wax ball so that it hits the house. If you can, try to throw it on the roof so that it will get trapped in the gutter. Turn your back on the house and return home. Take a cleansing bath with salt and hyssop herb, if you have it, but at least salt.

There's another variation if you're unable to get to your enemy's house. Grind up your peppercorns (or flies) and then mix this with your melted beeswax in a bowl lined with wax paper. While still melted, or soft, take and spread this on a photograph of your enemy, or on a paper with your enemy's full name and date of birth. Stick any identifying materials from them into the wax as well.

While the wax is still warm, fold the photograph or paper square into a small parcel and seal shut with some more melted wax. Let this bundle cool completely. Then, take this outside along with a hammer and a single nail. Find a dead tree, wooden fence, wooden fence post, or a black oak tree (*Quercus velutina*). Recite the verbal charm nine times, and after each recitation, hit the nail through the paper parcel and into the tree or fence.

When you're finished, return home and take a cleansing bath. Leave the work behind on the tree. There is no recharging necessary.

NOTES

The significance of the number nine used in this charm has mixed associations amongst Ozark charmers and magical practitioners. For most, nine is considered a cursing number as opposed to auspicious numbers like three, seven, and twelve. So, it's very common to see the number nine used in hexing or retribution rituals. For others, however, nine is a blessing number, being made up of three sets of the number three, which is by far considered the most auspicious number in Ozark folk belief. Some practitioners use the unlucky number thirteen.

☆ BINDING CHARM ☆

A variation on Gram Watson's charm against the demon. This verbal charm has traditionally been used to magically bind an enemy from doing any malign work against you or the person you are charming for. Specifically, the nature of this charm is oriented toward removing that person from your life altogether—in other words, sending them away. After performing this spell, your enemy might physically relocate, or they might just forget about you altogether. Generally speaking, as a result of this sending away process, the target will find it impossible to work against you. Likewise, they will not be able to successfully collect any identifying materials from you or your home.

The charming ritual utilizes a single apple seed to formulate the duration of the spell. The enemy who was targeted as part of the charming ritual will only be able to return to your life, either physically or metaphorically, when this apple seed has sprouted and borne apples of its own. By hiding the apple seed away and protecting it, you are ensuring that the infinity clause will not be able to come to fruition. In one case, I spoke with an informant who told me that she performed this apple seed curse on an enemy of hers only to find after a week that the apple seed had sprouted roots that poked through the bag that held it. This was a sure sign that her enemy was doing magical work to undo this curse. As an answer to this token, my informant packed the sprouted bag into a glass canning jar filled with alcohol, ensuring the apple seed wouldn't continue to sprout.

MAGICAL TIMING

Waning moon. Nighttime. Zodiac moon days in Aries (Mars, Tuesday, fire) or Scorpio (Mars, Tuesday, water) are good to use if the main purpose of this ritual is for protection; for specific binding and boundary work, use Capricorn (Saturn, Saturday, earth).

CHARM

Catch [him/her/them], crow! Carry [him/her/them], kite!
Take [him/her/them] away till the apples are ripe;
When they are ripe and ready to fall,
Home [he/she/they] come(s) back, apples and all.
(Repeat three times)

RITUAL INGREDIENTS

1 apple seed, cleaned and dried
Cloth bag with drawstring top, small
Ink pen or marker, black
5-inch paper square, white or red, or a photograph of your enemy

RITUAL ACTIONS

This verbal charm can be used as a standalone recitation whenever you see an enemy, or you can use it alongside an accompanying charming ritual. On its own, you can simply recite the verbal charm three times while in the presence of your enemy or the one you're working against, with the visualization that ghostly crows surround the person and slowly carry them away from you. You can replace the pronouns used in the charm with whichever identify your target.

You can create a longer-lasting effect using a charming ritual. In this case, you will begin by gathering a single apple seed. This can be store bought (as in one from a package of many), or you can gather it straight from an apple. Make sure the seed is whole, clean of any apple debris, and completely dried so that it won't mold. Perform this ritual on any of the zodiac moon days mentioned in the magical timing section. It's best if you have a photo of the one you're working against; better still is having identifying materials from them. If you don't have these things, you can use a square piece of paper upon which you have written your enemy's full name (first, middle, and last) as well as their date of birth.

Place the apple seed in the center of the photograph or the square of paper. Recite the verbal charm three times, blowing across the paper and the apple seed three times after each recitation. When you're finished, fold the edges around the seed to make a small parcel. However you choose to fold it, make sure that the apple seed cannot escape. Place this parcel into your small drawstring bag, pull the strings tight, then tie them together in three knots.

So long as your bag remains hidden and the apple seed remains intact, your enemy will not be able to work against you—and, in fact, you might find they now ignore you altogether. Place your bag in a secret location, somewhere no one else will see it besides yourself. You can feed this work every new and full moon by reciting the verbal charm over the bag three times.

✶ CONFUSING YOUR ENEMY ✶

This traditional tongue twister is used to magically twist up or confuse the mind of your enemy. The purpose of a ritual like this would be to prevent your enemy from being able to work against you or even think about you clearly. This ritual can work on behalf of yourself or another. The charmer who gave me this rite said that if your intention and gift are strong enough, you might even make your enemy forget you altogether. I can personally attest to the effectiveness of this charm; the enemy that I twisted up almost immediately was distracted away from me toward another project or person, never to return again.

String magic is particularly popular in the Ozarks because string is a household item that many people have on hand. In this specific case, ordinary string is used to symbolically represent the string of thoughts in a person's mind. When we work with string in this ritual, we are working with the thoughts of our enemy, wadding them up together, and tangling them into a confused chaotic mass. The fruit of our efforts is a confused mind that couldn't possibly work against us.

Just as string can be used in ritual cursing, it can be used to release curses as well. In one case I observed, a healer formed a rat's nest of strings for their client, alongside certain hidden verbal charms. Then, as part of the healing ritual, they took a thin, metal knitting needle and worked out every tangle and knot from the wad. By doing this, they were able to undo the work that was done to their client. They were able to untie and untangle the knots that had formed in the person's mind and body. By untangling these things, they were able to completely remove the underlying curse rooted in the body and soul.

MAGICAL TIMING

Waxing moon. Zodiac moon days in Gemini (Mercury, Wednesday, air) are excellent for working with magic to confuse, beguile, or enchant.

CHARM

When a twister, a-twisting, will twist them a twist;
For the twisting of their twist they three times doth in twist;
But if one of the twines of the twist do untwist,
The twine that untwisted, untwisted the twist.
Untwirling the twine that untwisted between,
They twirl with the twister, the two in a twine;
Then twice having twisted the twines of the twine,
They twisted the twine they had twined in twain;
The twain that, in twining, before in the twine,
As the twines were untwisted, they now doth untwine;
'Twixt the twain inter-twisting a twine more between,
They, twirling their twister, makes a twist of the twine.

RITUAL INGREDIENTS

Candle, black
Ink pen or marker, black
Lighter or matches
String, black, 13 feet
Paper envelope, black
3-inch paper square, red (or a photograph)

RITUAL ACTIONS

There's a quick way to enact this curse, which first involves memorizing the charm completely. It's said that if you are able to completely recite the charm from memory all the way through without stopping or correcting yourself, while looking at your enemy, that the curse will be successful. If not, the curse will fail, and it's said that you will have to try again on another day.

A much easier way of using this verbal charm, in my opinion, is pairing it with a simple ritual. Begin by gathering your materials. In an otherwise dark room, light your candle. Your candle can be any type as long as it is black. Write your target's full name (first, middle, last) and date of birth on the paper square. A photograph of the target will also work. Roll the paper square or photograph into a small tube and then tie one of the ends of your string to the middle. Begin reciting the verbal charm, and while you're speaking, wrap, twist, tangle, and knot the string around the paper. Work any identifying materials you might have from the target into this wad of string as you go.

The point is not to wrap the string in an orderly fashion, but to truly twist and tangle it up. This tangling action symbolizes the confusion that you want to cause your enemy. The more tangled the wad of string gets, the stronger the confusion will be and the more difficult it will be for the target to counter or reverse your work. Repeat the verbal charm as many times as needed to get through the entire length of string. When you're finished, place the bundle into the envelope and then seal it closed with wax from your black candle. Hide this away from prying eyes and in a location where your enemy will never be able to find it. For if they do find it, they will be able to use the materials to reverse the curse.

You can recharge this curse every full and new moon by reciting the verbal charm while holding the envelope in both of your hands. If at some point you wish to break this curse, all you have to do is unseal the envelope, take out the wad of string, and cut through all of the individual twines until you are able to retrieve the paper or photograph that is at its heart. This cutting through the strings symbolizes clearing the confusion from the person's mind. Burning the strings and the paper completely will release this curse.

NOTES

This rhyme was originally a cure for hiccups. The idea being that if you had hiccups, you would recite this charm, and by the end, your hiccups would be gone. It has also commonly been used as a humorous tongue twister amongst children and adults alike.

☆ **DISTRACTING YOUR ENEMY** ☆

The hex caused by this charming ritual can become quite unpleasant for the target, so be aware. The charmer who gave me this act of retribution said she only used it when she was being harassed by her enemies and needed to make an escape. As a distraction, this hex works on the basis that your enemy will be in so much discomfort that they won't even think about working against you anymore. They will have "bigger fish to fry," as the old saying goes.

MAGICAL TIMING

New or waning moon. Midnight. As this is considered an "earth hex" because of its elemental correspondences, Capricorn (Saturn, Saturday, earth) is a good zodiac moon sign to use.

CHARM

In [his/her/their] ear, in [his/her/their] nose,
Hey! Do you see?
Starts small but then it grows,
Wonder how you'll be?

RITUAL INGREDIENTS

Ink pen or marker, black
Meat, raw, any kind
3-inch paper square, red (or a photograph)
Plate (for the meat)
Shovel or spade
Knife (optional)
String, white, 3 feet (optional)
Tape, glue, or melted wax (optional)

RITUAL ACTIONS

You can work simply by holding a photo of your enemy (and/or identifying materials) in your left hand while repeating the verbal charm and imagining maggots growing bigger and bigger in their ears and nose. Having a direct line of sight to your enemy is preferable.

I was also given a more complex ritual. Prepare your ritual items before midnight. Write the full name (first, middle, last) of your enemy on the paper square, or you can use their photograph. At this time, attach any identifying materials you might have to the paper square or photo using some tape, glue, or melted wax. Fold your paper in half, then half again, to make a small, square parcel.

Next, prepare your meat. You can use any meat as long as it's raw. There are two ways you can attach your paper square to the meat, depending on what kind you purchased. If your meat is flat, add your folded paper square to the middle of the meat, fold the meat so that it's covering the paper, then tie closed using your string. If your meat is on the thicker side, you can take your knife and cut a small trench through the meat (butterflying the meat). Stuff the paper square inside, then tie the meat together with the string so that the paper is completely sealed inside.

At midnight, take your meat and shovel out to a secluded location. Seclusion is preferred with this work because of the belief that if your enemy is able to find your ritual objects, they can possibly reverse the work. Find a place where you can dig a hole big enough to fit your chunk of meat. In the Ozarks, cursing materials are traditionally buried beneath black oak trees (*Quercus velutina*), which have long associations with Saturnian work and hexes.

Once you have your hole dug, add the meat. Then, repeat the verbal charm. Fill the hole back in with dirt, then return home. Immediately after the ritual, take a cleansing bath. As the meat rots in the earth, your enemy will begin sensing the insects (in particular, maggots) on their skin or inside their body, causing them a great deal of discomfort.

In order to break this curse, should you need to, you will need to know the exact location where you buried the meat. If you know where this is, you can cleanse the spot—and thereby cleanse the hex. Pour water mixed with salt and hyssop over the spot while reciting Psalm 51:7 seven times: "Purge me with hyssop, and I shall be clean; wash me, and I shall be whiter than snow." When you're finished, sprinkle three pinches of salt over the spot, then return home.

NOTES

There are many Ozark hexes that involve live things growing inside a person's body. "Live things" is sometimes considered a disease or curse of its own that can be sent to unsuspecting victims by both practitioners and otherworldly beings. In many of the ritual procedures, the target has to actually eat or drink the cursed materia, often made from the dried, crushed-up bodies of certain insects, reptiles, or other small creatures. But, as seen with this verbal charm, live things can grow spontaneously through nothing more than the sympathetic connection created by simply possessing a person's full name or identifying materials. Live things also appear in the traditions of Southern Rootwork, Conjure, and Hoodoo. It's possible that these were a historic source for the Ozark folk belief.

☆ FIGHTING HEX ☆

This hex is intended to cause a fight between two different people. In the case of the charmer who offered me this work, they preferred using it to make their enemies fight against each other and therefore forget all about them. This charming ritual can provide a very useful distraction so your enemies cease working against you. It's based on a well-known nursery rhyme included in many collections from Mother Goose.

MAGICAL TIMING

Waning moon. Nighttime. Zodiac moon days in Aries (Mars, Tuesday, fire) or Scorpio (Mars, Tuesday, water).

CHARM

There were once two cats of Kilkenny.
Each thought there was one cat too many;
So they fought and they fit,
And they scratched and they bit,
Till, excepting their nails,
And the tips of their tails,
Instead of two cats, there weren't any.

RITUAL INGREDIENTS

Heat-safe dish, small grill, or incense burner

Incense charcoal, 3 pieces

Lighter or matches

Paper, red

Paper, white

Scissors

RITUAL ACTIONS

There are two different rituals that you can use alongside this verbal charm. Both make use of paper dolls, one cut from the white paper and the other cut from the red. Write the full name (first, middle, and last) of Person #1 on the white doll, then do the same for Person #2 on the red doll. Recite the verbal charm while visualizing the faces of each person on their corresponding dolls. When you begin the last two lines, take the two dolls, place them together, and then rip them into small pieces.

For the simpler ritual variation, you can throw these pieces into the garbage, bury them, or toss them into running water. For the longer ritual variation, burn all of the pieces on three hot incense charcoals until they, along with the charcoals, are completely reduced to ash. Once everything is cool, take the ash and throw some at each person's front door. By burning the dolls, you are ensuring that the targeted individuals will never be able to find them and reverse the hex.

✫ LIAR CHARM ✫

This simple verbal charm is used to enact retribution specifically upon a liar or slanderer. This could include someone who has lied to or about you or someone you're working for. The goal of this charming ritual is that the liar receive divine retribution against them as a result of your petitioning. The hope, of course, is that the slanderer will eventually awaken to their wicked ways and change. Because this verbal charm requires a burning ritual, it's hardly ever used on its own. However, there's nothing stopping a charmer from using this as a very good and fast reactionary spell—in the moment, in front of the enemy that you're targeting.

MAGICAL TIMING

Waning moon. Nighttime. Zodiac moon days in fire signs, specifically Aries (Mars, Tuesday, fire) or Sagittarius (Jupiter, Thursday, fire).

CHARM

Liar, liar, lickspit,
Turn about the candlestick;
What's good for liars?
Brimstone and fires!

RITUAL INGREDIENTS

Taper candle, black, with holder
Lighter or matches
Paper, red
Scissors
Ink pen or marker, black (optional)
Photograph of the liar (optional)

RITUAL ACTIONS

In a completely dark room, light your candle. Take and cut out a human shape from the red paper. If you have a photograph of the liar, cut it so that the person's form will fit on the torso of the paper doll, or so a photograph of their face will fit over the face of the doll. If you don't, simply write the target's full name (first, middle, and last) and date of birth on the torso of the paper doll. You can stick any identifying materials you might have to the paper doll with a few drops of wax from the candle.

Hold your paper doll in your left hand and face the candle. Recite the first line of the verbal charm. As you recite the second line, rotate the paper doll around the candle flame in a counterclockwise direction three times. Continue with the third line. As you finish the last line, hold the paper doll in the candle flame and then burn it completely to ash in a heat-safe dish or bowl. If the paper doll does not burn completely the first time, use tweezers or metal tongs and hold the remainder in the flame. Take any of the ash that you were able to collect and flush it down the toilet or throw it into a moving body of water. Blow out the candle and use it for another ritual in the future.

NOTES

This surprisingly harsh nursery rhyme lends itself well to being used as a retribution curse, and I suspect this was one of the original purposes of the rhyme itself. In one interesting ritual variation I collected, the charmer connected to the words of the charm in a very different way. In her work, when she roasted chickens using a rotisserie, she would name the chickens after her enemies. While she watched the rotisserie spit turn, she would recite this rhyme, imagining the entire time that it was actually her enemy that was slowly roasting in the fire.

☆ PARANOIA HEX ☆

This useful verbal charm curses an enemy with illusory paranoia specifically related to their house and home. Fire is invoked in the wording of the charm itself, but the destruction that manifests in the mind of the enemy can include many different things. The charmer who gave me this rhyme and ritual said he only ever used it once, but it was in a situation where his enemy was relentlessly slandering him to the community at large. As part of the ritual work, he drove his enemy crazy with paranoia until, at last, they came to him and asked for forgiveness. At this point, the charmer lifted the curse and the paranoia subsided.

MAGICAL TIMING

Waning moon. Nighttime. Zodiac moon days in Aries (Mars, Tuesday, fire), or use Gemini (Mercury, Wednesday, air), which is embodied with the power of illusion and enchantment.

CHARM

An old [woman/man/person] lived in Nottingham town,
Who owned a small house, and painted it brown;
And yet this old [woman/man/person] grew crazy with fright,
Lest someone should burn [her/his/their] house in the night.

RITUAL INGREDIENTS

Bowl

Olive oil

Optional Variation:

Black pepper, ground

Candle, red or black, any type

Ink pen or marker, black

Lighter or matches

Paper envelope, black

5-inch paper square, red (or a photograph)

RITUAL ACTIONS

There are two different variations on this charming ritual. In the first variation, begin by pouring some olive oil into a bowl. Recite the entire verbal charm once, then blow across the surface of the oil three times. Anoint your hands with this oil before coming into physical contact with the one that you're charming—this might be difficult if they're an enemy who you're strongly averse to being around. Contact can include a handshake, a hug, or simply touching the person's clothing or possessions. The point of this variation is that the oil will come into contact with the person (or something that they come into contact with) on a regular basis.

Be sure that you don't come into contact with anyone else while wearing this oil, otherwise the target of your charming ritual will also include them. To remove the oil, simply wash your hands with salt water or water that includes a pinch of salt and hyssop herb. Reciting Psalm 51:7 while washing is a traditional way of cleansing for rites like this: "Purge me with hyssop, and I shall be clean; wash me, and I shall be whiter than snow."

This oil can be bottled and used again as many times as needed. You can orient the oil to a specific person by adding identifying materials from them to the oil itself, or you can write their full name (first, middle, and last) and date of birth on a small piece of paper that you put into the oil once bottled.

The second variation involves a lengthier charming ritual. Begin with either a photograph of the person or a square of red paper upon which you have written the target's full name (first, middle, and last) and date of birth.

In an otherwise dark room, light your candle. Any variety of candle will work as long as it is red or black.

Place the square of paper or photograph in your envelope and add three pinches of ground black pepper. At this time, add any identifying materials you might have for the person. Seal the envelope with wax from the candle—do not lick to seal, as this will connect *you* to the results of the work.

Recite the verbal charm three times. While holding the envelope in your left hand, move it in a counterclockwise, circular motion around the candle flame for the entire recitation. When you're finished, blow out the candle, then hide the envelope in a location where no one else will be able to find it.

You can recharge this work on the full and new moons by reciting the verbal charm three more times and moving the envelope around a lit black/red candle in a counterclockwise circle. This work will continue until your enemy is able to find their envelope or until you break the work.

The charmer who gave me this rite cautioned that I must be very careful with handling the ritual materials. He believed that if you were to burn the envelope, the paranoia would come to fruition and the target's house would burn down—or metaphorically, their life would burn down. Unlike other rituals in the Ozarks, this spell shouldn't be broken using fire. Instead, open the envelope, retrieve the materials, and either give them to the person who was the target of the work or separate out all the elements completely before throwing them into different bodies of moving water. For example, throw the paper square into one river and all of the black pepper into another.

NOTES

The crazed paranoia invoked in the original nursery rhyme would have been a much more realistic fear for our ancestors, who often lived in wooden cabins or homes with thatched roofs. In the Ozarks, there are many protective rituals and charms specifically against house fires because of this very reason—fire was once a far more ominous threat. It's interesting to see in this charm how the very real threat of a house fire has been transformed into a metaphorical fire within the life of the victim.

While the charm might not actually burn a person's house down, it's believed even amongst modern practitioners that curses like this can be just as destructive to a person's livelihood, family, or emotional state. For this reason, I caution my students to consider their actions before enacting such a curse. The paranoia that is caused by a curse like this can lead to many unexpected outcomes, as in one old story I heard: the victim, driven mad by a hex, finally located their hexer and killed them in their home.

☆ SILENCING A SLANDERING ENEMY ☆

This verbal charm is used specifically in retribution work that targets a slandering enemy of the charmer or another. The tongue of the enemy—both physical and metaphorical, as a representation of the voice and, therefore, power—is the target of the spell work. By separating the tongue, the slanderer is unable to focus their malign magic on their intended victim. This charm then acts as a protection spell as well.

MAGICAL TIMING

New moon. Midnight. Zodiac moon days in Aries (Mars, Tuesday, fire) or Scorpio (Mars, Tuesday, water).

CHARM

[Target's name]
Tell, tale, tit,
Your tongue shall be split,
And all the dogs in town,
Shall have a bit!

RITUAL INGREDIENTS

Animal tongue—beef is commonly used, as it can be purchased from
    many butchers
Plate or bowl (for the tongue)
Ink or paint, black
Knife
Paintbrush, small

Optional Variation:
Glue or melted wax
Ink pen, black
5-inch paper square, white or red

Plate or bowl
Scissors

RITUAL ACTIONS

There are two variations associated with this verbal charm. Traditionally, an animal's tongue is used as the major ingredient of the ritual. Beef tongue is commonly used today because it can be purchased from many butchers and even some grocery stores. Other animals have been used as well, normally animals that were already slaughtered for food.

Begin by purchasing an animal tongue. Place it on a plate or platter with the top of the tongue facing up. Take your bottle of black ink or paint. With a paintbrush, write the name of your enemy (or the slanderer you are working against) down the length of the entire tongue. The more specific you can get, the better, so first, middle, and last name is preferred, as well as birthdate. If you happen to know their zodiac sun, moon, and rising signs, draw them on the tongue as well. This is even better, as it helps identify the specific individual that you are working against. If you have identifying materials from the individual, like hair or fingernail clippings, cut a trench down the length of the tongue with a sharp knife and stuff them into the cavity.

When you have your name painted and any other identifying information present, begin the charming ritual by saying the target's name aloud. Then, repeat the first two lines. With your sharp knife, make slash marks (as many as you want) across the top of the tongue. When you're finished, complete the verbal charm with the final two lines. After this, cut up the tongue (and any identifying materials inside) into pieces with the knife. Beef tongue can be very tough, so make sure your knife is sharp, and work slowly. You can cut it into however many pieces you'd like. Thirteen would be appropriate for a curse like this.

Once your tongue is cut into pieces, take the plate or bowl outside to a secluded wooded area and toss the pieces toward the west. If you used identifying materials like hair or fingernail clippings, they will likely be loose at this point. Toss them alongside the meat. When all the meat is gone, return home and take a cleansing bath. You can repeat Psalm 51:7 while you bathe for added benefit: "Purge me with hyssop, and I shall be clean; wash me, and I shall be whiter than snow."

The second variation of this ritual involves using paper instead of a physical tongue. In my experience, if your intention is focused, either variation will work just as well. Take your paper square and turn it so that it is in a diamond shape. There should now be one corner of the square facing away from you and another facing toward you. Write the full name of the slanderer as well as their birthdate and zodiac sign(s) in the center of the paper square. You can use identifying materials along with this ritual—just make sure they are fixed to the paper square with a little glue or candle wax.

Once everything is on the paper square, begin the ritual by reciting aloud the name of the target, then the first two lines. Take your scissors and cut a straight line away from you, from the corner pointing toward you up through the slanderer's name and identifying materials, stopping about an inch from the other corner. Over a plate or bowl, cut the paper square and identifying materials into tiny pieces while reciting the final lines of the charm. As you do this, visualize that you are cutting up the physical and metaphorical tongue of the slanderer.

Finish this variation by throwing the pieces of the paper tongue at a crossroads to confuse the slanderer, in a river to make them go away from where you are, at the gate of a cemetery to haunt them with memories of what they've done, or at the base of a red cedar tree to help them heal and change their slandering ways.

NOTES

This nursery rhyme curse appears in several different Mother Goose collections. The charmer who gave me these words said he had received them as a child from his mother, who told him that if anyone on the playground ever said anything bad about him or his family, he could repeat these words and they would be punished. As an adult, the charmer was still using the same rhyme, albeit with some added rituals pulled from other spells in the Ozark folk magic tradition. This just shows how simple childhood rhymes and verses can become such powerful spells.

The dogs listed in this charm are represented in the animals who will consume the beef tongue or the paper square in the charming ritual. Many Ozark verbal charms call upon the aid of animals to help take away illnesses, hexes, evil spirits, or, in this case, a slanderer's voice. This pact between humans and the animal world is an ancient one, and the close relationship our ancestors formed with canines is reflected in the many verbal charms that feature dogs as a magical helper.

✷ SPITE DOLL CHARMING ✷

This is one of my favorite examples of repurposing Mother Goose's rhymes for magical use. I received this ritual from a practitioner who held many other cursing rhymes, which she often used as part of her work. This example is used to magically silence or distract your enemy using a spite doll or poppet made to represent your target. The goal of this work is to distract your enemy from working against you, or to punish them until they change their wicked ways.

MAGICAL TIMING

New moon. Nighttime. Zodiac moon days in Aries (Mars, Tuesday, fire) or Scorpio (Mars, Tuesday, water) are good for this charming work.

CHARM

Here's Sulky Sue,
What shall we do?
Turn her face to the wall
Till she comes to.

RITUAL INGREDIENTS

Ink pen or marker, black
Nail or honey locust thorn (*Gleditsia triacanthos*)
1 sheet of paper, red
Scissors
String, white
Candle, black (optional)
Photograph of the target (optional)

RITUAL ACTIONS

As you will be magically "birthing" your spite doll, I recommend performing this charming ritual on the new moon.

Begin by cutting out a human shape from a piece of red paper. (You can craft a more complicated doll from cornhusks or cloth.) When you have your doll cut out or made, draw a face on one side, or you can take and cut out your target's face from a photograph and glue it on one side. On the same side of the paper, in the center of the doll's chest, write the target's full name (first, middle, last) and birthdate, if you know it. If you have any identifying materials from them, you can stick them in the same spot using some wax from a black candle.

After this, take your nail or honey locust thorn and pierce a hole through each hand and each foot. Then, take one piece of string, slip it through the hand holes, and tie them together. Take the other piece and slip it through the feet holes and tie them together. Knot the string tight in both areas.

Once you have your doll prepared, locate a spot away from casual glances; make sure you can face the doll toward a wall. I've found that the backs of unused cabinets are a great place to house these spite dolls.

When you've found your spot, take the doll in your left hand and recite the verbal charm. When you're finished, fold the paper doll at the waist so that it will be able to sit, then place it with its face toward the wall. If needed, you can lean the doll's head against the wall itself for stability. In my experience, the pronouns used in the verbal charm don't need to be changed to correspond to the targeted individual—Sulky Sue can remain as she is.

Leave the doll in its location for as long as needed. It's believed that as long as the doll faces the wall, your enemy won't be able to work against you and will be distracted toward different projects. You can renew the doll's energy on the new and full moons by feeding it with three drops of cinnamon or clove essential oil anywhere on the doll itself. Both of these herbs are considered to have hot natures and will therefore add more wood to the fire you've started, so to speak. In the event you'd like to break the work, take and cut the strings binding the doll's hands, then burn everything.

The charmer who gave me this ritual said there are specific tokens you can look out for to make sure your spite doll is still working:

- If your doll is still facing the wall, or still has its head leaning against the wall, then the work is continuing normally.

- If your doll is bent backward at the waist or lying flat on their back or front, repeat the verbal charm and fix the doll back in place.
- If the strings are broken, or if the hands/feet are no longer bound, your enemy is working spells to try and escape. Tie new strings to bind the hands and feet; you might need to make new holes if the old ones have ripped through.
- If the doll begins to mold or mildew, the curse is beginning to overtake the target. At this point, you can break the work and give them some relief, or you can continue.

CHAPTER 8

To See in Dreams
and Visions Too ...

At sixty-six years old, Ann Ganter had finally earned a community title of respect and was now known as Granny Ganter. Her more famous name, Granny Thornapple, was used whenever folks in Nelson's Holler were talking about the old woman behind her back. She got the pseudonym one summer after scaring away a bunch of teenagers who had snuck onto her property to go swimming in the creek. Normally the old woman didn't mind youths, but this group was known to toss beer bottles into creeks and listen to terrible music at deafening volumes. After the group ran back home to safety, they started saying she was as mad as a pig eating thornapples. Granny didn't mind it, though—she enjoyed the air of mystery it gave to her. Besides, who could mind being associated with a magical plant said to have driven many famous witches crazy throughout the centuries?

Granny Thornapple was considered the best midwife around by most of Nelson's Holler. Even Doc Winthrop's son, who had taken over the family clinic and drugstore, sent most of his pregnancies up the mountain to Granny Thornapple's house. While she never managed to settle down with any kids of her own, Granny Thornapple considered all the babies she helped birth to be part of her extended family.

One autumn, just after Granny Thornapple's sixty-sixth birthday, she got a call just as she was about to crawl into bed. The panicked voice on the other end of the line belonged to a local pregnant woman, Alice Blackwell, who Granny Thornapple had been working with for almost three months now. "Granny? You there?" she asked in a hushed, strained voice.

"I'm here, child," Granny Thornapple said loudly.

"I think somethin's wrong with the baby."

"You hold on, I'll be right over."

Granny Thornapple threw the phone down without even returning it to the receiver. She grabbed a coat and threw it on over her nightdress, tied up her heavy boots, and left the cabin. Shortly after Gram Watson had passed, Granny Thornapple was given an old pickup truck so she could be quicker about her deliveries and rounds visiting folks. She firmly refused the offer at first, as she didn't have a license and didn't trust any vehicle that went faster than a bicycle. Eventually, she was worn down and decided she'd use it for emergencies only. Within a month she'd reupholstered the entire cab in lush, pink velvet, installed a sleeping perch for her cat Buckles, and had even given the truck a name: Matilda.

In a fury, Granny Thornapple threw her bag of essentials into Matilda's passenger seat, hopped in behind the steering wheel, and tore down the mountain. The creek was high this time of year, so the low-water bridge was covered by the current. That was no trouble for Matilda, who splashed happily across the bridge and back onto the dirt road on the opposite side. In only about fifteen minutes, Granny Thornapple had arrived at Alice Blackwell's house.

Granny Thornapple hurried in as fast as her stiff back and arthritis would allow. Alice was in the front room on the couch. Her grandmother, Sissy Blackwell, was near her, wringing out a blood-covered towel into a bucket of water. Granny Thornapple's heart beat fast and she started her examination. Alice was covered in sweat and blood. She passed out just as Granny Thornapple knelt down beside her.

Granny Thornapple spent most of the night in her examination. She got a few minutes of sleep around four in the morning when she sat in a rocking chair near the fireplace. The next morning, Alice was feeling better. Despite the pain and amount of blood, the baby was still alive and healthy. Alice had had a miscarriage about three years before, so Granny Thornapple feared the worst at first sight. "You got a strong one in there," she said with a smile, wiping sweat from Alice's forehead with a damp rag.

Sissy Blackwell offered the midwife breakfast, but Granny Thornapple refused. "Got to get back home to feed Buckles," she answered, gathering items back into her bag. "If anything else suspicious happens, you call me."

Alice nodded, then drifted back to sleep. Granny Thornapple saw herself out, returned to Matilda, and made the trek back up the mountain.

Almost a week to the hour later, Granny Thornapple got another frantic phone call from Alice Blackwell. The same exact thing had happened again, but this time Alice was sure she'd lost the baby. Granny Thornapple threw on some clothes, hopped into Matilda, then sped off down the mountain. While the situation was similar, the child was fortunately still alive and growing. "You're just gonna be a difficult one, aren't you?" Granny Thornapple said with a grin, holding her hand against Alice's belly.

While Alice slept, Granny Thornapple had a cup of tea with Sissy Blackwell. "You don't think it's some witching, do you?" Sissy asked in a whisper.

At first Granny Thornapple dismissed the notion. She had a lot of strong feelings about curses and hexes, which more often than not were just scared people looking for answers to problems that could easily be fixed with the right knowledge. "What makes you think that?" she asked Sissy.

"It's just..." Sissy hesitated, then walked over and made sure the door to the living room was shut, even though Alice was fast asleep and snoring on the couch. "The father... it was a terrible divorce. You know he used to hit her?"

"I didn't know that, Sissy. I'm so sorry."

"Well, it's done now. But he had a lot of strange relations, you know."

Granny Thornapple gave Sissy a confused glance as she sipped her tea.

"His mother, for instance," Sissy continued, "I'm sure she was a witch. She had these cold eyes. They used to scare me somethin' terrible. Do you think she might have thrown somethin' on the baby?"

Granny Thornapple shook her head, "No, Sissy. I wouldn't worry about that." But she secretly wondered if there wasn't something else happening here. After all, Alice already saw Younger Winthrop, which is what Nelson's Holler had taken to calling old Doc Winthrop's son. While he had given her a clean bill of health, Granny Thornapple decided it might be worth it to divine what might be hidden beneath the surface.

Granny Thornapple waited four days until the following full moon to perform her rite. She'd never done any dream magic before, but she remembered Gram said that psychic power was highest on the full moon. It would have been better if she could

have waited for a full moon in Pisces—the sign that rules over dreams and trances—but that was too far away. If she waited any longer, there might be more than one life lost.

She gathered up what she could remember of the ingredients for the ritual, including a white candle in an old brass holder, some mugwort that was still growing in the cottage garden from when Gram planted it almost three decades ago, and a strip of thick, black wool that she'd use as a blindfold. As the full moon rose high into the sky, Granny Thornapple lit the white candle, which she placed on the nightstand beside her bed. She held a wad of mugwort into the flame, then dropped it in a small, stoneware bowl. A trail of bitter smoke snaked into the air. Then, she relaxed back onto the bed, placed the black wool across her eyes and ears, and recited a charm: "I go out to see, I go out to hear…" The words appeared in the dark void around her. She didn't know the charm by heart, but some power within her created it as she spoke. "I go out and back again…" Slowly, slowly, she felt her body grow heavy as the words continued.

"For sight and sound, near and far, I go out among the stars…" she felt as though she were floating in a warm ocean.

The bed beneath her had disappeared. In front of her, lights like stars began to flicker and flash. "From here to there, from there to here, let me fly out, let me fly out…"

She felt a sudden pull, and her body flew through the stars so fast that they merged into walls of brilliant white fire around her. "Let me go out, then back again—for sight and sound—to find and bring back—what is hidden, be illuminated."

The fiery light around her grew until she was completely consumed. For a moment, Granny Thornapple thought she'd been destroyed by the fire. But then her senses began to come back to her. She slowly opened her eyes and found herself sitting at the kitchen table of her cabin, like it used to be when Gram was still alive. Hearing a clanging sound in the kitchen, she turned and saw Gram pulling a cast-iron skillet full of hot biscuits out of the oven. She felt a tear run down her face. It had been so long since she'd seen Gram. "Get one of these in you while they're hot!" Gram said happily as she sat the skillet onto the kitchen table.

"Gram…I…" Granny Thornapple tried to speak but kept getting choked up.

"Now, don't start that," Gram replied, wiping her apprentice's face off with a tea towel. "We've got work to do."

"Work? I don't understand."

Granny Thornapple had become immersed and distracted in the details of the dreamworld around her. Gram gave her a light smack right across the cheek. "This ain't your home, child," she said sternly. "You're only visiting."

Granny Thornapple saw her wrinkled hands. She remembered Alice and her baby. She remembered she was dreaming. "Gram!" she shouted at the realization.

Her mentor just smiled and rubbed Granny's sore cheek with her soft hand. "I'm glad you came," she said gently.

"Me too, Gram. I need your help."

"Right, I was hoping you'd show up so I could deliver my message. The woman's in trouble, Ann."

Granny Thornapple's heart sunk. It was what she'd feared the entire time. "What sort of trouble?"

"She's got a nasty hex on her. From that deadbeat ex-husband of hers."

"From the mother?"

Gram looked pleasantly surprised. "Yes, from the mother. I guess you've got some good wits about you. I always knew I taught you right."

"What can we do?"

Gram shook her head. "You've got to find the hex and break it."

"Find the hex?"

"Hexes are so powerful because we believe in the power they hold. That power gets bigger when we know the hex is out there, but we can't see it. Hiding hexes means the nastiness will continue on until someone finds it and breaks it apart."

"How can I find the hex pieces to reverse them?"

"You've got to use your sight, Ann. We've talked about all this before."

A loud pounding sound interrupted their conversation. The walls shook. Pictures fell to the wooden floor and shattered. Granny Thornapple could see Gram trying to say something but couldn't make out the words. Her vision became blurry and all at once, she sat bolt upright in bed with a gasp of air. While she reoriented herself to the waking world, a banging noise sounded at the front door. She grabbed her house-coat and rushed to the front room. She didn't bother looking out the window, but just opened the door with a jerk. Outside stood Alice Blackwell's brother, Henry. He was pale and shivering despite the fact that it was a warm night. "What's wrong?" Granny Thornapple asked in a panic.

"Alice got taken to the hospital over in Washburn," Henry answered, holding his chest with a shaking hand. "It's bad, Granny."

★ ★ ★

The boy tried explaining the best he could, but it was clear that what little learning about human anatomy he had at the local high school had completely gone over his head. Granny Thornapple sent him away, then slammed the front door behind him. The white candle had blown out, despite there not being any moving air in Granny Thornapple's room. She relit the candle, ignited some more mugwort, then returned to her trance.

Granny Thornapple repeated the verbal charm over and over in her mind. Her world went dark and her body floated in the void like a leaf on a still pond. Stars flashed around her as she was pulled headlong through the darkness. "Find the pieces … find the pieces …" she whispered to herself.

Her feet suddenly landed hard on a soft surface. She fell forward into dewy grass. As she looked up, her eyes adjusted to a golden morning light. Apart from a few birds chirping in the trees around her, the world was completely silent. Granny Thornapple struggled to her feet and glanced around her. She was standing in the old Nelson's Holler cemetery, just across the holler from her cabin. The sunlight that poured in amongst the headstones had a strange quality to it. Her cheek burned and she remembered the slap Gram had landed there earlier. "I'm just visiting," she laughed to herself as she began searching around the graveyard.

She didn't know what she might be looking for at first. She wondered what her sight might offer her in a dream-vision like this one. Will I even be able to recognize it when I find it? she thought to herself. Then, as she paced back and forth between the stones, she saw a sparkling light out of the corner of her eye. She turned in that direction, and the sparkle hung onto one of the gravestones not too far from where she was standing. As she hurried through the dewy grass and dead leaves, the sparkle vanished.

The headstone was an old one. Unassuming, with simple carved letters, not like some of the fancier ones in the cemetery. Granny Thornapple couldn't make out the name but noticed someone had placed a single rose on the ground at the base of the stone. She reached down and dug around the rose. The soil was loose, wet, and cold to her fingertips. Only a few inches down, she found something buried. She pulled out the object and found a small bundle wrapped in black cloth and tied up with string. It made her remember the incident with Gram and Otho years ago. She pocketed the object in a hurry, then ran toward the streams of sunlight.

Granny Thornapple thought she was starting to get the hang of traveling through the dream-vision. The world began to stabilize quicker. She managed to locate the second bundle buried underneath the hearthstone of the old Blackwell homestead—just a ruin these days. The final bundle was in the cash register of Marcum's Mercantile over on Main Street. Granny Thornapple had to sneak around Lily-Kate Marcum, sweeping off the front stoop, and around the patrons shopping inside. Not a soul noticed her presence, and the old woman wondered if she was still in the real world or some other place altogether. She didn't have time for such contemplations. She grabbed up the bundle, stuffed it into the pocket of her housecoat with the others, then hurried back into the shifting void.

Believing she was returning to her body, Granny Thornapple flew through the stars and walls of brilliantly colored lights. Forward, ever forward. But the dream had different plans for her. As though someone flipped a light switch, all the stars turned off and she was dropped into some deep darkness. She heard a baby wail and scream. A lamp turned on beside her, illuminating a scene of Alice Blackwell, reclined back in her bed. Her grandmother, Sissy, wiped her forehead with a towel. Granny Thornapple saw herself standing at the bedside, removing the caul from the baby's head and face. "He's got the gift in him!" she heard herself say. The old woman couldn't help but cry tears of joy at the brief vision of the future she'd been given.

Granny Thornapple woke with a jump that nearly threw her sideways out of bed. The telephone was ringing. She tore off her blindfold and rushed to the kitchen, toward where her telephone hung on the wall. "Hello? Yes? Are you there?" she said, desperately trying to catch her breath.

"Granny? It's Henry," the voice on the other line said. "I've got good news. Alice and the baby are just fine."

Granny Thornapple closed her eyes and smiled. Her heartbeat finally calmed to a normal pace. "That's wonderful, darlin'. You tell her to hang in there."

Granny Thornapple hung up the phone and returned to bed. For now, she'd sleep soundly. There wasn't any reason for dreaming.

SEEING WHERE OTHERS CANNOT

In the old Ozarks, individuals who could sense or see things that other people in the community couldn't were said to have the "sight" or "second sight." For some, the sight meant that the individual was able to see spirits or perhaps even glance into the future. These are the associations many of us still have today, but those possessing the sight experienced their gift in a variety of ways. Yes, for some it meant having a close connection to the otherworld, but this didn't just mean seeing spirits of the dead. In Ozark folk belief, the word *spirit* could encompass ghosts, the Little People (as well as other varieties of Ozark fairies), angels, land spirits, and hidden entities. Having the sight could mean being able to physically see these beings, or it could point to a general feeling of their presence.

Sometimes having the sight means being able to locate areas where the veil between worlds is thin. As with one of my healer friends, who sees these thin spots as shifting, watery surfaces, almost like mirages. Others use their sight in order to locate diseases and hexes inside the body. In some cases, the sight manifests as a talent for divination in general. Whether it's cards, pendulums, dowsing rods, or another method of divination, the sight isn't just a *physical* ability, but can manifest in dreams, trances, and visions as well.

I was once told by an Ozark seer that for her, the sight only came through dreaming, and that she was able to see things that hadn't happened yet as well as look into the bodies of her clients to find hidden illnesses. Dreaming is traditionally seen as being a powerful form of diagnosis amongst Ozark healers and magical practitioners. In this realm, one's own gifts and abilities are magnified in infinite proportions. Contacting spirits is said to be much easier while in the dreaming world, which means accessing timeless knowledge is as easy as finding and learning from your departed teachers in that other place.

DREAMING AS DIVINATION

Dreaming up remedies and cures is common amongst Ozark folk healers and practitioners, even those who might seem very traditional. As one healer told me, "The Bible is filled with dreamers—why should I think all that just stopped happening?" Dreams have traditionally been one of the only forms of divination accepted by more conservative healers who, of course, would never call it divination; dreams are seen as being gifts from God or angels, delivered almost like prophecies to those who are honest and pious.

One client of mine had a string of terrible bad luck and believed that they had been cursed by someone close to them. I decided to take their situation with me into the dreaming world to find a solution. In my dream, I was sitting at a small table in a busy café. I watched nervously as people pushed past each other trying to find open seats. Through the crowd, I could see my client standing at the counter arguing with a barista. They were both so angry their faces were turning a very unnatural shade of red. I tried standing up to intervene in the situation, but I was pushed back down by the crowd. I watched on, finally recognizing that this was a dream. At the height of the argument, the barista picked up a glass of water on the countertop and threw it into my client's face, drenching him. To my surprise, my client started laughing wildly, followed by the barista. As this happened, the crowd began dispersing quickly like they were afraid of the water that was thrown. Soon, it was just myself, my client, and the barista left in the café.

I spent much of the next day pondering this mysterious dream. I knew it was relevant, I just didn't immediately know how. In speaking with my client about the dream, I learned that he had severe crowd-related anxiety. I asked whether his perceived bad luck occurred during these times of heightened anxiety and confirmed that it did. This connection, which he hadn't previously been able to make, was a sort of cure in and of itself. I took another tip from my dream and recommended he take weekly herbal baths with cold water as a way of cleansing off the anxiety that he was feeling build up as a result of dealing with crowded areas.

Tokens, or omens, often come from within the culture itself. You can see this around the globe with almost every group that attaches value to dreams—the interpretations are going to change depending on the culture. For example, amongst Christian groups, dreaming of a white dove might be a universal symbol of peace and hope, especially if it is carrying an olive branch in its mouth. Likewise, seeing a red figure with horns and hooved feet holding a pitchfork might have very specific symbolic connotations for evil. It's important to keep in mind the religious and cultural symbols you carry in your own mind.

Many of the dream interpretation guides on the market are based on very specific (and, often, outdated) symbols from a Western, Christian point of view. These guidebooks can be an aid, but I recommend using them only as a starting point. How would you personally interpret a dream's meaning? In my experience, personal symbols are far more meaningful.

There's very good reason for this. Our dreams are made up of thoughts, images, feelings, emotions, etc., all of which come from within ourselves. How you feel about something is going to have a significant effect upon the dreams you have. If you have a strawberry allergy, for example, you might approach strawberries in a dream in a very different way than I would, as a person who doesn't have this allergy. Let your dreams guide you, but keep in mind how your own view of the world might shape and form the symbols within your dreams.

DIVINING AND CHARMING

Divination and the second sight are often closely linked in Ozark folklore. Both rely on the ability to see where others cannot. Charmers have found their own forms of divination using their words and special sight.

Counting charms are quite common in the Ozarks, many of which were once gleefully recited by children as entertaining nursery rhymes. While many of these might seem like games to us today, the origins of counting charms were most likely in actual divinations used to determine the auspiciousness, or luckiness, of a specific time, place, and situation.

Take, for instance, this famous bird-counting charm that was a divinatory method turned nursery rhyme: "One's unlucky, / Two's lucky, / Three's health, / Four's wealth, / Five's sickness, / Six is death." The method for this charm would be to count the number of birds in a flock, then count through the numbers in the charm. So, for example, if there were four birds, you would have "Four's wealth," signifying good luck, or auspiciousness, at that particular moment, or as an answer to a specific question asked before the counting began. Or, if you had eleven birds, that would be one set of six then another of five, landing on "Five's sickness," an inauspicious or unlucky token. There are hundreds of these counting charms, all of which use objects or animals that occur in nature. I've seen charms that count everything from eggs a group of hens lay overnight, to a handful of dried beans grabbed out of a sack, to the number of blackberries gathered from a single cane.

Auguries like these represent an interesting intersection between the charming tradition and other Ozark magical practices. Amongst the charmers I've met who had examples of these divinatory charms, it was important to recite the specific words of the counting charm while you count. In this way, there is often a magical link drawn between the words and the auspiciousness of the resulting divination. For example, the healer who gave me the bird-counting charm said that if you just went out and counted some birds, nothing would happen, but if you recited the verbal charm *while you counted*, then the counting would actually be empowered.

As with other verbal charms in the tradition, what might seem very juvenile and simplistic on the outside actually hides a fascinating foundation of belief and magic at its core. We shouldn't write off counting charms and traditional forms of divination any more than we should write off Mother Goose rhymes repurposed as healing or protective charms. With the right intention, a charmer can spin golden threads even from straw.

THE CHARMS

In general, Gemini (Mercury, Wednesday, air) and Pisces (Jupiter, Thursday, water) are great for all types of divination and dreaming. Aquarius (Saturn, Saturday, air) is traditionally used for work to reveal secrets or things that have been hidden.

☆ BRAMBLE BUSH CHARM FOR SCRYING ☆

This verbal charm was given to me for use primarily alongside scrying. In the Ozarks there are many different varieties of this method of divination. Gazing into bowls and bottles of water, mirrors, clear quartz crystals, flames, and even smoke are just a few of the many scrying methods found within Ozark folk magic. And all of these methods are highly specific to the individual themselves.

Reciting this charm before the actual scrying session is believed to heighten the second sight of the charmer to be able to see the proper tokens or omens. Additionally, you can use this charm alongside any divination method, as well as to see tokens in dreams.

MAGICAL TIMING

Full moon. Zodiac moon days in Gemini (Mercury, Wednesday, air) and Pisces (Jupiter, Thursday, water) for general divination, or Aquarius (Saturn, Saturday, air) for revealing secrets or things hidden.

CHARM

There was a man in our town,
And he was wondrous wise,
He jumped into a bramble bush,
And scratched out both his eyes;
But when he saw his eyes were out,
With all his might and main,
He jumped into another bush,
And scratched 'em in again.

RITUAL INGREDIENTS

Bowl, dark colored
Candle
Water

RITUAL ACTIONS

The charming itself doesn't involve much of a ritual at all, but your scrying method might be more involved. If you're new to scrying, an easy way to get into it is to use water and a candle flame. Find a dark-colored bowl, lower than the candle you are using. The candle should be tall enough to allow the flame to appear on the surface of the water when standing on the table; a taper candle in a holder is best for this.

Fill your bowl with water, then light your candle. Position the candle on the tabletop so that the flame reflects near the center of the bowl of water. Next, begin the charming procedure. It's best if you can memorize this charm beforehand, as you will be covering your eyes.

Position your hands over the bowl of water, palms facing down. Recite the first two lines of the charm. Then, cover your eyes with your hands, each palm covering an eye, and recite the next two lines. Continue the next two lines of the charm with your eyes covered. Then, with your eyes still closed, move your hands away from your face and position them on either side of your head with your palms facing forward. Finish the charm, then open your eyes and gaze into the bowl.

Let your eyes become unfocused but remain gazing into the candle flame reflected on the surface of the water. What images appear to you? Perhaps you see people dancing around the water like a movie is playing on the surface. Try not to focus too strictly; let the images appear as they want to without trying to make sense of them at first. Scrying is an art, so if you don't see anything at first, try and try again. As with dream interpretation, let yourself gather the images that seem most important *to you*, for the situation at hand, at this specific time. You can always quickly write down or record what you see and then interpret the images later on.

✭ COUNTING CHARM FOR SOMETHING LOST ✭

Another common counting charm, this ritual work is intended to help you find something that is lost or hidden. This can have many different meanings. On the surface, this charming ritual can be used to locate physical objects or items that have been lost. The charmer who gave me this work told me it can be used to uncover hidden treasure, if you're particularly lucky. Underneath the physical, one can also use this verbal charm to uncover secrets or information that is intentionally being withheld.

I've personally used both of these ritual variations. One client was trying to find a pocket watch that belonged to his recently deceased grandfather. He couldn't find it anywhere in the house and didn't want to approach his grandmother, so he decided to come to me for a divination session before he continued his hunt. As a result of the charming ritual, we landed on "Four in the ground." The man approached his grandmother about the watch, and she told him she had buried it with the man's grandfather.

In another case, a client believed her boss was secretly trying to fire her. We did this charming ritual and landed on "Eight with a friend." The woman looked very surprised by this answer. Later, she reported back to me that she had talked to her best friend at work about the situation, and her friend revealed the boss had indeed been talking to her in private about firing my client.

MAGICAL TIMING

Full moon. Zodiac moon days in Gemini (Mercury, Wednesday, air) are great to use when uncovering hidden information or lost items.

CHARM

One forever lost,
Two soon found,
Three look around,
Four in the ground,
Five all bound,
Six a lie,
Seven truth to find,
Eight with friend,
Nine with foe,
Ten with a stranger,
Eleven is danger,
Twelve leave it alone.

RITUAL INGREDIENTS

Counting objects, such as flower petals, chunks of bread, dried beans
    or corn kernels, etc.

RITUAL ACTIONS

Begin by identifying what you are trying to find as well as what counting object you'd like to use as part of the ritual. I find it helpful to be very specific in imagining what I'm looking for and to write it down on a piece of paper. If you're looking for your lost car keys, for example, don't say, "I'm looking for a key," but instead be specific and say, "I'm looking for the key that works with my [insert car type]." Remember to be specific when you're looking for information as well.

Note that even when your question is very specific, the answer that is given by the ritual is oftentimes only a suggestion and might need some time to process. As with the case of the missing pocket watch I mentioned at the beginning of this charm—my client figured out the answer a couple weeks after our initial divination session.

As far as counting objects go, you can use anything really, as long as you don't already know how many you have. I like to use dried beans or corn kernels because I can easily grab a handful without knowing how many there are. Flowers with lots of small petals are great to use for this ritual.

Begin the ritual by asking your question, then count out your objects while reciting the verbal charm. If you reach twelve, start over again until you don't have any of the counting objects left. This number is the answer to your question.

I'd like to take some time and explain the answers you might receive in a little more detail.

- **"One forever lost"**: Indicates that what you are searching for will either take a long time, won't ever be found, or will require a lot more divination work to locate.

- **"Two soon found"**: Means that your efforts will soon be rewarded but that another divination session might be needed. Try, try again!

- **"Three look around"**: Calls for you to physically search or hunt for what is lost, and indicates that an answer might be right under your nose.

- **"Four in the ground"**: Points to the earth as concealing the object that is lost. In the case of secrets, I interpret this number to mean that I should look to the root of the problem or situation for my answer.

- **"Five all bound"**: A good indicator that something is interfering with the work you're doing. I take this as a sign that someone is magically working to conceal the answers that I'm seeking.

- **"Six a lie"**: Meaning that there's some amount of illusion or enchantment surrounding the situation that is leading you or the querent away from the truth. Perhaps you swear you had your wallet or purse when you left your house but, in fact, your mind was playing tricks on you.

- **"Seven truth to find"**: Shows there's some underlying truth that needs to be uncovered, perhaps using an additional divination session. Unlike "Six a lie," this number points to the fact that some information is missing from the situation, not necessarily that there is a lie or illusion present.

- **"Eight with friend"**: Indicates that what you are seeking—or information about what you are seeking—is with a friend.

- **"Nine with foe"**: As opposed to "Eight with a friend," this number indicates that the item/object or secret is currently with an enemy of yours, or they know something more about the situation.

- **"Ten with a stranger"**: Similar to eight and nine, this indicates that what you are seeking is with a stranger. I take this to mean that some additional ritual work might need to be done to draw the stranger to me or my client.

- **"Eleven is danger"**: Acts as a warning that what has been lost is in a dangerous location or that the result of revealing the secrets you seek might mean some danger for you or others involved in the situation.

- **"Twelve leave it alone"**: For me, this is a clear indication to stop the divination, but not necessarily forever.

NOTES

Counting rituals for divination are common in Ozark folk magic. Most of the examples I've collected are divination charms to find one's true love, but there are examples of divining for other situations as well. The simplest of these rituals is to take a handful of dried beans and count out one and two with the charm "One is yes, two is no." This variation limits your work to yes or no answers only. In another variation, you use *yes* to mean auspicious or good and *no* to mean inauspicious or bad. Of all of the counting charms I've found in the Ozarks, this simple divination is by far the most used by folk healers and magical practitioners.

✸ DREAMING OF A CURE ✸

This verbal charm was given to me by a healer who used it frequently as part of her diagnosis routine for clients. Her process involved reciting the verbal charm three times before going to bed—the idea being that she would then dream of the cure or solution for her client. This charming ritual isn't limited to dreaming up remedies but can be used to help resolve any difficult or hidden situations.

Dreaming processes can vary from practitioner to practitioner, so feel free to develop your own. In many cases, you might be physically told the remedy by an angel or entity within the dream, or you might see yourself in the dream performing some ritual action, like gathering certain plants that can be used in the cure. This is a very straightforward approach to the dreaming process.

In my experience, though, dreams often deliver coded messages that need to be parsed out while awake. Dream symbols are highly personal, and what is meaningful to me might not be for you. I'm not a proponent of universal dream symbols like you might see in dream interpretation books—I prefer to let the dreamer themselves decipher the symbols hidden within their dreams.

MAGICAL TIMING
Full moon. Gemini (Mercury, Wednesday, air) or Pisces (Jupiter, Thursday, water) are great zodiac moon days for divination and dreaming.

CHARM
For every evil under the sun,
There is a remedy or there is none.
If there be one, seek till you find it;
If there be none, never mind it.
(Repeat three times)

RITUAL INGREDIENTS
Cup or mug
Ink pen or marker, black
3-inch paper square, white
Passionflower leaves (*Passiflora incarnata*) or chamomile flowers
Water

RITUAL ACTIONS

In my own use of this verbal charm, I like to add a few ritual elements to assist with the dreaming process. The first element is drinking a small amount of hot tea made from passionflower leaves (*Passiflora incarnata*). Passionflower is not only a pleasant sedative but also assists in generating dream activity. If you don't have access to passionflower leaves, you can use chamomile flowers. Make an infusion by pouring boiling water over a tablespoon of dried leaves (or chamomile flowers) in a coffee cup or mug. Let this steep for four to eight minutes. Strain and then drink the tea. Do this thirty minutes before going to bed.

While you wait, write the full name (first, middle, and last) of the person you are dreaming for on the small paper square. If you're dreaming for yourself, you can skip this step. When you go to bed, put this paper square underneath your pillow, then recite the verbal charm three times. I like to keep a notepad next to my bed so that I can record my dreams as soon as I wake up in the morning, or if I happen to wake up in the night. Dreams can then be interpreted much easier during the waking hours.

If no dreams occur, or if you can't remember what you dreamed, this could be a sign that there is no current solution to the problem at hand. Personally, I will try the ritual at least one more time before drawing that conclusion, just in case.

✮ DREAMING OF YOUR LOVE ✮

The first use of this charm is to identify someone who might be in love with you—or, in a more traditional usage, someone who is meant to be your spouse. I will say, using this charming ritual for the goal of finding your true love often has very unexpected results—I know from personal experience. In my true love dream, which was surprisingly vivid and detailed, I was approached by an enormous walrus while casually walking through a zoo. We both stopped and met gazes, then the walrus kissed me on the cheek before diving into a nearby river. I'm still unable to interpret this message. Remember, dream divinations often require some pondering.

The second use of this charming ritual is to identify a cheating spouse or partner. In this variation, the dream will reveal information surrounding the situation. In some cases, it might even show you a sort of real-time image of the act itself. I will say, take all dream divinations with a healthy amount of skepticism. This is especially important when the symbols revealed might lead to anger, hurt feelings, and unnecessary confrontation.

MAGICAL TIMING

Full moon. Zodiac moon days in Gemini (Mercury, Wednesday, air) and Pisces (Jupiter, Thursday, water) for general divination, or Aquarius (Saturn, Saturday, air) for revealing a suspected cheater.

CHARM

When I my true love want to see,
I put my shoes in the shape of T.
Full moon, bring them close to me.

RITUAL INGREDIENTS

2 rose petals, red, dried or fresh
Salt
Shoes, pair

RITUAL ACTIONS

Begin by placing a pair of your shoes into the shape of a T under your bed, beneath where your head will be while you're sleeping. To form the T shape, your left shoe will be the vertical line and your right shoe will be the horizontal top line. If you can't access underneath your bed, then you can place your shoes on the side of your bed. If your shoes are underneath your bed, the top of the T-shape should be parallel with the head of your bed; if your shoes are on the side, the top of the T should be parallel with the side of your bed. Place a pinch of salt underneath each shoe. Then, place a rose petal inside of each shoe, near the toe.

Recite the verbal charm once, then go to bed. I like to keep a notepad and pen next to my bed to quickly record any dreams that I might have. The ritual for identifying a cheater is exactly the same, only the interpretation of the resulting dream will differ.

NOTES

I've yet to identify why the shoes are made into a T shape as part of this charming ritual. Even the charmer who gave this ritual to me had no idea, but suspected it might be connected to the tau cross (named after the Greek letter), which symbolizes Jesus of Nazareth's crucifixion and has ancient origins amongst early Christian groups. A Roman Catholic friend of mine identified this shape as being Saint Anthony's Cross, which has been used as a symbol of the saint since at least the twelfth century. In my friend's intriguing interpretation, perhaps the shoe shape is a callback to Saint Anthony as the patron of lost or hidden things.

⭑ DREAMING OF LOVE WITH THE NEW MOON ⭑

This is another love divination that utilizes the power of the moon to produce prophetic dreams. This verbal charm aims to show the charmer the identity of their true love—namely their hair color, clothing, and a date when the two shall be wed. Many Ozark love divinations work in a similar manner to reveal key elements from the individual, but not necessarily their full appearance. It's up to the charmer to interpret the symbols that manifest within the dream.

MAGICAL TIMING

New moon. Nighttime. Zodiac moon days in Gemini (Mercury, Wednesday, air) or Pisces (Jupiter, Thursday, water).

CHARM

New moon, new moon, do tell me
Who my own true lover will be,
The color of their hair,
The clothes that they will wear,
And the happy day they will wed me.
(Repeat three times)

RITUAL INGREDIENTS

None

RITUAL ACTIONS

Go outside somewhere you can see the new moon in the sky. If it's a cloudy night, do your best to find where the moon is located, or else pick another new moon night. While looking at the moon, recite the verbal charm three times. After each recitation, turn around in a clockwise circle, then return to looking at the moon. When you're finished, return home and go immediately to sleep. The symbols that appear in your dreams will point toward your true love. This charming ritual can be repeated as often as needed, but only on the new moon.

NOTES

In charming rituals similar to this one, the moon is invoked to deliver all kinds of useful information. In particular, it's the new moon that is used in these charming rituals, although the full moon is often associated with dreaming and divination in Ozark folk magic. I've collected several of these variations, including a verbal charm that petitions the new moon to aid in finding a lost object: "New moon, new moon, shine on me, / Bring this lost thing back to me, / Bring it back from high or low, / Bring it back, or tell me no!" The resulting dream is believed to reveal the location of the lost object.

⭑ EGGS TO FIND ILLNESSES AND HEXES ⭑

This egg ritual bears a great deal of similarity to other Ozark egg cleansing rituals, like the "Pregnancy Blessing" in chapter 4 of this work. There is another egg cleansing ritual offered in my *Ozark Mountain Spell Book*. This is more of a divination ritual than a cleansing, however, and only aims to locate or diagnose illnesses and hexes, not necessarily cleanse them out immediately.

This divination requires observing tokens or signs, the symbolic patterns and forms produced by the cracked egg are essentially left open to interpretation. Trusting your intuition will allow you to see things that perhaps aren't listed amongst the common tokens that have traditionally been looked for by Ozark healers.

MAGICAL TIMING

As it was taught to me, this diagnosis divination can be used at any time; my teacher never waited for auspicious moon phases or zodiac moon signs. However, if you do wish to use magical timing, full moons in Gemini (Mercury, Wednesday, air) or Pisces (Jupiter, Thursday, water) are very auspicious.

CHARM

Hickety, pickety, my black hen,
She lays eggs for the gentlemen;
Gentlemen come almost every day,
To see what my black hen doth lay.

RITUAL INGREDIENTS

Bowl
Egg(s), any color
Glass or cup, clear
Water

RITUAL ACTIONS

There are two ritual variations that you can use, depending how deep you want to go with this work. Begin either variation by first gathering your materials. You will need a clear drinking glass, wine glass, or cup—any shape will work as long as it is completely clear, with no colored tint. Fill the glass with water, stopping about half an inch from the lip to allow for expansion when the egg is cracked into the water. You will also need an egg for this ritual. If you're doing the first variation, you'll only need one egg. If you're doing the second variation, you will need twelve.

For the first variation, you will have your client stand facing the east. (Or you can perform this charming ritual on your own body.) Take the egg and begin gently rubbing it along your client's body from head to toe while reciting the verbal charm quietly—or even silently, in your head.

Direction and number of passes is very important in this ritual. You will work in a downward direction, beginning at the crown of the head and ending by rubbing the egg gently on the soles of the feet (with shoes on is fine).

Do this entire motion a total of three times on the front, then walk around behind your client—making sure they still face east—and repeat three more times on the back. Repeat the verbal charm for the entirety of the rubbing process. You can either physically touch their body directly or pass it over the body a few inches above the skin.

When you're finished, take and crack the egg into the glass of water. Put the eggshell in a bowl and place it to the side. You will now begin interpreting the egg yolk and white suspended in the water. I will list some common symbols looked for by Ozark healers, but remember to watch for other things that might jump out at you as important tokens.

- **Whole, Yellow Yolk (No Spots) and Clear Egg White:** No illnesses or hexes are present.
- **Yolk with Red Blood Dot or Smudge:** Indicates there is an illness or hex present in the body, but it isn't severe.
- **White Circular or Spherical Spot Attached to the Yolk or on the Surface of the Yolk:** Specifically indicates the presence of the Evil Eye. Sometimes healers will associate dark-colored shadow spots inside the yolk as the Evil Eye.
- **Cracked or Broken Yolk:** The reading has been magically interfered with by someone on the outside—cleanse and then try again.
- **Black or Dark-Colored Shadow Spots on the Yolk:** Severe illness or hex is present. These shadow spots are sometimes associated with the Evil Eye.
- **Cloudy Egg White Around the Yolk:** Something is clouding the reading—cleanse and then try again.
- **Sharp Knife/Spear Shapes in Egg White:** Presence of hex work against the person who is being diagnosed. If there is blood or shadows on the yolk, this could indicate the need for immediate cleansing. If no blood or shadows appear, the work has been stopped before reaching the person being diagnosed.
- **Rotten or Foul Smell/Appearance:** Dire illness or hex is present—begin a cleansing process immediately.

After interpreting the egg, end the charming ritual by throwing the water, yolk, white, and eggshell into a running body of water or by burying everything underneath a strong, living tree.

The second ritual variation is a little more involved. The Zodiac Man features heavily in many aspects of Ozark folk healing and magic; the basic idea is that the twelve zodiac houses can be found inside the human body as well as up in the sky. Each of the zodiac signs appear from head to toe, in order, and rule over specific bodily systems. You can read more about the Zodiac Man in the introduction to chapter 4 as well as in my first book, *Ozark Folk Magic: Plants, Prayers & Healing*.

If working with the houses, your charming ritual will begin just like the first variation, except here you will need twelve eggs—one for each of the zodiac houses. I recommend working through one house at a time, from Aries in the head to Pisces in the feet. You will need access to multiple clear glasses, or you can use a single glass that will be washed between readings.

In this ritual, the person being diagnosed will lie down on their back with their head facing east. (This ritual is a little difficult to perform on yourself, but it can be done.) Begin by filling a glass with water, as in the first ritual variation. Take and rub an egg on the person's body from head to toe three times while quietly (or silently) reciting the verbal charm. End by rubbing three counterclockwise inward spirals on the corresponding zodiac house location while visualizing the egg sucking out whatever illnesses or hexes might be present there. As with the first variation, you can either physically touch the person's body or hold the egg a few inches from the skin.

Once the spiraling motion is complete, crack your egg into the glass of water and begin the interpretation. In this ritual variation, whatever appears in the yolk and white corresponds to each house alone and will provide a much more in-depth look at where exactly the illness or hex might be "rooted," as Ozark healers often say. After you're done with your interpretation, you can throw the contents of the glass into a large bowl or pitcher for disposal later on, or you can do what I've seen many healers do after each reading: flush the egg and water down the toilet and toss the shell into the trash or compost heap. If you are using separate glasses for each house, you can change them out now. Otherwise, wash your glass with salt water before proceeding to the next reading.

Continue with the same ritual procedure through each of the twelve houses. I highly recommend having a notepad present to record your observations. When you're completely finished with the reading, you can thoroughly wash your glass(es) as you would any other dish. If you haven't yet disposed of the eggs used in the reading, along with the bowl of shells, they can be taken outside and buried beneath a strong, living tree. You can also throw them in a moving body of water or even flush them down the toilet.

NOTES

Cleansing rituals using eggs are also found in traditions of Curanderismo and Hoodoo. It's certainly possible that either of these traditions is the origin of our Ozark egg practices. There are a significant amount of examples of eggs being used as containers to collect and hold illnesses and hexes from across Europe as well. It's most likely that egg cleansing is the result of blended traditions, each one influencing the other through interactions between healers from all of these communities.

The most prominent feature of this verbal charm is the specific naming of a black hen. This links to another significant piece of shared folk knowledge found throughout the Americas as well as the Old World: from an Ozark perspective, all-black or all-white animals are considered highly auspicious and oftentimes believed to be otherworldly creatures who have just disguised themselves as ordinary animals. Unlike other all-black animals in Ozark folklore, black chickens aren't considered evil or inauspicious, but are seen as powerful healers.

It's believed that black chickens can absorb illnesses and hexes without taking on the effects of the malady themselves. For this reason, black chicken feathers and eggs are commonly used in Ozark folk magic. Black chicken feather brooms are often used in cleansing rituals, as they can absorb and sweep off hexes without needing to be destroyed or cleansed at the end of the ritual process. They can be reused again and again.

As part of this charming ritual, it isn't necessary to have a black chicken egg. A primordial example of the black chicken is instead invoked to add auspiciousness to the work whether or not specific materials are available.

✴ FINDING SOMETHING LOST OR HIDDEN SECRETS ✴

Another verbal charm used as a traditional form of divination, though this one involves an intriguing visualization ritual. This charm can be used to locate lost objects as well as hidden information. In one particular usage I observed, a charmer wished to know the identity of a person who was magically working against him, so he used this charming ritual and was shown their face in a dream he had that night.

MAGICAL TIMING

Full moon. Nighttime. Before going to sleep. Zodiac moon days in Gemini (Mercury, Wednesday, air) are great to use when uncovering hidden information or lost items.

CHARM

[Ask your question]
Snail, snail!
Come out of your hole!
Or else I'll beat you black as coal.

Snail, snail!
Put out your head!
Or else I'll beat you till you're dead.

One, two, three, four,
A knock at my door.
Don't walk, but run,
And now we're done!

RITUAL INGREDIENTS

Candle, white
Matches or lighter

RITUAL ACTIONS

Light your candle and let it be the only light in the room. While facing the candle, ask your question aloud, then recite the verbal charm. When you reach the word *done*, blow out the candle.

The charmer who gave me this ritual said that at the point of the candle flame being blown out, you might receive an immediate visualization that links to the answer to your question. In one ritual I performed, I did in fact see a flashing image—for just a moment—of a person's face. As it turned out, this person was someone who my client knew and had the answer we were seeking. Your answer might come in the dream that follows the ritual, and this has been the case for me most of the times I've used this charm. For this reason, I like to go to sleep immediately after blowing out the candle.

NOTES

This verbal charm is a repurposing of a famous nursery rhyme, with the snail being a symbolic representation of the answer you're seeking in the ritual. In a similar variation of the same theme, one Roman Catholic healer I met gave me a charm that invoked Saint Anthony as the patron of lost items: "Tony, Tony! / Poke out your head, / And get yourself out of bed!" The verbal charm is then followed by a question like, "Where are my car keys?" or "Where is my wallet?" What is missing, of course, are the threats launched at the poor little snail in our version.

☆ TRAVELING IN SPIRIT FORM ☆

This traditional Mother Goose rhyme is steeped in mystery. It reads like a verbal charm from the very beginning, and it isn't difficult to imagine how it might have originally been born from a much more ancient charm. This charming ritual focuses primarily on spirit flight, especially while in a trance or while dreaming. At its core, this verbal charm is used to induce lucid dreaming, whereby the practitioner can explore the otherworldly spaces—or even real places in our own world. This lucid trance or dreaming session can be used for diagnosis, for divinatory purposes, or even to curse your enemy while shrouded in magical invisibility.

CAUTION

Do not consume mugwort essential oil. It contains a chemical compound called thujone, which can be lethal when ingested in highly concentrated forms like an essential oil. Be cautious when using this essential oil on your skin, as it can cause contact dermatitis in some people, and in high concentrations can be poisonous.

MAGICAL TIMING

Full moon. Nighttime. Moons in Gemini (Mercury, Wednesday, air) or Pisces (Jupiter, Thursday, water) are very auspicious to use for this charm—especially Gemini, whose mercurial nature works with all forms of spirit flight, trance, and vision work. I was taught that Gemini's twins can be a symbol for the practitioner's dual nature: body and spirit.

CHARM

How many miles is it to Babylon?
Threescore miles and ten.
Can I get there by candlelight?
Yes, and back again.
If your heels are nimble and light,
You may get there by candlelight.

RITUAL INGREDIENTS

Candle, white
Matches or lighter
Incense charcoal and burner (optional)
Mugwort (*Artemisia vulgaris*) (optional)

RITUAL ACTIONS

Whether you're using a trance or dreaming while asleep, both methods will involve the same process. I once asked an Ozark teacher of mine what the difference was between a trance and dream, and she just smiled and answered, "Words." In Ozark magical theory, waking dreams, daydreams, trances, whatever you'd like to call them, are all made up of the same stuff.

Find a comfortable spot where you can be free from distractions, or as best you can be. If you're going to be sleeping, you can use your bed for this ritual. If you're wanting to cause a trance or waking dream, choose a spot where you can sit propped up instead of lying down; this will prevent you from unknowingly falling asleep. Sensory deprivation tools can be used in either method and actually help in the beginning stages, when you're still adjusting to the process. These can include eye masks, earplugs, or noise-canceling headphones. This process is going to be yours, so choose tools that aid in your work, whatever they might be.

When you're ready to begin, light your white candle, then turn off all the lights in the room. I like to position the candle far enough away that the light won't distract me from the trance or keep me awake. For safety purposes, I like to use a votive or tealight candle that won't burn the entire night, since it will be left unattended while you sleep. You can also place the candle in a large bowl to keep it away from other objects. At this point, you can also light your incense charcoal and add a pinch of dried mugwort leaves. Mugwort is an excellent facilitator for trances and lucid dreams. If you're sensitive to smoke, you can use mugwort essential oil with a diffuser or even add a few drops to a cotton ball and keep it next to you.

With everything together, begin repeating the verbal charm. You will repeat the verbal charm either until you fall asleep or until you slip into a trance state. From here, the visions may begin. I recommend not to try and control what you are seeing, but allow yourself to be carried through whatever visions or dreams might be produced.

Observe your surroundings. How do you feel? What do you see? Hear? Smell? Taste? Observe what symbols or tokens might appear, especially if your intention is divination. If you wake up out of the trance or dream, begin repeating the verbal charm again. Continue for as long as feels right.

I will say that with trance work, the longer you can sit still, the easier it will become. Take some time in the beginning, before you repeat the charm, to sit quietly and calm your thoughts down. Image them beginning as a rushing river, then slowly—slowly—they calm to just a trickle, or become like soft, rolling waves on a calm ocean.

One process for dreaming that I've found very helpful is to curate your lucid dreaming experience. With this method, you will set an alarm for sometime in the middle of the night, then go to sleep like you normally do. For example, when I work this method, I'll go to sleep at 10:00 p.m. and set an alarm for 3:00 a.m. When the alarm goes off, wake up, light your candle, then settle back into bed. While your eyes are closed and you're repeating the verbal charm, set your intention that you will wake up to the dreaming experience. You can add your other intentions here as well—divination, diagnosis, etc.

NOTES

Ozark folklore is filled with tales of witches who could fly out as spirits and plague their victims. In the past, many traditional healers lived with their patients while ritual work was being performed so that they could watch out for these spirits, coming to suck the life out of the one who was sick. There's a story I heard once about a boy who was lost in the woods and was eventually helped home by a kind old lady who lived next door to him. When he got back to his family's cabin, he told his parents the tale, and his mother jumped all over him for lying. "Stop telling tales, child. I was just with her next door borrowing some flour!" The boy swore up and down that it was their neighbor who had helped him. From then on, the family suspected the old woman of being a witch.

While many of us today can see some humor in these old tales, the truth was much more dangerous for hillfolk healers and magical practitioners, who often had to fiercely hide their practices to avoid such accusations of witchcraft. Having practiced many of the old methods myself, I firmly believe many of the folktales are likely based on some amount of truth. That said, the intentions behind the practice of flying out in spirit form were likely far more benign then communities were willing to admit. In my own collected accounts, I've found far more practitioners using such gifts to heal remotely, or to gain knowledge from the otherworld, than to harm anyone or suck the life force from the sick and infirm.

CHAPTER 9

To Pass Beyond
and Back Again ...

Paul Blackwell was born just after midnight on May Day. At the time of his birth, a storm had rolled into Nelson's Holler and was pelting down a hard, cold rain. The storm flooded ol' Paul Landry's mill for the second time in sixty-six years, causing so much damage that his grandson later sold the ruins and moved away to Washburn to start a fancy restaurant. The storm killed at least twenty cows out on Buffalo Ridge, causing the ranchers to reconsider putting livestock out there in the first place.

Granny Thornapple was present as midwife, as she had been for many of the children born in Nelson's Holler. She reported two unusual tokens, or omens, at the birth of Paul Blackwell. 1) He was born in the caul, and 2) he was born completely silent, until he let out a banshee wail that shocked even Granny Thornapple. As this powerful cry was released into the world, lightning struck the hundred-year-old burr oak tree down on Main Street, splitting it completely in twain. "He's got the gift in him!" Granny Thornapple laughed as she handed the child over to his mother.

Paul Blackwell grew up fast and strong. He was beloved by all who knew him. Even strangers couldn't help but be pulled into his magnetic field—especially when he smiled, showing off his naturally straight teeth and the dimple in his chin. At seventeen years old, he'd been able to graduate high school early. While the boy was an academic wizard, he hated the way school made him feel so trapped; he'd rather be out running through the woods or brewing up potions with his mentor, Granny Thornapple.

Paul had started his apprenticeship the moment he was born and Granny Thornapple was able to stare into his icy-blue eyes. An instantaneous connection was made—one that would last for years. As a child, Paul loved climbing the mountain to

233

Granny Thornapple's house. She always had sweets ready for him when he arrived. Sometimes they would walk the woods and fields and the old woman would point out plants and share their associated remedies with him. Sometimes they would cook up yarb broths and love potions together, and Granny Thornapple would remind the child how dangerous it was to play with matters of the heart.

The Blackwell family loved Granny Thornapple and considered her to be a surrogate grandmother to little Paul. They never said anything when he ran out of the house to see her, or when he came home stinking to high heaven of bitter herbs, woodfire, and red cedar smoke. They all knew Paul had the gift in him, and they all knew the best person in Nelson's Holler to address that gift was Granny Thornapple.

One morning, as Paul sat at Granny Thornapple's kitchen table grinding herbs in a big mortar and pestle, a loud knock sounded on the front door. The sound made Paul jump in his chair. He'd been in his own head all morning, trying to make sure he performed all the tasks his mentor had given him with precision. Granny Thornapple was taking her mid-morning nap in the back of the cabin, so Paul stood and ran over to answer the front door. Standing on the other side was Younger Winthrop, the local doctor. He was clearly shaken by something—he wrung his hands nervously together, and his face was deathly pale. "Mornin', Paul," he said in a raspy voice. "Sorry not to call, but I was in the area. Is Granny Thornapple at home?"

Paul nodded. "She's in the back, asleep."

"Could you tell her that I stopped by? And that Rachel Lynn Osburn down in town is real sick. We could use her ... expertise."

Paul agreed, and the doctor rushed back to his truck in the driveway. Paul hurried to Granny Thornapple's bedroom. She was already dressed and putting her boots on when the boy arrived. "I know, I know," she mumbled as she grabbed her cane. "Could you load my bag into Matilda, darlin'?"

It took longer than usual to get down the mountain and into Nelson's Holler. Paul hated driving Matilda, but Granny Thornapple insisted he get used to her. "She'll be yours when I'm gone, after all," she'd always say to him.

Despite her prodding to go faster, Paul crept the truck down the old dirt roads off the mountain. They got to the Osburn place slower than Granny Thornapple had wanted. "But we got here in one piece," Paul said as he helped the old woman out of the truck.

Younger Winthrop met them at the front door. He led the two into the house, then to one of the back rooms, where Rachel Lynn was sick in bed. Paul had never seen someone look so bad in all his days. She'd lost a lot of weight over the past week, and her cheeks were sunken into her face. She was pale as death and covered in sweat despite the fact that the room was cold. Rachel Lynn shifted between lucidity and some dream world every few minutes. As the healer and her young apprentice entered the room, her eyes softened with joy. She reached a boney hand out to Granny Thornapple.

"It's all right now, Rachel Lynn," Granny Thornapple said, sitting herself down in a wooden chair beside the bed.

Younger Winthrop and Paul sat down on a small couch on the opposite side of the room. The doctor began explaining all the symptoms he'd recorded, but Granny Thornapple held up her hand, silencing him without really even trying. At eighty-three years old, she'd seen more illnesses, maladies, hexes, and harm than Younger Winthrop could even imagine. She immediately knew this was no virus, cancer, or contagion. Her sight showed her the hexes deep in Rachel Lynn's stomach, causing her emaciation, and those in her throat, which had taken the woman's voice. "Has she said anything strange, Doc?" Granny Thornapple asked, turning to where Younger Winthrop was sitting. "I mean, strange to you, I guess."

"When I got here," the doctor said, "she said the crows were bothering her, but when I looked outside I didn't see anything, so I didn't pay much attention to it."

Granny Thornapple nodded silently, then turned back around to Rachel Lynn. "Darlin', listen to me, were them crows trying to get inside the room?"

Rachel Lynn's eyes grew wide and she managed to nod slightly. Granny Thornapple was reaching for her bag when a loud thump hit the roof right above them. "What was that?" the doctor whispered.

Granny motioned with her hand for the man to keep quiet. She looked up to the ceiling and waited. A clawing noise started on the roof. It was barely audible at first, then grew louder and louder as it moved toward where the smoke pipe for the woodstove exited through the ceiling. Younger Winthrop stood up quickly, his hands clasped and shaking as he looked toward where the clawing was increasing. "What is that?" he whispered.

Granny Thornapple grabbed her bag and reached inside. She pulled out a bottle of salt along with a few other items. She placed a pinch of salt on the center of Rachel Lynn's chest, then hurried over to where Paul and the doctor were standing.

"Open your mouths," she barked, and they followed her orders. She took a pinch of salt and put it into each of their mouths. *"Close your mouth, but keep the salt in there. You hear me?"*

The doctor and Paul both nodded, then sat back on the couch. Paul winced and contorted his face from the lump of salt currently drying out his mouth. Younger Winthrop was too shaken from the whole situation to notice any discomfort.

The clawing sound finally reached the smoke pipe on the roof. With the clanging of metal and the scraping of sharp claws, Granny Thornapple heard something fall down into the cold woodstove with a thump. She threw a pinch of salt toward the sound, and the stove shook in place. The three watched as the door to the woodstove slowly started to open. Granny Thornapple's heart began to beat faster. She hadn't had to do anything like this in many years. *I hope my nerves can take it,* she thought to herself.

The woodstove opened. A thick, black smoke poured into the room. Granny Thornapple took another pinch of salt and threw it at the smoke cloud now suspended in the shape of a human body, towering over the woodstove beneath it. The cloud retreated slightly, as though the salt had hurt it somehow. It made a low rumbling sound, like an old, worn-out truck engine. *"This is the third time I've seen you, demon,"* Granny Thornapple laughed, holding out the chunk of wood she still wore as an amulet around her neck.

The smoke's fiery eyes grew brighter as it growled and then flew toward Rachel Lynn. It reached a long, black claw toward the woman. Just as it almost touched her, a white light flashed and the demon recoiled, repelled by the salt Granny Thornapple had placed on Rachel Lynn's chest. *"And twice now you've vexed me, human,"* the demon hissed.

Granny Thornapple laughed and began reciting her charm. *"Three rings of white fire, come down off the mountain!"*

The demon rolled in agony as a faint, fiery glow held its spectral arms in place.

"Three rings of white flame, come!" Granny Thornapple continued. *"Come for healing! Come for blessing! Come for cleansing!"*

The smoke demon cried out, the sound piercing into Paul's head, making him shove his fingers into his ears to block it out.

"As wax melts in this fire, so will you and your darkness melt away!"

The demon shape began to change as the smoke condensed into a thick, black ichor that fell to the floor.

"As dust blows in the wind, I will blow you away!"

The ichor solidified into gray dust that swirled through the room and around Granny Thornapple. Paul could tell she was beginning to falter—the demon was taking too much from her. He started to rush forward but was pushed back into his seat by the wind.

"I blow you into the west, your home, the home of all evil and sickness!"

The window beside Rachel Lynn's bed flew open with a crash, and the dust began flying outside.

"I seal you in the west until the stars fall from the sky above!"

The black dust began screaming again as it swirled in a twisting cyclone out the window.

"I seal you until all good things pass from the world!"

Granny Thornapple collapsed onto the floor. The last remainder of the demon vanished out the window and the world was silent again. Rachel Lynn gasped, then began breathing normally. She blinked her eyes and moved her fingers, and Younger Winthrop thought some color had definitely come back into her cheeks.

Paul rushed over to Granny Thornapple on the floor. She was weak but still aware. He grabbed her hand in his own. "Are you all right?" he asked, holding her gently.

"Rachel?" Granny Thornapple wheezed softly.

"I think she'll be all right. Doc's with her."

Granny Thornapple smiled. "Good."

"Are you all right?" Paul repeated, but again his mentor ignored his question.

Granny Thornapple reached under her dress and took off her wooden amulet, handing it to Paul. "The circle is unbroken," she said softly before her eyes closed. Her breathing slowed, then stopped completely.

Paul wiped the tears off his face with the back of his hand and then slipped the amulet around his own neck.

In the coming days, Rachel Lynn Osburn made a full recovery, much to the surprise of most of Nelson's Holler. When asked what had happened in her room that day, Younger Winthrop would simply reply, "A miracle," and leave it at that. He would go on to further build up his father's office and pharmacy on the hill, and he forged vital partnerships with many of the healers in the area.

Paul never fully recovered from what he experienced that day, but he keeps Granny Thornapple's work and memory alive through his own healing practice. He was left the cabin, land, Granny Thornapple's black book, and, of course, her most prized possession, Matilda. Every now and then, when the moon was full and shining down through the trees outside the cabin, Paul would see Granny Thornapple tending to her garden and couldn't help but smile.

WORKING WITH THE SPIRIT WORLD

One of the most closely guarded secrets within Ozark traditional healing and folk magic has been work with the spirit world. In the old days, working with spirits was seen as being very close to the dreaded witchcraft, especially for those who had spirit familiars who helped them in their work. Tall tales abound about workers who fell into dabbling with spirit boards and seances. These were often used as cautionary tales, especially for those who were gifted with healing abilities. In many cases, healers who did work in this way often hid their practices behind work with angels, a term that has come to include a host of spirit entities here in the Ozarks.

While for many Ozarkers this is still a taboo subject, there have always been traditional healers and workers who have derived power from interactions with the spirit world. Spirit work is often especially powerful for those with the sight or second sight who can sense the invisible world around them. Working in these liminal spaces between the worlds can include a variety of practices—from healing, to divination, to exorcism.

In some cases, interactions with the otherworld are initiatory, as with one healer I met who learned all of her verbal charms from a spirit that spoke to her out of an old oak tree stump. She only ever interacted with the spirit during these training sessions, and their meetings stopped completely when they were finished. I've met several healers who invoke the power of specific angels or saints as a main feature of their work, and I've met healers who employ spirit beings as helping familiars. Whatever the work, all methods involve interactions with beings known as *spirits*, but that word has come to mean many different things over the years.

WHAT IS A SPIRIT?

On many occasions, I've heard Ozarkers refer to spirits by a plethora of different names: angels, fairies, the Little People, ghosts, wights, haints—just to name a few. Some names, like *angel*, have been used both as traditional forms of devotion as well as clever ways to hide personal practices in order to avoid accusations of being a witch. *Fairy* is another popular grouping of all spirit beings, sometimes even angels.

All of this can get very complicated, mind you. As in the case of angels, who can be considered spirits of the dead who are now allowed to intercede on behalf of us humans. Additionally, they are often their own type of spirit entity—one who has never actually had any human form. In this case, they are very similar to the fairies (or the Little People, as they are called in the Ozarks). But, the Little People can also refer to a very specific type, or species, of fairy being. Ghosts can refer to shades of the dead, as well as to spirit entities in general. So, the question is raised—*what the heck is a spirit?*

In my work, I've tried desperately to answer this question. The best definition I've been able to come up with is that a spirit is a being (a personality, an individual, etc.) who originates in, or spends the majority of their time in, the otherworld. The otherworld is, well, that *other* place that's not here.

There are many images of the otherworld. In Ozark folklore, it's most often depicted as a mirror image to our own world, but with a different *quality* to it—usually only distinguishable by those with the sight. In some tales, the otherworld takes its form from the heart of the observer, leading to many traditional beliefs about Heaven and Hell being situated in the otherworld. For a good soul, the otherworld might appear as a paradise, while for those who were evil in life, it might appear as a fiery hell. Any differentiations between the two worlds occurs solely based on the state of the individual soul.

Let's take a brief look at some individual spirit beings and their roles within Ozark folk magic and healing.

ANGELS

Angels are common features of Ozark folklore and religious life. Unlike those named angels of the Roman Catholic, Orthodox, and Anglican traditions, Protestant Ozarkers often refer to angels simply as a group of divine beings, or in some cases, you might hear reference to one's own "guardian angel."

Amongst healers and magical practitioners, work with angels is very common, and they are often invoked in verbal charms and rituals. Sometimes an angel will be a departed loved one, especially if they were also a healer. Most commonly, though, angels go unnamed. Angels are often teachers, bringing divine gifts to their apprentices. In other cases, angels can be summoned to add power or auspiciousness to the work at hand. Angels are often invoked within traditional exorcisms as beings who can easily overpower evil entities—unlike us mere mortals.

GHOSTS

Ghosts also go by the traditional name of *haint*, derived from the word *haunt*, as in *haunted*. *Ghost* or *haint* commonly refers to an entity who was once in a human body, then died, and is now appearing in their spirit form. These words carry a very negative weight with them. Loved ones who were kind and pious in life are hardly ever called *ghost* and never referred to as a *haint*. These are, instead, called *angels* or *beloved dead* as opposed to ghosts and haints, who carry with them a sense of suspicion or even caution. Haints are almost always associated with hauntings; in particular, spirit activity that is noisy or disturbing.

Ghosts and haints are the targets of most Ozark exorcisms, many of which aim at helping the spirit heal or "elevate." Much of the language surrounding our spirit work actually derives from a combination of traditional beliefs mixed with nineteenth century Spiritualism and Spiritism, both of which were once very popular in the Ozarks. As one medium and healer explained to me, ghosts or haints are weighed down by their guilt or evil deeds, and that's why they roam the earth. Angels, on the other hand, are light and able to fly because they bear no burdens.

Workers rarely use haints in any practices, as these beings are often confused and unable to keep focused. There are stories, however, of mountain magicians summoning up ghosts and forcing them to reveal where they might have buried treasures. In most cases, this practice is frowned upon by healers as being cruel; to the general public, it's seen as a humorous tall tale.

FAIRIES

Fairies include a variety of otherworldly beings, all of whom have deep connections to the natural world, as opposed to angels and haints. Land spirits are sometimes lumped in alongside fairies in more traditional accounts, but I like to separate them into their own category.

Fairies can include many different species or types, but by far the most common in the Ozarks are the Little People. Some might avert their eyes at the mere mentioning of their name. Here in the Ozarks, still to this day, matters of the Little People are never taken lightly. They are fierce and often capricious protectors of nature, especially natural land features like waterfalls, springs, creeks, boulders, caves, ancient trees, etc. These auspicious places of power are considered to be where the Little People make their villages. Only those with the sight are able to pierce the veil between worlds and see them, however.

Usually between six inches and a foot tall, the Little People are said to look exactly like human beings, the difference being that the Little People come from the otherworld and are much closer to the flow of magic through the world. The Little People are most often described as a smaller version of humankind; similarly, the Little People have their own language, religion, laws, customs, etc. One healer told me that the Little People are how humans are *supposed* to be—protectors of nature. According to her, the Little People only became little when humans no longer cared about the same things as their otherworldly cousins. As our love for nature diminished, so too did its protectors.

Many of our descriptions of the Little People have come from early interactions with Indigenous peoples while Ozarkers were still in Appalachia. In particular, Cherokee beliefs around the *yunwi tsunsdi* have influenced these fairy beliefs to a large extent. The Cherokee still also use the English phrase *Little People* today, and this is likely where our own term comes from. It should be noted, however, that Ozark beliefs surrounding the Little People are not completely Indigenous in origin and, for the most part, utilize symbology and folklore from across Northern Europe rather than from the New World.

Interactions with fairies and the Little People have created the most Ozark cautionary tales. Generally speaking, if you're kind to the Little

People, or kind to nature, they will be kind to you. In some cases, such positive interactions can result in gifts of power. For those who have bad intentions, who don't keep their end of fairy agreements, or who needlessly harm the land, the Little People are known to deliver powerful and often incurable hexes. Gifts from the fairies require an equal exchange; I once met a healer who, in his youth, made a deal with one of the Little People and exchanged his right eye for the power.

Land spirits are often called *fairies*, but in my experience they have distinctive characteristics and behaviors. These spirits tend to be formless, or they take the form of their natural container, whether that's a tree, boulder, spring, etc. Unlike other fairy varieties, if you destroy the land spirit's home or container, you destroy the land spirit themselves. In some accounts, the land spirit will flee back to the otherworld, but I've also heard that they can disappear from existence altogether. These entities can be petitioned and worked with like other spirits but are slow to make friends and take their time with any work agreed upon. It might be years before you see any pacts come to fruition. Their gifts, however, are as deep as the wellsprings of power that course through nature and as strong as the rock foundations of the earth. They tend to be more neutral than other spirits. They rarely act out of aggression, unless they are acting as nature acts; for example, a tree falling on your house or a creek swelling outside its boundaries. Land spirits are honored for what they are—the life force of nature itself.

HOUSE AND HOME

Traditionally, Ozark hillfolk had many magical practices and beliefs based within the home itself. It's no surprise, considering how much time would have been spent inside the cabin—especially in the old days, where homesteads were far apart from each other and from town. The tradition of repurposing household objects for use in healing rituals comes from this deep connection to the home. Families often cleansed their houses using smoke from powerful plants like red cedar (*Juniperus virginiana*) and tobacco, or through intricate rituals of magical sweeping and washing. Spirits are often the target of these cleanses, such as general, unnamed entities like the "spirit of sickness" or evil spirits. Ghosts and haints often become the target of cleansing exorcisms, especially lost and wandering relatives who've found their way back to ancestral abodes.

There are several spirits that are specific to the home and can be powerful helpers and protectors. The first are called *house brownies*, who are generally considered to be fairies but are quite different from the Little People. These useful beings were brought to the New World with settlers from the British Isles, then mixed with fairy beliefs while in Appalachia. House brownies appear whenever the hearth is lit inside a home for the first time, and they will remain until the house is completely destroyed. To apply this to the modern world, I usually tell people that if there are walls, a floor, and a roof, then there will be house brownies living there. One of my students once asked what the modern equivalent of lighting the hearth for the first time would be; I think it could be turning on the heat or air conditioning for the first time, or lighting up the stovetop and oven.

What attracts the house brownies to us? None can say for sure. They enjoy spending time with humans, though, and will be fierce protectors of those inside the home—as long as they are taken care of. This usually involves two things: 1) giving food and drink offerings on a regular schedule, 2) making sure to invite them to all parties, large meals, and gatherings held inside the home (they don't like being excluded), and 3) notifying them before any furniture is moved or any new furniture is brought inside the home. With an exception of the first item, it's wise to treat house brownies like you would treat a roommate.

Another protector spirit found in Ozark homes is called the *house chicken*. In form, the house chicken appears as a ghostly white hen. Most of the time, however, only those with the sight will actually see these spirits. As with house brownies, the house chicken can be offered food and drink—usually dry grains and water—in exchange for watching over the house. I have two anecdotes to share about this spirit.

One of my informants was adamant about leaving out food and drink for the house chicken, which she did every Saturday. One night, as the story goes, she and her husband were woken up from a deep sleep by the loud cry of a hen somewhere in the house. They both sat straight up in bed and listened, but they didn't hear the sound again. Then they smelled smoke. My informant ran to the hallway and saw flames inside the kitchen. Luckily, they were able to grab their daughter and the family cat and escape the home before the fire spread. My informant insisted that their house chicken had warned them of the fire.

Another informant told me this story: Once, his house was robbed while he was out of town visiting family. He'd long been a believer in his own house chicken, and so he put out some dry oats and water and asked for the house chicken to please help him. About two weeks later, he heard a knock at his front door. Standing outside was a young man who was pale, sweating, and shaking. At his feet were four large cardboard boxes. It was the thief, come back to return what he'd stolen from the house. He apologized profusely to my informant, telling him that he hadn't been able to sleep since he'd broken into the house. Every night he'd dream of chickens pecking at his eyes and face, then wake up in a cold sweat.

There are too many varieties of house spirits to go into great detail here. Like the kitchen spirit, who will keep food stores high and can be petitioned using burned toast. Or the outhouse imp, a spirit who moved indoors when hillfolk started modernizing their homes. Or one of my favorites, the bed goblin, who lives off eating dust bunnies, who steals single socks in every pair, and who can scare away ghosts and demons.

GRABBING THE DEVIL BY THE TAIL

Exorcism has occupied an interesting position in traditional Ozark healing and folk magic. Many of the rituals and verbal charms to cast out devils and spirit entities were inherited from much older European traditions; others are reworkings and evolved practices unique to the Ozark region.

Amongst modern practitioners, there are two main approaches to exorcism. The first is the traditional "kick them to the curb" method, using rituals and charms that will forcibly remove the targeted entity from the home or person they are currently inhabiting. This method sometimes involves a sort of spiritual death for the entity, whereby they aren't only removed but sealed back in the otherworld. There are many different practices that fall within this category. Among them, the rites I myself have encountered include: binding, tying, sealing in knots, trapping, cutting apart, nailing as a form of sealing, slaying, burning, drowning, and several others.

For many healers and magical practitioners, traditional forms of exorcism come with a certain degree of wrath, anger, or even cruelty. While there aren't any formal vows or creeds that Ozark healers and magical practitioners adhere to, I have found that the majority of gifted individuals I've met feel that compassion is at the heart of their work. As one healer told me, "Our gift is for everyone—alive or dead." This sense of altruism extends not only to what we traditionally think of as healing practices, but can include exorcism as well.

One of my favorite teachers gave me a great term to use for this kind of compassion-led spirit work. She called it a *kinder exorcism*. In this work, spirits, ghosts, demons—whatever you might be dealing with—aren't harmed, banished, or sealed. Instead, the worker aims at healing or elevating the spirit itself. Much of the foundation for this practice comes from nineteenth-century Spiritualism and Spiritism. Books, theories, and practices from both of these areas seeped into the Ozarks around the turn of the twentieth century and became very popular amongst city folk and rural Ozarkers alike.

While more traditional forms of exorcism are still popular amongst Ozark healers and practitioners today, in my experience, these practices are used as a last resort only. Compassion toward all things, both visible and invisible, helps maintain a proper balance within the individual themselves. This need for maintaining equilibrium can be found in nearly all Ozark healing and magical practices. As one of my teachers taught me, "If you show kindness to nature, nature will be kind to you." This idea extends not only to nature, but to all things in the world—the innate flow of magic flows through us all.

THE CHARMS

As with human beings, Cancer (Moon, Monday, water) is great to use as a general auspicious sign for all healing and cleansing rituals related to spirits or otherworldly entities. Leo (Sun, Sunday, fire) and Sagittarius (Jupiter, Thursday, fire) are both traditionally used for spiritual elevation, illumination, or working with spirits as helpers and familiars. Boundary-building

Capricorn (Saturn, Saturday, earth) is excellent for exorcism, banishing, and elevation rituals. Aquarius (Saturn, Saturday, air) can be used for general spirit work or contacting spirits for divinatory purposes.

☆ ANSWERS FROM A SPIRIT ☆

This verbal charm is used as an accompanying ritual for any divinatory methods involving summoning spirits. For example, these words can be used as an invocation before using a Ouija or spirit board, before a séance, etc. As I talked about in the introduction to this chapter, the types of spirits that are used as helpers in the Ozarks not only include spirits of the dead, but a whole host of nonhuman entities from the otherworld. So, in the case of this specific ritual, our imagining of spirit communication should be broadened to include these beings as well.

As a spirit worker and medium myself, let me offer a couple pieces of advice that have served me well over the years in my practice. First, it's easier and safer to work with spirits *whom you know*. These can be trusted ancestral spirits, guides or patrons, saints, or even your own guardian angel. And second, if you are going to work with spirits you don't know, make sure to have one of your trusted spirits present during the work to act as a filter for the spiritual influences. Not everything that comes across from the otherworld has your best interests in mind. Having a personal guiding spirit, guardian angel, saint, or even a deity present will help your spirit working sessions immensely. Some of these entities can be summoned with a simple prayer, or if you already have specific invocation methods you work with, try performing these before you begin your spirit-working session.

MAGICAL TIMING
Full moon. Zodiac moon days in Aquarius (Saturn, Saturday, air) are great for general spirit work or when using spirits for divinatory purposes.

CHARM
[Name the spirit—or else say "Spirit"]
Awake, arise, pull out your eyes,
And hear what time of day;
[Say the current time, day of the week, month, and year number]

And when you have done,

Pull out your tongue,

And see what you can say.

RITUAL INGREDIENTS

Candle, white

Glass or cup, clear (no colored tinting or pattern)

Matches or lighter

Spirit board, Ouija board, tarot cards, or other tools of divinatory spirit
   communication

Water

RITUAL ACTIONS

I like to begin any spirit-working session by putting out traditional offerings associated with this type of work. Amongst Ozark Spiritualists and mediums, this includes a lit white candle and a glass/cup of water next to it. As one of my teachers taught me, the glass and water should be completely clear and clean. This is for three reasons: First is so that the candlelight can reflect through the water, which is why they are placed side-by-side. This aids in the summoning of spirits, who are said to manifest easier through the mediums of light and water. The second reason is that the water can act as an offering to soothe the spirit's thirst—should they have any. And the last reason is that the water is often observed by mediums to judge the temperament or presence of the spirit itself. There are certain tokens or signs that are looked for to provide this information. For example, many tiny bubbles on the inside of the glass indicate the presence of spirits, or a sudden cloudiness to the water might mean that there is some outside influence that is hindering the summoning process.

Once you have your candle and water placed, take out whatever divination tools you're using for the session. This can be any method you're attuned to, including Ouija or other spirit boards, pendulums and dowsing tools, or even tarot cards. Next, recite the verbal charm slowly and clearly. After the charm has been recited, continue with your divination session with whatever tool you have selected.

When you're finished, return the spirit back to the otherworld by snuffing (not blowing) out the candle. You can do this at any time if you feel like the spirit you have summoned is becoming angry or even trying to trick you.

☆ BANISHING CHARM ☆

This Ozark exorcism is based in a tongue-twisting Mother Goose rhyme. It can be used to banish any of a variety of aggressive or troublesome spirits including: devils, haints, Little People (and other fairies), boogers, etc.

I frequently am asked by students whether banishing charms like this one could inadvertently send away beneficial or protecting house spirits. The simple answer is yes, it could, if your intention isn't focused while enacting the charming ritual. The easiest way to avoid this problem is to state your intention clearly. For example, you could begin the ritual by saying something like, "May those evil, harmful, or troublesome spirits of this home be banished by this ritual." In this way, you are clearly stating that evil spirits will be the target of the charming ritual and nothing else.

This verbal charm can be used both as a reactionary measure or as a preventative ward. I often recommend incorporating banishing rituals like this one into a weekly house-cleansing practice. As a method of cleansing, this charm will remove both evil entities and the stagnant energies of sickness and curses that might linger inside the home.

MAGICAL TIMING

In Ozark folk belief, spirits are at their most powerful on the full moon and least powerful on the new moon; a new or waning moon in Scorpio (Mars, Tuesday, water) would be a highly auspicious time for this banishing.

CHARM

Aena, deena, dina, duss,
Kattle, weela, wila, wuss,
Spit, spot, must be done,
Twiddlum, twaddlum, twenty-one.
O-U-T spells out!

RITUAL INGREDIENTS

Candle, white

Matches or lighter

Metal handbell, or a small cookpot and wooden spoon

Incense charcoal and burner (optional)

Red cedar leaves and / or berries (*Juniperus virginiana*) (optional)

RITUAL ACTIONS

Begin this charming ritual in the center of the home, which in Ozark folk belief is the kitchen. Light your white candle and place it on your dining table, or you can place it in the center of your stovetop. At this time, light your incense charcoal, if using, and let some red cedar leaves and berries smolder as a purifying smoke. If you prefer, you can use traditional cleansing materia like frankincense resin, camphor, or juniper leaves and berries. The smoke is an optional part of this particular ritual.

In addition to smoke, this rite uses the cleansing sound from a metal handbell. If you don't have a bell, you can use a wooden spoon banged against the bottom of a metal cookpot or skillet. One of my teachers informed me that this was a very old Ozark way of working, since people weren't likely to have bells lying around their cabins.

Moving now into the charming ritual, open your front door and stand inside your home, facing outside. Recite the verbal charm. While you're reciting the words, ring the bell or bang on your cookpot.

The charmer who gave me these words pronounced them in a very specific way. When I asked him if the pronunciation mattered, he said he didn't know, but it couldn't hurt to be exact. For this reason, I will give my pronunciation of the charming words here:

Ae-na ("Ae" rhyming with *pay*, "na" rhyming with the "blu" in *bluff*)

Dee-na ("dee" rhyming with *knee*)

Di-na ("di" rhyming with *eye*)

Duss ("du" rhyming with the "blu" in *bluff*)

Kattle (rhyming with *rattle*)

Weela ("wee" rhyming with *knee*, "la" rhyming with the "blu" in *bluff*)

Wila ("wi" rhyming with *eye*)

Wuss ("wu" rhyming with the "blu" in *bluff*)

Spit, spot, must be done,

Twiddlum ("twi" rhyming with *knee*; entire word rhymes with *bedlam*)

Twaddlum ("twa" has the same vowel sound as *at*; entire word rhymes with *bedlam*)

Twenty-one.

O-U-T spells out!

When you reach the end of the verbal charm and begin to spell O-U-T, place your bell or cookpot on the floor, then clap loudly on each letter. After this, close your front door and then move to the next exit from your home. Repeat this same ritual at every door that exits your home directly to the outside; you don't have to include doors that, for example, open into a garage.

When you're completely finished, snuff out the candle. If you're using smoke as part of this ritual, you can carry it throughout the house for added benefit.

NOTES

The words of this verbal charm originate with a nonsense rhyme from Mother Goose. There are, however, many other charms that I've collected that also have seemingly magical words whose meanings are cryptic or unknown. As with familiar magical phrases like *abracadabra* and even the words in the famous "Sator Arepo" square, charming words are thought to have once had very specific meanings, but as they were passed down from one charmer to the next, the words changed, were misinterpreted, or were simply misunderstood altogether, as in cases where charms spoken in one language are passed to an individual who doesn't speak that language.

S	A	T	O	R
A	R	E	P	O
T	E	N	E	T
O	P	E	R	A
R	O	T	A	S

✯ FUNERAL CHARM ✯

This verbal charm is used to prevent attachment from spirit entities and ghosts while attending funeral services, especially those located inside a cemetery. There's another exorcism that involves taking a person who is possessed by a spirit to a cemetery and having them recite this charm while walking backward out the cemetery gate; this is believed to detach the spirit entity as well as leave it in the graveyard, considered the abode of the dead in Ozark folklore.

MAGICAL TIMING

This verbal charm is recited upon leaving a cemetery, especially after a funeral service. Traditionally, the charm is recited as soon as you step across the boundary of the cemetery, returning back to the world of the living.

CHARM

The death bells ring,
And with them I sing,
What stays behind,
I leave behind,
And what's left behind,
Peace and joy will find.

RITUAL INGREDIENTS

Payment item(s): penny, dime, buckeye nut, loose tobacco, dried beans,
    dried corn kernels, food items, etc.

RITUAL ACTIONS

This simple charming ritual is performed whenever you are leaving the boundaries of a cemetery, usually as you walk through the gate. The charm is recited once while still in the cemetery, one more time at the threshold of the gate, and a third time on the other side—beyond the boundary. For some, the verbal charm is enough to prevent any restless dead from attaching themselves to you. Others will leave behind a small payment of some sort to the spirits of the place; in some traditions, this payment is to the

King or Queen of the Dead—often the spirit of the first person buried in the cemetery.

Payment items don't have to be anything large or expensive. Traditional Ozark payments include food items like dried beans or corn kernels, loose leaf tobacco, or coins like pennies and dimes. As this is a form of sacrifice, the payment need only be something symbolically significant to you. I recommend not leaving behind things that will pollute the land or be considered litter. I've seen whole cigarettes left behind as payment or offerings as well as packaged food items. While I'm sure the proper sentiment was there when these items were left behind, it's important to remember how we interact with the land spirits as well as the spirits of the dead. Polluting the land is not maintaining a good relationship with the land spirits. For this reason, if you're able to, leave things that are out of packaging, especially food items that the animals of the place will consume. Avoid chocolate or overly sugary/salty items, as these are bad for most fauna. If you want to leave behind tobacco or other herbs, make sure to leave the dried leaves only.

Leave your payment items at the cemetery gate during the first recitation of the verbal charm. In some cases I've seen, individuals will leave payment offerings as they enter the cemetery as well as when they exit.

NOTES

I've managed to collect quite a few funeral or death charms in my travels. Many of them focus on honoring the dead or remembering their lives in some way. Such charms harkened back to the keening tradition from Gaelic countries. Others focus on more magical purposes. In Ozark folk belief, spirits of the dead—especially those who are considered to be restless—can attach themselves to mortal individuals in cemeteries. These restless dead are especially active immediately after dying, which is why such charms are often used to prevent attachment after funeral services.

There are other methods of detaching such spirits, including one of my favorites, which involves a bath made with horsemint (the name given to several species of the *Monarda*, or beebalm, genus). Taking one of these baths after visiting a cemetery or attending a funeral service is believed to detach any wandering entities or spiritual influences from the body, thereby preventing any of the negative effects from such possession.

✳ HOUSE CHICKEN'S SONG ✳

The house chicken's song has been repurposed from an old rhyme. In my practice, I recite it whenever I'm leaving out offerings for my own house chicken. It's a way of honoring this unique spirit as well as describing some of the tasks you want this familiar spirit to perform for you. Feel free to add your own tasks to the charm provided here.

MAGICAL TIMING

Recited whenever offerings are made to the house chicken. This is traditionally on the full and / or new moons, as well as on holidays and gatherings.

CHARM

I had a little hen, the prettiest ever seen,
She washed me the dishes and kept the house clean;
She went to the mill to fetch me some flour,
She brought it home in less than an hour;
She baked me my bread, she brewed me my ale,
She sat by the fire and told many a fine tale.

RITUAL INGREDIENTS

Bowl
Food offering: dried corn kernels, dried beans, fresh vegetables,
     bread, etc.
Cup
Drink offering: water, whiskey, milk, tea, coffee, etc.
Silver coin or other silver item

RITUAL ACTIONS

This ritual will take place in whatever spot in your home is designated as your offering location. Traditionally, offerings for the house brownies and house chicken were left in the kitchen, considered the center of the home. If you have animals in the home, you might want to keep your offerings in a high place; I've found that placing them inside an upper kitchen cabinet keeps out my furry friends quite nicely. Offerings could also be placed on a bit of open countertop, on the dining table, or even on the stovetop (in between the burners). In this way, we symbolically invite our house guardians into our family by inviting them into the heart of our living space and feeding them a good meal in the same place we ourselves are nourished.

Choosing your offering time is completely up to you, but I recommend a regular schedule that you know you can keep. If you can only maintain offerings on holidays, then that's what you should do. I maintain a new and full moon schedule—twice a month is easy for me to accomplish. Many practitioners I've met do weekly offerings, in which case it's just a matter of picking which day you want to use. In my experience, house guardians don't necessarily care about the frequency of our offerings, but they do want to be remembered on a regular schedule. I recommend my beginner students to write down their offering dates and place this piece of paper near their offering spot; this helps them be mindful of their timing.

Food and drink offerings can really be anything you have on hand, but I recommend offering fresh foods and drinks, not stale or moldy items. Ozark offering items I've personally seen used include fresh bread (wheat or cornbread), dried beans and corn, fresh vegetables, water, milk, whiskey, or moonshine; in some cases, offerings are whatever the family is eating at that time.

You'll begin this ritual by gathering your food and drink items. This can be as simple as a piece of bread and glass of water. Remember, intention is key. Once you have your food and drink, place them on your offering spot. As you place your items, set your intention that you are offering these things for the nourishment not only of your house chicken, but of all your guardian spirits, then recite the verbal charm. It's traditional to leave a silver dime or other silver item as payment for the work done on your behalf.

These items can be taken away in between offering rituals. I recommend leaving them out overnight, but no longer than that, as they might begin to rot and mold—a very offensive gesture to the spirit world. Offerings can then be thrown outside for local fauna to feast on. Try to use food items that are nourishing for animals as well, which means avoiding things that could be harmful, such as chocolate and food items that are high in salt or sugar.

NOTES

Offering services were once much more common in the Ozarks than they are today. There are few families left who still have such devotion to the land

and its invisible inhabitants. Even amongst religiously conservative Ozarkers of the past, offerings left outside for the Little People or placed inside for house brownies were quite common, especially on Christmas Eve, when the veil between worlds is believed to be at its thinnest. Offerings might have been left out in the springtime to ensure a good harvest; at harvesting, or the "first fruits" time of the year, as gratitude for a good harvest; or on other occasions, especially those that involved parties or feasting. You never want to leave your house guardians out of the fun!

Offering rituals in the Ozarks are generally very simple and mesh into daily life, as in one ritual I observed, where an old-timer would place a small plate of breakfast items on the cold stovetop every Sunday morning for her own house brownies. Others might use the mantelpiece over a fireplace or woodstove as their offering location; this connects us back to our ancient roots, when we used to cook our meals over open flames. The hearth and modern kitchen still remain intimately linked. In one ritual I observed, my informant would place a shot glass of whiskey and three cookies (or sometimes a chunk of homemade bread) on the mantelpiece every new and full moon night. He would then throw these offerings into the woods the next morning.

☆ SUMMONING HOUSE GUARDIANS ☆

This Mother Goose rhyme makes a perfect charming ritual for welcoming in house brownies, a house chicken, or other guardian spirits. I usually recommend this ritual when moving into a new home, especially one that was recently built and might not already have guardian spirits within its walls. You can do this ritual at any time, however, as a way of connecting with new guardian spirits or even ones already present.

In my experience, all homes and dwelling places have house guardians of some sort—either house brownies, house chickens, or another kind. Older houses in particular often come with an entire host of spirits that dwell there, including some very old and well-established families and clans. For this reason, I recommend offering practices when moving into a new house to show goodwill to the spirits who might be there. There's an interesting belief I've encountered amongst several Ozark healers and magical practitioners that maintaining good relationships with your house guardians will ensure that malicious or trickster entities won't be able to enter. As one healer I met told me, "Where there are good spirits, evil can never take root."

If you're unable to make regularly scheduled offerings, that's okay! Again, it's all about intention. Taking the time to remember and thank the guardians of your home is just as good of an offering. Remembrance and thankfulness is key.

MAGICAL TIMING

Nighttime or at dusk. A full moon at a time of the year when the veil between worlds is thin is most auspicious for this ritual. These times of the year amongst traditional Ozark practitioners include May Day and Christmas Eve, but Halloween, the solstices and equinoxes, and even holidays on the Wheel of the Year (in its many forms) work as well.

CHARM

Cross patch, draw the latch,
Sit by the fire and spin;
Take a cup and drink it up,
Then call your neighbors in.
(Repeat three times)

RITUAL INGREDIENTS

Bowl

Food offering: dried corn kernels, dried beans, fresh vegetables, bread, etc.

Candle, white

2 cups (1 for your drink offering, 1 to toast your drink)

Drink offering: water, whiskey, milk, tea, coffee, etc.

Matches or lighter

Red cedar berries (*Juniperus virginiana*) or juniper essential oil

Salt

Shot glass to toast drink (optional)

RITUAL ACTIONS

I recommend first placing all your ritual elements on a table. This could be your dining table to symbolically represent welcoming your guardian spirits to be nourished alongside your family. Light your white candle, then crush up your red cedar berries and add them to the wax. This is easiest if you use a jar or votive candle, but you can also slightly melt the wax on the sides of a taper (before lighting) and then roll it through the crushed red cedar berries. Juniper essential oil works as well. The combination of the light from the white candle and the scent of the red cedar (or juniper) creates a cleansing and protective field around the work about to be performed.

For added protection, since you will be welcoming spirit entities into the home, put a line of salt across the bottom of your closed front door. This is the door you will be using later in the ritual. Making the line on the inside of your house will be easier to clean up later on. Make sure the line is solid, with no breaks, and extends the full length of the doorway. This salt will act as a spiritual filter, allowing entrance to spirits that are pure while denying entrance to anything that might bring harm to us or our homes.

Next, gather together your offering items. These will be food and drink offerings that you will be giving to the spirits that enter your home. These can be placed on the dining table or in a designated offering spot in your home.[9] In addition to your food and drink offerings, pour yourself a small glass or cup of any drink you want to be a toast during the ritual. Make sure you have enough to take three drinks (or three shots).

With your items together, you can begin the charming ritual. While at your front door, begin the first line of the charm, "Cross patch..." and with these words, make an X shape on your front door with your right forefinger. To form the X, begin on the left with a downward \ motion, then repeat on the right with a downward / motion. Then repeat the words "...draw the latch," then unlock and open your front door.

Return to your candle and say, "Sit by the fire and spin," making three clockwise spinning motions as you recite. Then, say the words "Take a cup and drink it up," after which you will take a sip or shot of your toasting drink. End with the words "Then call your neighbors in" and clap three times.

---

9. You can learn more about these offering locations and the types of food and drink to use in the "House Chicken's Song" earlier in this chapter.

Repeat this entire verbal charm and ritual three times in total. After the first time, you don't need to repeat the X motion or reopen the front door.

After your charming ritual, I recommended leaving your front door open for seven minutes (a number sacred to Ozarkers). Some people like to do divination readings regarding their house guardians while the front door is still open—this is a highly auspicious times for such readings. After seven minutes have passed, you can close your front door, snuff out your candle, and clean up the salt you put down. Don't clean up the salt until you've shut the front door! If you put the salt line outside of your house, you can leave it there until the next day, then clean it up. Leave out your food and drink offerings overnight, then dispose of them outside.

☆ SUMMONING SPIRITUAL AID ☆

There are many variations within the category of summoning charms, so many I could probably publish a book on just this theme. Many are based on children's rhymes, which are a common feature of the Ozark charming tradition. This one in particular was passed to me for summoning spirits to aid in ritual work or to provide answers through divination. The spirits that are summoned aren't just any ordinary spirits—Ozark folk magic warns against flippant summoning of anything that might be hanging around. The spirits we call here are friendly spirits: angels, guides, guardians, kindly ancestors, etc. Basically, the spirits who want the best for us and truly want to help in our work. Everyone else is left at the door. Or, as the charm says, "Come with a whoop, come with a call, / Come with a good will or not at all."

MAGICAL TIMING

Full moon. Day and zodiac moon sign corresponding to the magical work you want empowered by the presence of spirits.

CHARM

Girls and boys, come out to play,
The moon doth shine as bright as day;
Leave your supper, and leave your sleep,
And come with your playfellows into the street.
Come with a whoop, come with a call,

Come with a good will or not at all.
Up the ladder and down the wall,
A half-penny roll will serve us all.
You find milk, and I'll find flour,
And we'll have a pudding in half an hour.

RITUAL INGREDIENTS

Divination tools, or other ritual items

Plate, big enough for your food and drink offerings

Food and drink offerings: as simple or complex as you'd like, but a basic
offering usually includes a bread, a soft drink (milk, tea, coffee, water,
soda, etc.), and a hard drink (beer, wine, whiskey, moonshine, etc.)

RITUAL ACTIONS

This verbal charm is used to empower any magical ritual or divination reading. It summons the presence of your guiding spirit entities to aid in your
work. Additionally, you can use this ritual as a way of contacting and identifying these spirits. Either way, you will begin by assembling your food and
drink offerings on a plate. This can be placed on your home altar or shrine.
You can also use locations mentioned elsewhere in this chapter—the kitchen,
for example.

Once you have your offering plate assembled and placed, repeat the verbal charm. When you've finished reciting the charm, you're now ready to
begin your divination reading or magical ritual. Know that those spirits who
watch over you and your practice are now present to empower your ritual
work.

After your work is completed, take your offerings outside and dispose of
them at the base of a tree or in a moving body of water.

NOTES

Summoning helping spirits to aid in ritual work or divination isn't uncommon in Ozark folk magic practice. In the old days, healers and magical
practitioners would have had to hide these practices lest they be associated
with witchcraft. Often, workers hid their spirit practices behind the guise of
working with angels, which was much more acceptable to the religiously

conservative hillfolk. Still to this day, Traditionalists—those still connected to the older, more conservative way of working—will use the term *angel* to cover a variety of spirit types and categories.

✱ TAMING DEVILS ✱

This is an interesting transformation of a Mother Goose rhyme—traditionally, it uses *scholars* rather than *devils* as part of the lyrics. Doctor Faustus is, of course, related to the literary figure of Faust, who was a bit of a demon summoner himself. In this way, the charmer is able to harness the power of a more skilled conjurer in order to tame his devils.

This verbal charm can be used in two different ways. The first is as an exorcism, in which the devils would be rounded up as part of the charming ritual and then whipped out of the house—or out of the person, depending on the situation. The second ritual allows the charmer to utilize the power of these devils for their own benefit. In this case, the charmer would be whipping their devils into shape—meaning subjugating them. The charmer who gave me these words and ritual used them in both ways. For some of his devils, he recited this charm as a way of returning them back to their spirit homes after using them in a ritual. He told me, "Devils don't like going back home—you have to whip them there like a stubborn mule."

I should warn you, though, that not all spirits enjoy benefiting mortal beings—in particular, those entities that are considered to be devils or demons. While in my opinion not supremely powerful, these devils are still trickster beings and are certainly able to misguide and cause trouble for an unsuspecting charmer. Take great care when working with any spirits. I recommend having a powerful guide or guardian spirit, deity, patron saint, or guardian angel close beside you while doing any of this work. In the event that something goes wrong, these higher-order beings will be able to intercede on your behalf.

MAGICAL TIMING

In the Ozarks, ritual work to tame or exorcise spirits is usually performed on the new moon, as this is believed to be a time when spirit entities are at their lowest energetically. New moons in Aries (Mars, Tuesday, fire) or Leo (Sun, Sunday, fire) are good for overpowering and subjugating spirit entities.

CHARM

Doctor Faustus was a good man.
He whipped his devils now and then;
When he whipped, he made them dance
Out of Scotland into France,
Out of France into Spain,
And then he whipped them back again!

RITUAL INGREDIENTS

Bowl

Salt

Pliable branch for the whip, usually made from willow, redbud,
or witch hazel; at least 2 feet long

Optional Variation:

Bowl

Salt

Canning jar with lid, or a wooden box with a lid

Pliable branch for the whip, usually made from willow, redbud,
or witch hazel; at least 2 feet long

Sulfur or charcoal powder

RITUAL ACTIONS

The first ritual variation is to be used as an exorcism for the home or for an individual. Begin by finding a branch that will act as your magical whip. This branch can be any length, but I recommend at least two feet long. You want it to be pliable enough so that it whips rather than bends or breaks. Green wood from most trees will work for this purpose; in the Ozarks, willow, redbud (*Cercis canadensis*), or witch hazel are used, as these trees yield naturally flexible branches.

Once you have your whip, fill a small bowl with salt of any kind. You can begin this ritual at the front door of the home, or in the spot where the most haunted activity has taken place. You can also determine the proper spot using any divination method you choose. Once you've found your starting position, hold the whip in your right hand and the bowl of salt in your left.

In a counterclockwise direction, move through this room and every room of the home, finally returning to the front door (or wherever you began).

As you move through these rooms, recite the verbal charm constantly. As you recite the charm, make a whipping motion through the air three times with the branch, then throw a pinch of salt toward the wall, which should be on your right-hand side if you are moving counterclockwise. Do this entire route a total of three times, ending wherever you began each time. Once finished, open the front door, make three whipping motions across the threshold, and throw a pinch of salt outside. At this, your exorcism is complete. The salt that was thrown during the ritual can be swept or vacuumed up and disposed of outside the home.

If you are doing this exorcism for a person who believes they are possessed by a devil, you will have the person face the west. Then, while facing them, make a whipping motion through the air three times, once at the beginning of the verbal charm, another in the middle, and finally a third at the end. Take care that you don't actually whip the person with the branch. After each of the three whipping motions, you will throw a pinch of salt toward the person. While they are still facing west, you will repeat this entire process again at their back. After this, I recommend doing three full counterclockwise circuits of the home as in the first part of this variation to exorcise any lingering entities that may now be in the space. For added benefit, make sure the person who is on the receiving end of this ritual takes a cleansing bath after this work.

The second variation of this charming ritual is for trapping devils inside a container or spirit trap. Begin in the same exact way as the first variation by finding a proper whip and filling a small bowl with salt. You will need more salt for this variation than for the first. You will also need to prepare a spirit trap, which is made from a glass canning jar with a lid, or any other container of your choosing that has a tight lid on it. You really do want a container that seals tightly because according to this ritual process, if the spirit container is opened with a spirit inside, they will be released again.

For the purposes of this charming ritual, the spirit trap is simple yet very effective. Once you have your container selected, add three teaspoons of either sulfur or charcoal powder. The charmer who gave me this ritual said that the sulfur or charcoal powder reminds the devils of their home in Hell and will attract them toward the trap. You can use either powder or a combination of three teaspoons of each powder.

Place your spirit trap on the floor in the middle of the central room of your home, or in the room where there is the most haunted activity. Next, place a line of salt across the bottom seal of every exiting door as well as every window in your home; an exiting door is any that leads directly to the outside. The salt line acts as a seal against spiritual influences and will prevent the devils who are inside the home from being able to exit through the windows and doors. It's important that your line of salt is solid and runs the entire length of the seal. If you don't have a way of placing the salt at the bottom of your doors and windows, you can make a spray by mixing salt and warm water in a spray bottle; spray this along the bottom seal of all the doors and windows.

Now, proceed with the ritual as in the first variation. The difference is that instead of returning to the front door after each round, you will return back to the spirit trap. After three rounds, seal the lid on your jar. Once sealed, clean up any of the salt at your doors and windows.

In essence, what is happening with this ritual is that you are coercing the devils out of their hiding places with the whip and the verbal charm. Because the doors and windows are sealed with salt, the devils are not able to escape from the home, and so they are spiraled inward, toward the spirit trap, as you work in a counterclockwise direction. After three rounds of this whipping and verbal charm, you will have driven your devils to the spirit trap, into which they will happily jump, believing it to be their home in Hell.

From here, you can use your spirit jar in a number of ways. It can be used as a magical battery of sorts to charge work that you might be doing, especially works aligned with the elements of fire and the zodiac signs Aries or Scorpio. As these are devils that you have trapped, they do prefer work that is aligned with retribution, wrath, vengeance, revenge, or subjugation. To use the spirit jar as a battery, simply place it in your space whenever you are performing a ritual or allow it to touch the ritual elements as you practice. You can place it alongside amulets as they charge with magical power to receive extra auspiciousness. I would like to note again that if the spirit jar is opened, the devils will be released back into your home, and I highly doubt they will be in a good mood.

NOTES

It's interesting that in Ozark folk magic, there are similar verbal charms that use the character of Jesus or another saint—usually one of the apostles—as a devil-taming figure. Certainly, in the Christian Bible, Jesus is seen as a demon-exorcising wizard of sorts, able to tame devils at will. It's no surprise that Jesus has become a figure in many of these exorcism charms as well as ritual work for subjugating or taming spirit entities. This is the only charm example I've encountered that uses Faust as this figure, and I suspect it's more so because the original rhyme utilizes this character.

Conclusion

For many Ozark healers and magical practitioners today, the power of our traditions and practices lies in the idea of simplicity. For me, this is one of the foundational ideas at the heart of all healing and magical practices here in the mountains. However, simplicity, in practice, doesn't mean *making do without*, but rather a deeper connection to *working from within*. Simplistic practice doesn't exclude rituals, ingredients, or tools, but says that these things are enhancements to what is already present within the practitioner.

This idea of simplicity likely has its origins in mountain life, where life was once much more difficult than it is today. Surviving in the wilderness meant having a very close relationship with the idea of impermanence. Attachments weren't easily made in a world where at any moment, nature could destroy your crops, your home, or even your family. For this reason, Ozarkers began to connect themselves to beliefs and practices that were closer to their own bodies and minds. Storytelling is one of these areas, as is the charming tradition. These things could be carried with you no matter where you went, and they were protected as long as you were alive.

Over the years, I've received a lot of criticism for teaching such simple practices. Many people crave ritual work these days; they fixate on things that can be touched and described. However, these criticisms, by and large, haven't come from Ozarkers. For mountain folk, even those living in big cities or away from the mountains altogether, *simplicity feels like home*. This is one of my favorite descriptors of our magic, given to me by an Ozarker now living in California. For her, as for many of us, Ozark magic is carried in the heart, not in the hands. It moves with us, no matter where we might go.

Our real power lies in the cunningness we cultivate—the ability to think and speak ourselves through (and around) any situation we might come across. The power lies in our connection to the land. Not in an exploitative relationship, but with the realization that although we live very different lives today, our survival still depends upon the well-being of nature and its unseen inhabitants.

Our charming tradition isn't unique to the Ozark Mountains but can be found across the world as a product of oral folk culture. Because so much of our life and culture is now depending less and less upon storytelling through remembrance, many of our verbal charms and prayers are being lost. Despite this, I believe that our connection to the power of simplicity is actually growing. I've encountered many young people who have taken to Ozark folk practices, now embracing highly internalized forms of work. Reasons behind this vary, but I think a big contributing factor is increasing economic hardship, climate change, and loss of the natural world around us. The equilibrium of our lives has been thrown out of balance. Like our ancestors, connecting back to the land—and back to our innate power, which doesn't rely on outside manifestations—has allowed many practitioners to feel at home in any situation.

All of us carry the power with us, as we ourselves are carried with the current of nature's magic. This isn't a cultural or religious inheritance but a *human* one. Let this magic carry you. This is the heart of the Charming Way. Feel yourself falling back into this river, the cool water healing your body and soul. Close your eyes. Feel yourself pulled in the direction life would have you go. You are the water and the water is you. Inseparable from the flow, you are the current; you are the magic. No holder, nothing to hold on to. From this place of deep, interconnected bliss, grab at some words and breathe new charms into the universe. May Granny Thornapple be a good guide for you, and may all charmers both in this world and in the world of spirits give you magical words when you need them.

Bibliography

Breatnach, Liam. "Satire, Praise, and the Early Irish Poet." Ériu 56 (2006): 63–84. https://www.jstor.org/stable/30007051.

Davies, Owen. *Cunning-Folk: Popular Magic in English History*. London: Hambledon and London, 2003.

de Blécourt, Willem, Ronald Hutton, and Jean La Fontaine. *The Twentieth Century*. Vol. 6, *The Athlone History of Witchcraft and Magic in Europe*, edited by Bengt Ankarloo and Stuart Clark. London: Athlone Press, 1999.

Greenaway, Kate, ill. *Mother Goose or the Old Nursery Rhymes*. London: Frederick Warne & Co, 1881.

Halliwell, James Orchard, ed. *The Nursery Rhymes of England*. London: Frederick Warne & Co., 1886.

Harris, J. Rendel. *Origin and Meaning of Apple Cults*. Manchester: Manchester University Press, 1919.

Parler, Mary Celestia. University Folklore Collection. University of Arkansas Libraries.

———. *Folk Beliefs from Arkansas*. Self-published, 1962.

Randolph, Vance. *Ozark Magic and Folklore*. New York: Dover Publications, 2003.

Rayburn, Otto Ernest. Papers. Special Collections Department, University of Arkansas Libraries.

———. "The 'Granny-Woman' in the Ozarks." *Midwest Folklore* 9, no. 3 (1959): 145–48. https://www.jstor.org/stable/4317804.

———. *Ozark Country*. New York: Duell, Sloan & Pearce, 1960.

Stark, Laura. *The Magical Self: Body, Society, and the Supernatural in Early Modern Rural Finland*. Helsinki: Suomalainen Tiedeakatemia, 2006.

Weston, Brandon. *Ozark Folk Magic: Plants, Prayers & Healing*. Woodbury, MN: Llewellyn Publications, 2021.

———. *Ozark Mountain Spell Book: Folk Magic & Healing*. Woodbury, MN: Llewellyn Publications, 2022.

"What Coins Are Silver?" *Top Cash Buyer* (blog). Accessed June 8, 2023. Americash. https://topcashbuyer.com/blog/what-coins-are-silver/.

Wright, Blanche Fisher, ill. *The Real Mother Goose*. Chicago: Rand McNally & Co., 1916.

TO WRITE TO THE AUTHOR

If you wish to contact the author or would like more information about this book, please write to the author in care of Llewellyn Worldwide Ltd. and we will forward your request. Both the author and publisher appreciate hearing from you and learning of your enjoyment of this book and how it has helped you. Llewellyn Worldwide Ltd. cannot guarantee that every letter written to the author can be answered, but all will be forwarded. Please write to:

Brandon Weston
℅ Llewellyn Worldwide
2143 Wooddale Drive
Woodbury, MN 55125-2989
Please enclose a self-addressed stamped envelope for reply,
or $1.00 to cover costs. If outside the U.S.A., enclose
an international postal reply coupon.

Many of Llewellyn's authors have websites with additional information and resources. For more information, please visit our website at http://www.llewellyn.com.

Notes